PRACTICE & REVISION KIT

pens
pencils
eraser
passport
letter

Advanced Certificate in Market and Social Research Practice

BPP Professional Education
February 2005

First edition 2005

ISBN 0 7517 1695 2

British Library Cataloguing-in-Publication Data
A catalogue record for this book
is available from the British Library

Published by

BPP Professional Education
Aldine House, Aldine Place
London W12 8AW

www.bpp.com

Printed in Great Britain by W M Print
45-47 Frederick Street
Walsall, West Midlands
WS2 9NE

We are grateful to the Market Research Society for permission to reproduce
the syllabus and past examination questions. The suggested solutions to past
examination questions have been prepared by BPP Professional Education.

We are also grateful to Dr Bob Foley of Hot-Spots Multimedia Ltd (www.hot-
spots.co.uk) for his help in the preparation of this book.

CONTENTS

QUESTION AND ANSWER CHECKLIST/INDEX

The headings indicate the main topics of questions, but questions often cover several different topics.

Tutorial questions, listed in italics, ease the transition from study to examination practice.

ALL questions other than tutorial questions are worth a third of the total marks for the exam. You have 2.5 hours (150 minutes) to complete the exam and you should therefore **spend no more than 50 minutes** on any question.

MINI-CASE QUESTIONS

ABOUT THIS KIT

You're taking your MRS Advanced Certificate exam in a few months' time. You're under time pressure to get your revision done and you want to pass the exam first time. Could you make better use of your time? Are you sure that your revision is really relevant to the exam you will be facing?

If you use this BPP Practice & Revision Kit you can be sure that the time you spend revising and practising questions is time well spent.

The BPP Practice & Revision Kit for the MRS Advanced Certificate in Market and Social Research Practice

The BPP Practice & Revision Kit has been specifically written for the Advanced Certificate syllabus.

- We offer vital guidance on revision, question practice and exam technique.

- We show you the current syllabus and analyse past papers.

- We give you a comprehensive question bank containing:
  - *Tutorial questions* to warm you up
  - *Exam-standard questions*
  - *Full suggested answers* - with summaries of the examiner's comments where available

- We include two Test Papers consisting of the February 2004 and June 2004 exams, again with full suggested answers, for you to attempt just before the real thing.

Help us to help you

Your feedback will help us improve our study package. Please complete and return the Review Form at the end of this Kit; you will be entered automatically in a Free Prize Draw.

BPP Professional Education
February 2005

To learn more about what BPP has to offer, visit our website: www.bpp.com

---

REVISION

This is a very important time as you approach the exam. You must remember three things.

> Use time sensibly
> Set realistic goals
> Believe in yourself

Use time sensibly

1 **How much study time do you have**? Remember that you must EAT, SLEEP, and of course, RELAX.

2 **How will you split that available time between each subject**? What are your weaker subjects? They need more time.

3 **What is your learning style**? AM/PM? Little and often/long sessions? Evenings/ weekends?

4 **Are you taking regular breaks**? Most people absorb more if they do not attempt to study for long uninterrupted periods of time. A five minute break every hour (to make coffee, watch the news headlines) can make all the difference.

5 **Do you have quality study time**? Unplug the phone. Let everybody know that you're studying and shouldn't be disturbed.

Set realistic goals

1 Have you set a **clearly defined objective** for each study period?

2 Is the objective **achievable**?

3 Will you **stick to your plan**? Will you make up for any **lost time**?

4 Are you **rewarding yourself** for your hard work?

5 Are you leading a **healthy lifestyle**?

Believe in yourself

Are you cultivating the right attitude of mind? There is absolutely no reason why you should not pass this exam if you adopt the correct approach.

- **Be confident** - you've passed exams before, you can pass them again

- **Be calm** - plenty of adrenaline but no panicking

- **Be focused** - commit yourself to passing the exam

QUESTION PRACTICE

Do not simply open this Kit and, beginning with question 1, start attempting all of the questions. You first need to ask yourself three questions.

> Am I ready to answer questions?
> Do I know which questions to do first?
> How should I use this Kit?

Am I ready to answer questions?

1   Make sure that you can answer the questions in the textbook and that you are familiar with all the material.

2   If you are happy, you can go ahead and start answering the questions in the Question Bank. If not, go back to your study material and revise first.

Do I know which questions to do first?

1   **Start with tutorial questions**. They warm you up for key and difficult areas of the syllabus. Try to produce at least a plan for these questions to ensure your answer is structured so as to gain a good pass mark.

2   Don't worry about the time it takes to answer these questions. Concentrate on producing good answers. There are eight tutorial questions in this Kit.

How should I use this Kit?

1   Once you are confident with the short questions, and the tutorial questions, you should try as many as possible of the exam-standard questions.

2   Try to **produce full answers under timed conditions**; you are practising exam technique as much as knowledge recall here. Don't look at the answer, your study material or your notes for any help at all.

3   **Mark your answers to the non-tutorial questions as if you were the examiner**. Only give yourself marks for what you have written, not for what you meant to put down, or would have put down if you had had more time. If you did badly, try another question.

4   Take note of the advice given and any **comments by the examiner**.

5   When you have practised the whole syllabus, go back to the areas you had problems with and **practise further questions**.

6   Finally, when you think you really understand the entire subject, **attempt the test papers** at the end of the Kit. Sit the papers under strict exam conditions, so that you gain experience of selecting and sequencing your questions, and managing your time, as well as of writing answers.

EXAM TECHNIQUE

Passing professional examinations is half about having the knowledge, and half about doing yourself full justice in the examination. You must have the right approach to two things.

> The day of the exam
> Your time in the exam hall

The day of the exam

1   Set at least one alarm (or get an alarm call) for a morning exam.

2   Have something to eat but beware of eating too much; you may feel sleepy if your system is digesting a large meal.

3   Allow plenty of time to get to the exam hall; have your route worked out in advance and listen to news bulletins to check for potential travel problems.

4   Don't forget pens, pencils, rulers, erasers.

5   Put new batteries into your calculator and take a spare set (or a spare calculator).

6   Avoid discussion about the exam with other candidates outside the exam hall.

Your time in the exam hall

1   **Read the instructions (the 'rubric') on the front of the exam paper carefully**

Check that the exam format hasn't changed. It is surprising how often examiners' reports remark on the number of students who attempt too few - or too many - questions, or who attempt the wrong number of questions from different parts of the paper. Make sure that you are planning to answer the right number of questions.

2   **Select questions carefully**

Read through the paper once, then quickly jot down key points against each question in a second read through. Select those questions where you could latch on to 'what the question is about' - but remember to check carefully that you have got the right end of the stick before putting pen to paper.

3   **Plan your attack carefully**

Consider the order in which you are going to tackle questions. It is a good idea to start with your best question to boost your morale and get some easy marks 'in the bag'. Don't feel constrained to answer questions in the order in which they appear in the paper.

4   **Check the time allocation for each question**

You have to attempt three questions, each of which accounts for one third of the final result. The exam is two and a half hours long (150 minutes) and so you should complete each question within one third of the total time available (50 minutes). When this time is up, you must go on to the next question. Going even one minute over the time allowed brings you a lot closer to failure.

5   **Read the question carefully and plan your answer**

Read through the question again very carefully when you come to answer it. Plan your answer to ensure that you keep to the point. Two minutes of planning plus eight minutes of writing is virtually certain to earn you more marks than ten minutes of writing. Make sure that you can link each point you make to the question being asked. Put a line through any rough notes or plans that you don't want the marker to take into consideration.

6   **Produce relevant answers**

Make sure you answer the question set, and not the question you would have preferred to have been set.

7   **Gain the easy marks**

Include the obvious if it answers the question and don't try to produce the perfect answer.

Don't get bogged down in small parts of questions. If you find a part of a question difficult, get on with the rest of the question. If you are having problems with something, the chances are that everyone else is too.

8   **Produce an answer in the correct format**

The examiner will state in the requirements the format in which the question should be answered, for example in a report or memorandum.

9   **Follow the examiner's instructions**

You will annoy the examiner if you ignore him or her. The examiner will state whether he or she wishes you to 'discuss', 'comment', 'evaluate' or 'recommend'.

10 **Present a tidy paper**

Students are penalised for poor presentation and so you should make sure that you write legibly, label diagrams clearly and lay out your work neatly. Markers of scripts each have lots of papers to mark; a badly written scrawl is unlikely to receive the same attention as a neat and well laid out paper.

11 **Stay until the end of the exam**

Use any spare time checking and rechecking your script.

12 **Don't worry if you feel you have performed badly in the exam**

It is more than likely that the other candidates will have found the exam difficult too. Don't forget that there is a competitive element in these exams. As soon as you get up to leave the exam hall, forget the exam and celebrate!

13 **Don't discuss an exam with other candidates**

After the exam, put it out of your mind until the day of the results and relax!

ASSESSMENT AND THE EXAM PAPER

Assessment

There are two compulsory components of assessment:

- One coursework assignment of 3,500 words ✓
- A 2 ½ hour written examination

The Integrated Assignment

The Integrated Assignment is a practical project of 3,000 to 3,500 words which integrates learning objectives from the various units of the Advanced Certificate syllabus.

BPP offers an e-tutor programme covering the preparation of the Integrated Assignment. For more information, visit our website at www.bpp.com/mrs or email your MRS queries to mrs@bpp.com.

The Written Examination

The examination paper will require you to answer:

		Weighting
Section 1:	A compulsory mini case study containing three tasks	One third of the total
Section 2:	Two essay questions from a choice of six	One–third of the total each

The time given for the examination will be 2.5 hours.

Answers will not receive a numerical mark, but will be given a band mark (Distinction, Merit, Pass, Fail). In order to achieve a Pass overall, candidates will normally need to achieve a minimum of a Pass in each question. If one answer is awarded a Fail grade, candidates will normally be expected to achieve a Merit band or above in one of the remaining two questions in order to Pass.

Analysis of past papers

There are three examination sessions per year in February, June and October (usually in the second week of the month).

Prior to 2004, the exam was slightly different and the exam had three sections, one of which consisted of ten multiple choice questions, but this is no longer included.

June 2004

Section 1 (compulsory mini-case)
RenAid: problems of face-to-face interviews; questionnaire design; collecting qualitative information

Section 2 (answer 2 questions only)
1   Strengths and limitations of various quantitative methods
2   Using the Internet to conduct research
3   Sampling/recruitment in qualitative research
4   Secondary research
5   Concepts in the analysis of quantitative data
6   Setting research objectives

(The June 2004 paper forms the second test paper at the end of this Practice and Revision Kit.)

February 2004

Section 1 (compulsory mini-case)
LiveSport!: benefits and drawbacks of centrally-conducted international telephone survey; sample recruitment issues; reporting results

Section 2 (answer 2 questions only)
1   Limiting research projects to control costs
2   Qualitative and quantitative research
3   Email surveys
4   Explain statistical terms
5   MRS Code of Conduct and ethical considerations
6   Evaluating the quality of a research report

(The February 2004 paper forms the first of the test papers at the end of this Practice and Revision Kit.)

September 2003

	Question in this Kit
Section 1 (compulsory mini-case) Eduweb: online training courses in a new market. Re-organise a table of published data; summarise findings after re-organising table; identify other useful information	58

Section 2 (answer 2 questions only)

	Question in this Kit
1 Why are market research reports ignored by clients?	5
2 Data fusion problems and how to minimise them	16
3 Differences between individual interviews for qualitative and quantitative research; how to ensure quality of data generated	35
4 Measuring attitudes: difficulties and response formats	46
5 Quota sampling: reasons for growth in use; limitations and how to overcome them	27
6 Strengths and weaknesses of extract from a questionnaire; how should it be amended and why	42

June 2003

March 2003

September 2002

BPP
PROFESSIONAL EDUCATION

June 2002

March 2002

SYLLABUS

Introduction

The Advanced Certificate is designed to provide a practical grounding in the principles and techniques which underpin effective research.

The ten units of the syllabus follow the steps in the research process. Successful candidates will be able to demonstrate that they meet the learning outcomes attached to each unit.

Syllabus

Unit 1: Introducing the research process and its context

Content summary:	
▪	Role of market research in industry, commerce and the public sector
▪	Ethical issues - MRS *Code of Conduct* and *Data Protection Act*
▪	Role of agency and client - role of in-house researcher
▪	Problem definition, hypothesis development and testing, prioritisation, cost-benefits, risk analysis, identification of action to be taken as a result of research - the crucial role of research briefs and the research proposal in effective research. The stages of the research process and the writing of the research brief

Learning outcomes: candidates will be able to:	
▪	Demonstrate knowledge of the role of market research
▪	Demonstrate knowledge, understanding and application of MRS *Code of Conduct* and *Data Protection Act* to the practice of research
▪	Define the contribution of market research in the social and corporate context
▪	Demonstrate an awareness of problem solving and information management and its limitations

Unit 2: Types of data and categories of research

Content summary:	
▪	The different roles of primary and secondary data; knowledge of searching the paper and electronic systems including the Internet
▪	The fundamental differences between qualitative and quantitative data
▪	The uses of exploratory, conclusive, ad hoc and continuous research
▪	The uses of in-house data, Management Information Systems and Decision Support Systems - understanding the sources and uses of databases, data mining and concepts and problems of data fusion. With particular reference to the electronic methods of collecting and storing of data

Learning outcomes: candidates will be able to:
▪ Collect secondary/desk research data available from hard or electronic sources
▪ Understand and analyse the different types of data and research required
▪ Understand the concepts of data management, marketing information systems and decision support for different types of decisions

Unit 3: Writing a research proposal and selecting a research design

Content summary:
▪ Elements and structure of research proposal
▪ Exploratory, descriptive, conclusive, multi-method research designs
▪ Test designs, causal or inferential data, before and after tests, with and without controls
▪ Commercial designs - panels, audits, simulation studies, omnibus surveys
▪ Continuous research - the role of continuous research within the context of market monitoring, tracking studies, planning and exploration

Learning outcomes: candidates will be able to:
▪ Begin to write a research proposal including information requirements and research objectives
▪ Understand the connections between a brief and proposal in the context of the research process
▪ To select research design for data collection, for a given research brief
▪ Understand different types and levels of research design, continuous and ad hoc etc and apply them to appropriate problems

Unit 4: Sampling

Content summary:
▪ Steps in the sampling plan - identifying the population of interest and selecting a sampling frame
▪ Sampling method and sampling size - probability based methods of random sampling and types of non-random sampling
▪ Sampling and non-sampling error
▪ Understanding the sampling plan

Learning outcome: candidates will be able to:
▪ Select appropriate sample type, sample size and sample frame, and apply this in constructing a sample plan for a research proposal

Unit 5: Collecting qualitative information

Content summary:

- Planning for qualitative information collection, specification of information required

- Qualitative research techniques and types of data: group discussions, depth interviews, observation

- Advantages and disadvantages of discussions and interviews

- Undertaking a group discussion and individual interview: role of the moderator, use of stimuli, projective techniques

- Validity and reliability of qualitative data. To understand the strengths and weaknesses of qualitative work

Learning outcomes: candidates will be able to:

- Select the appropriate qualitative method, or combination of methods, aware of their strengths and weaknesses, for a given research problem

- Conduct a focus group or individual interview

Unit 6: Quantitative data collection

Content summary:

- Types of survey: on street, in-home, postal, at-work. Face-to-face, telephone, Internet interviewing

- Observation as a quantitative technique: electronic and manual: bar-coding and mystery shopping

- Uses and methods of all issues related to on-line interviewing

- Appropriateness of methods to research and budget constraints

Learning outcomes: candidates will be able to:

- Understand the advantages and disadvantages of different quantitative data collection methods

- Select an appropriate quantitative data collection method for task in hand

- Understand how electronic measurement works and what data it produces

Unit 7: Designing and planning questionnaires

Content summary:

■	The role and structure of a questionnaire
■	Relationship to data input: editing and coding
■	Wording and phrasing - pitfalls of question construction and flow, response formats, question sequencing and layout
■	The questionnaire planning process
■	Piloting and revisions

Learning outcomes: candidates will be able to:

■	Prepare questions that collect the data required by the research objectives
■	Understand the different types of data that can be collected and their relationship with wording and phrasing
■	Understand the questionnaire plan and process
■	Be able to design and execute a questionnaire plan

Unit 8: Measuring attitudes in research

Content summary:

■	The concepts of attitudes, beliefs, motivations and the problematic connection with behaviour
■	Problems of measurement and elicitation of attitudes and motivation and the role of qualitative research
■	Quantitative techniques available and their limitations: Likert and semantic differential scales
■	Creating and testing scale items
■	Response format of scales
■	Types of scales and types of response format: dichotomous, balanced, forced, etc

Learning outcomes: candidates will be able to:

■	Understand the difficulties associated with ascertaining and interpreting attitudes and behaviour
■	Create and test a pool of items for a Likert Scale and descriptors for a semantic differential scale
■	Understand the connection between scales, the responses and attitude/behaviour theory

Unit 9: Analysing information and data

Content summary:

■	Analysis of qualitative information: transcribing and recording of verbal and non-verbal responses, respondent types and varied responses identified; theoretical frameworks to be used in interpretation, hypotheses generated identified and justified
■	Analysis of quantitative data: understanding, editing, coding and data inputting
■	Specifying output: cross tabulations and bi-variate analysis, filtering and use of different bases, principles of weighting, dealing with non-response
■	Use of summary and descriptive statistics, confidence intervals and significance testing

Learning outcomes: candidates will be able to:

■	Transcribe and record accurately examples of qualitative research
■	To code, input data for analysis and undertake examples of different kinds of quantitative analysis
■	Know about and be able to interpret different weights and filters

Unit 10: Reporting the results

Content summary:

■	Approaches to report writing
■	The principles of interpreting and reporting data
■	Methods of presenting and displaying data and qualitative information
■	Approach to report writing and oral presentation, bearing in mind the audience and the objectives of research
■	Understanding the concepts of reliability, validity and the bases for evaluation of research results

Learning outcomes: candidates will be able to:

■	Write all types of marketing documents eg briefs, proposal etc
■	Prepare a written report based on analysis of data
■	Give oral presentation of results
■	Evaluate research proposals, secondary data, and research findings from primary field surveys

Question Bank

BPP
PROFESSIONAL EDUCATION

1 Tutorial question: Marketing research process

Your organisation is concerned to improve customer service through better distribution of its product lines to retail stores. Currently the computer ordering system is linked directly to major retail customers (who represent more than 70% of your total business) through Electronic Data Interchange. Using this technology your firm is able to supply 90% of its product lines in less than three working days and 50% within 24 hours. You have been given the responsibility of conducting specific marketing research with the aim of identifying areas of possible improvement in the distribution and logistics function. You are asked to provide a report to your marketing manager that clearly outlines:

(a)   The key stages necessary in conducting such research

(b)   What the specific objectives of the marketing research should be and how you propose to conduct the research

2 Tutorial question: Market research industry structure

You have been asked to prepare an in-house presentation for your firm's training day. Your audience are the sales executives and members of the sales administration team. You are to outline to them the nature and structure of the market research industry.

3 Background report (06/02)   50 mins

How could a researcher develop a comprehensive background report on a global industry that her/his research agency had no previous experience or knowledge of? Choosing one example, identify the main elements necessary for this type of report.

(Total weighting: one third of the marks for the whole exam)

4 Choosing a market research agency   50 mins

Your line manager has decided to investigate the merits of using a market research agency service and he has asked you to write a report to him on the matters that need to be considered and the procedures for choosing a market research agency.

(Total weighting: one third of the marks for the whole exam)

5 Left on the shelf (09/03)   50 mins

Many research projects are commissioned, only to have the reports left on the client's shelf.

(a)   Describe the main factors which can limit the usefulness of a piece of research to a client.

(Weighting: 33%)

(b)   Describe the steps which can be taken to ensure that a client can make full use of research findings. Illustrate your answer with examples.   **(Weighting: 67%)**

(Total weighting: one third of the marks for the whole exam)

6 Research techniques and legal issues (06/02)   50 mins

Describe and analyse the research techniques used in customer relationship management. Identify what legal issues are important to bear in mind when using these techniques.

(Total weighting: one third of the marks for the whole exam)

7 MRS Code of Conduct (09/02)   50 mins

Evaluate the usefulness to each of the following of the MRS Code of Conduct.

(a)   A fieldworker
(b)   A questionnaire designer
(c)   A focus group moderator
(d)   A respondent

(Total weighting: one third of the marks for the whole exam)

8 Ethical issues (03/03)   50 mins

What are the key ethical issues in market research which relate to the following?

(a)   The respondent
(b)   The client
(c)   The researcher

(Total weighting: one third of the marks for the whole exam)

9 Marketing ethics and social responsibility   50 mins

You are a marketing executive of Sarkey and Sarkey, a market research agency. Your client 'Dell Boy Enterprises Ltd', has commissioned you to research a new high alcohol 'alco-pop' drink for teenagers and to build up a personalised marketing campaign database by any means possible. Dell suggests that if we secretly video film taste sampling sessions, any favorable clips could be used in a subsequent advertising campaign.

During the course of the conversation, Dell indicates that once the database has been compiled the company propose selling on the details of the entire customer list to interested parties to defray your fees. They intend keeping the data on a laptop computer (which it transpires has been lost twice already).

The company indicates that a further opportunity for any data obtained could be to pass it on to Dell's cousin in the USA who has an international Internet sales organisation business based in America, which markets and sells medical supplies and personal services to various countries including the UK.

(a)   Indicate what broad ethical marketing issues you understand to be involved in this request.   **(Weighting: 20%)**

(b)   Indicate what legal and social issues would influence your views on your client's approach in this instance.   **(Weighting: 40%)**

(c)   Discuss any codes of conduct that would influence your approach and decisions in this case.   **(Weighting: 40%)**

(Total weighting: one third of the marks for the whole exam)

10 Tutorial question: Qualitative and quantitative

For an in-house marketing research training day with your team you have been asked to produce a handout that:

(a)   Explains the difference between quantitative and qualitative methods of marketing research

(b)   Provides a list of clear examples of the different tools used to gather different types of marketing research

(c)   Gives advantages and disadvantages of each example listed in (b)

(d)   Provides a clear illustrative example of how and why you would prefer a qualitative approach as opposed to a quantitative approach to conducting marketing research

11 Tutorial question: ICT and marketing research

For an organisation of your choice, write a report to define and explain some recent Information and Communication Technologies (ICTs) to present to the Marketing Team. In this context you have been asked to explore how the organisation could make use of these ICTs to improve the quality of marketing decisions.

The terms that you must define and explain in your written report are:

(a)   Internet
(b)   Intranet
(c)   Extranet
(d)   Data warehousing
(e)   Data mining

12 Continuous and *ad hoc* (03/02)   50 mins

A large national corporation of estate agents is updating its marketing research function. Give clear recommendations for a continuous marketing research agenda and also identify what ad hoc research may be required and for what purpose.

(Total weighting: one third of the marks for the whole exam)

13 Developments in research techniques (09/02)   50 mins

'Research methods have not improved since the 19th century.' Discuss this statement in the light of developments in research techniques over the past century, giving relevant examples.

(Total weighting: one third of the marks for the whole exam)

14 Marketing database   50 mins

You are the marketing manager for Luddite Ltd, a firm manufacturing and selling bathroom furniture by mail order and via retail outlets to the public and plumbing firms. Your boss, Tom Crapper, no longer in his first flush of youth, has heard that marketing databases are a good thing but, in his technological ignorance, he rather doubts that a marketing database would benefit Luddite.

Given his doubts and concerns, Tom has asked you to explain what types of information would be required to set up such a database. Tom is worried that once the database has been set up, the information would become out of date and contain and perpetuate inaccuracies. He says this is probably a good reason to stick with the good old information system.

You spend some time trying to tell Tom about the processes for setting up and maintaining a database. Regrettably he remains confused and asks you to explain, in a memo, the processes for setting up and maintaining a corporate database.

You are to write a memo to Tom explaining the processes for setting up and maintaining a database.

(Total weighting: one third of the marks for the whole exam)

15 Data mining
50 mins

(a) Explain the concept of data mining using firms or examples with which you are familiar to illustrate your answer. (Weighting: 40%)

(b) Describe the techniques with which you are familiar that are used in data mining.
(Weighting: 30%)

(c) Explain the benefits of data mining. (Weighting: 30%)
(Total weighting: one third of the marks for the whole exam)

16 Data fusion (09/03)
50 mins

Data fusion is the process of combining data from a range of different sources.

(a) Discuss the potential problems which a researcher might face when using data fusion in their research. (Weighting: 50%)

(b) Describe the steps which can be taken to minimise these problems. Illustrate your answer with examples. (Weighting: 50%)
(Total weighting: one third of the marks for the whole exam)

17 Proposal document (03/03)
50 mins

(a) Explain the role and importance of the proposal document to the research process.

(b) Outline the key sections which should be included in a proposal document.
(Total weighting: one third of the marks for the whole exam)

18 Research proposal
50 mins

You have recently been appointed marketing manager and a research proposal from a firm of market research consultants for a proposed new product range has arrived in your 'in tray'.

(a) Describe the features of the report that you would expect to find within the proposal.
(Weighting: 70%)

(b)   What questions would you, as marketing manager, want the proposal to answer?

(Weighting: 30%)

(Total weighting: one third of the marks for the whole exam)

19 Type of research   50 mins

Your organisation is a national provider of management training programmes aimed at middle and senior management executives across a number of industries. Training programmes typically include general open courses in a variety of specialist areas covering: financial management, sales management, marketing and general management. In addition bespoke training programmes are designed for a variety of clients in both public and private sector organisations. The organisation is currently considering entry into new overseas markets offering management training and has asked you to write a brief report outlining the type of marketing research that will need to be undertaken.

Your report should indicate:

(a)   The research objectives   **(Weighting: 25%)**
(b)   The type of research and why it is appropriate   **(Weighting: 25%)**
(c)   How you propose the research will be conducted   **(Weighting: 25%)**
(d)   The benefits you expect to realise through the research activity   **(Weighting: 25%)**

(Total weighting: one third of the marks for the whole exam)

20 Research plan   50 mins

You are newly appointed as a marketing manager in a publishing company and have been given specific responsibility for a new product launch. Your organisation wants to introduce a new magazine aimed at the teenage female market, as identified as part of last year's strategic review. In this respect you have been given a budget of £30,000 to conduct further market research prior to the launch. Explain how you would plan and conduct this research. You are required to give the specific stages in your research plan and evaluate and justify each of your chosen options.

(Total weighting: one third of the marks for the whole exam)

21 Tutorial question: Random and judgement sampling

(a)   You have been requested by a colleague to define clearly and explain the difference between a *random sample* and a *judgement sample*.

(b)   In the context of an organisation of your choice explain how a *random sample* may be drawn, and comment upon sample size in relation to:

(i)   The degree of confidence
(ii)   Cost and value of information

22 Tutorial question: Sample size determination

Although there are statistical methods for determining the size of a sample in marketing research, frequently other means are used. What means are these?

23 Sample selection (03/02)
50 mins

Identify how you would select a sample of respondents to collect data for a research project commissioned to identify trends in the uptake of financial services by lower income groups. Indicate differences in methods used if time and/or costs are limited.

(Total weighting: one third of the marks for the whole exam)

24 Sampling plan (06/02)
50 mins

A mail order 'office supplies' company wishes to establish a continuous research programme in-house that provides information on its customers, their likes and dislikes and their purchases. Provide them with a detailed sampling plan, identifying critical sampling issues that are pertinent to obtaining useful information.

(Total weighting: one third of the marks for the whole exam)

25 Sampling frame (09/02)
50 mins

(a) For what types of sampling is a sampling frame important, and why?

(b) What methods would you use to compile a sampling frame of purchasers for use by a manufacturer of airline seating?

(Total weighting: one third of the marks for the whole exam)

26 Voting behaviour and sampling plan (06/03)
50 mins

The Government wants to undertake research into voting behaviour amongst a nationally representative sample. How would you develop a sampling plan for this project? Outline the stages involved and discuss the factors which might affect your decisions at each stage.

(Total weighting: one third of the marks for the whole exam)

27 Quota sampling (09/03)
50 mins

Over the past 20 years, quota sampling has become the dominant sampling method used in commercial research.

(a) Discuss the reasons for this growth in the use of quota sampling   **(Weighting: 33%)**

(b) Describe the main limitations of quota sampling, and discuss how these limitations might be overcome within a research project. Illustrate your answers with examples.
(Weighting: 67%)
(Total weighting: one third of the marks for the whole exam)

28 Qualitative research and data collection (03/02)
50 mins

Discuss what considerations a researcher should take into account when designing qualitative research to develop new concepts for children's dolls. What data collection methods would you recommend and why?

(Total weighting: one third of the marks for the whole exam)

29 Data collection and analysis (03/02)   50 mins

What differences has modern technology made to data collection and analysis? Illustrate your answers with examples, fully explaining their relevance.

(Total weighting: one third of the marks for the whole exam)

30 The Internet and data collection (06/02)   50 mins

'In the long term the Internet will have little effect on data collection techniques'. Discuss this statement with reference to one area of applied research; agreeing or disagreeing with the statement and giving reasons for your answer.

(Total weighting: one third of the marks for the whole exam)

31 Panels (09/02)   50 mins

(a)   Describe briefly the roles of panels in the market research process.

(b)   Evaluate the usefulness of panels to researchers and identify any major problems associated with running them.

(Total weighting: one third of the marks for the whole exam)

32 Focus groups v in-depth interviews (03/03)   50 mins

When would you recommend the use of group discussions (focus groups) as opposed to in-depth interviews as a method of collecting qualitative data? Illustrate your answer with examples.

(Total weighting: one third of the marks for the whole exam)

33 In-home interviews (06/03)   50 mins

Personal interviewers, who are prepared to conduct interviews in respondents' homes, are becoming increasingly difficult to recruit.

(a)   Discuss the benefits and drawbacks of in-home data collection.   **(Weighting: 50%)**

(b)   What are the most appropriate alternatives to in-home interviewing? Describe when and why you might use them in preference to in-home interviewing.   **(Weighting: 50%)**

(Total weighting: one third of the marks for the whole exam)

34 Observation and interviewing (06/03)   50 mins

Both observation and interviewing are valuable research tools.

(a)   Compare and contrast the value of each approach to the researcher.   **(Weighting: 33%)**

(b)   Describe how observation can be used to collect:
(i)   quantitative data; and
(ii)   qualitative data.

Illustrate your answer with examples.   **(Weighting: 67%)**

(Total weighting: one third of the marks for the whole exam)

35 Individual interviews (09/03)

Individual interviews are an important data collection tool for both qualitative and quantitative research projects.

(a) What are the key differences between individual interviews undertaken for qualitative research studies and those undertaken for quantitative research studies? Illustrate your answers with examples. **(Weighting: 50%)**

(b) You have planned a series of individual interviews as part of a qualitative study. Describe the steps you would take to ensure that the interviews generate accurate and relevant data. Give reasons for your suggestions. **(Weighting: 50%)**

(Total weighting: one third of the marks for the whole exam)

36 Multinational quantitative surveys (06/02)

Discuss, with reference to multinational quantitative surveys, the issues that determine the delivery of sound information. Give appropriate examples illustrating themes over and above those relevant to domestic surveys.

(Total weighting: one third of the marks for the whole exam)

37 Hall tests and placement tests (09/02)

Discuss the similarities and differences between a Hall test and a Placement test. In what circumstances would each be more appropriate?

(Total weighting: one third of the marks for the whole exam)

38 Errors in quantitative surveys (03/03)

(a) You are planning a quantitative survey. Describe the major types of error which might occur during the research process.

(b) Describe some of the practical steps you can take to minimise these types of error occurring.

(Total weighting: one third of the marks for the whole exam)

39 Postal surveys (03/03)

"Postal surveys take too long and response rates are typically low. Therefore, it is not usually a worthwhile approach".

(a) Do you agree or disagree with this statement? Evaluate the usefulness of postal surveys, giving reasons for your decisions. **(Weighting: 50%)**

(b) Describe how you might overcome the disadvantages usually associated with postal surveys. Illustrate your answer with examples. **(Weighting: 50%)**

(Total weighting: one third of the marks for the whole exam)

40 Tutorial question: Research techniques

There are a number of specific marketing research techniques that may be employed to research consumer behaviour. An airline you are advising on marketing research is concerned to find out:

(i)   Why customers choose their airline, and

(ii)   What services customers value highly and are prepared to pay a premium price for

Required

Write a brief report on the three specific research techniques that are listed below and explain the appropriateness of the techniques listed to achieve the stated research objectives. You should provide a brief but clear explanation of each technique and discuss how it may be used in this context.

(a)   Shopping mall tests

(b)   Focus groups

(c)   Postal questionnaires

41 Questionnaire design (06/03)   50 mins

(a)   What factors need to be considered before beginning the process of designing a questionnaire? How does each factor influence the design decisions?

(Weighting: 50%)

(b)   Describe the key stages in the process of effective questionnaire design. Explain the importance of each stage to the overall design process.   **(Weighting: 50%)**

(Total weighting: one third of the marks for the whole exam)

42 Quality of a questionnaire (09/03)   50 mins

A large supermarket chain is considering expanding its range of organically-produced food, and wants to find out more about its customers' views. Below is an extract from the interviewer's copy of a questionnaire which the research department has produced.

Question 6:

How often do you buy organic milk?

a) **Every week**   b) **Once per month**   c) **Less than once per month**   d) **Never**

Question 7:

Why do you buy organic milk?

a) **Because it tastes better than non-organic**

b) **Because it is healthier for you**

c) **Because it is more expensive than other milk**

(a)   Identify the strengths and weaknesses in the extract shown.   **(Weighting: 33%)**

(b)   How would you amend the questionnaire to ensure that it meets the company's need? Give reasons for the changes you suggest.   **(Weighting: 67%)**

(Total weighting: one third of the marks for the whole exam)

43 Discussion guide and questionnaire design   50 mins

You have been asked by a new nightclub to create a discussion guide for use by an interview moderator, with a view to him/her exploring clubbers' attitudes towards the various attributes provided during clubbers' nights out. You have also been asked to design a questionnaire for use in a parallel survey to discover levels of customer satisfaction of the club go-ers. You may assume that for the interview, the participants have visited the club on one or more previous occasions.

(a)   Design a discussion guide that could be used by a moderator to explore the club go-ers' attitudes to the facilities offered by the disco/club.   (Weighting: 50%)

(b)   Using a range of techniques, design a questionnaire with the objective of obtaining feedback on the customers' satisfaction on the services likely to be provided by a club/bar/discotheque.   (Weighting: 50%)

(Total weighting: one third of the marks for the whole exam)

44 Opinion polls (06/02)   50 mins

'Opinion polls are more often wrong than right!' Discuss this statement and identify robust research techniques that should be used to measure attitude and behaviours of a population towards its political parties before a general election.

(Total weighting: one third of the marks for the whole exam)

45 Attitude research (06/03)   50 mins

A lot of money is spent each year on attitude research. What are the strengths and limitations of using:

(a)   quantitative research; and   (Weighting: 50%)

(b)   qualitative research   (Weighting: 50%)

to collect data on attitudes?

(Total weighting: one third of the marks for the whole exam)

46 Measuring attitudes (09/03)   50 mins

An attitude, which Allport (1935) defined as a "learned predisposition to respond to an object or class of objects in a consistently favourable or unfavourable way", is a complex construct and measuring attitudes presents the researcher with a wide range of difficulties and choices.

(a)   What are the main difficulties the researcher is faced with when measuring attitudes? Illustrate your answer with examples.   (Weighting: 50%)

(b)   Describe two response formats used in attitude measurement with which you are familiar. Evaluate the usefulness of each to the researcher.   (Weighting: 50%)

(Total weighting: one third of the marks for the whole exam)

47 Data coding and input (03/02) 50 mins

You have been asked to input data from a questionnaire dealing with local housing. Over five thousand questionnaires have been returned. Provide a data coding and input plan, clearly indicating the stages of data input: editing, coding and dealing with open-ended responses. How would you determine the reliability of your procedures?

(Total weighting: one third of the marks for the whole exam)

48 Pre-coding and post-coding (03/03) 50 mins

(a) Briefly describe the key differences between pre-coded responses to questions and post-coded responses. **(Weighting: 50%)**

(b) What should you take into account when deciding whether to pre-code or post-code responses to a question? Illustrate your answer with examples. **(Weighting: 50%)**

(Total weighting: one third of the marks for the whole exam)

49 Data editing (06/03) 50 mins

Data editing is an important part of the data analysis process for both pen-and-paper and computer-aided data collection methods.

(a) Explain what is involved in the process of data editing. **(Weighting: 33%)**

(b) Explain what is meant by the term 'missing data' and how it occurs. Describe ways in which missing data can be dealt with. Illustrate your answer with examples.

(Weighting: 67%)

(Total weighting: one third of the marks for the whole exam)

50 Tutorial question: Training handout

You have recently been appointed as Head of a new Marketing Research Section and your staff have only limited experience in marketing research. One of the first responsibilities your manager has delegated to you is to explain to your team the following terms:

(a) Lifestyle research
(b) Survey research
(c) Mall intercept interview research

Write a short training handout that defines each of the terms listed above, and then explain how each technique can be used in the context of an organisation of your choice.

51 Report and presentation 50 mins

Your market research team has been conducting research on a proposed new product. Your team have analysed the results and you have been asked to write the research report in support of your team's decision to recommend the launch of a new product. The board of directors has also asked you to make a verbal presentation of your findings to them at the forthcoming board meeting.

(a) Outline the characteristics of a good research report. **(Weighting: 20%)**

(b) Discuss the format you would use for your written research report, outline the headings you would use and the summarise the contents and rationale for each of those headings.
(Weighting: 40%)

(c) Assume your team has been asked to make the oral presentation of the market research report to the board of directors. You are advising your colleagues on a suitable format and range of presentation techniques to present the research report. Outline your advice to your colleagues. **(Weighting: 40%)**

(Total weighting: one third of the marks for the whole exam)

52 Presentation preparation (09/02)

50 mins

How would you prepare for a presentation of research findings to a client? Describe the different elements of preparation which you would need to consider and explain why each is important.

(Total weighting: one third of the marks for the whole exam)

53 Municipal council (03/02)

50 mins

The municipal councils of large cities in the UK have been told that they need to implement a number of measures as a result of recent government directives, namely they have to provide:

(a) An annual record of the council's effectiveness in providing services that the community wants and needs

(b) An annual record of providing services that are value for money

(c) An annual record of appropriate staff appraisal and relevant professional development support.

At yesterday's Monthly Meeting of the Council of one particular large city, it was agreed that the leader of the Council, Mrs Hadthorpe, and the Chief Executive, Peter Clodden, should produce a report to present to the Council at next month's meeting. This report should:

(a) outline what information already exists that the council might use to satisfy this directive; and

(b) make recommendations for further action.

No expenditure relating to this project will be approved until the next full council meeting.

Mrs Hadthorpe and Peter Clodden are to meet tomorrow to discuss these issues and how they might best advise the full council at its next meeting. You, as the only market research professional employed by the Council, are to attend the meeting tomorrow and have been asked to do the following.

(a) Advise Mrs. Hadthorpe and Peter Clodden on what research should be undertaken immediately to inform their report to the Council next month in relation to their first objective. **(Weighting: 33%)**

(b) Advise them on what regular research you would recommend if starting with a clean sheet to deal with each of the government measures to be implemented. **(Weighting: 50%)**

57 Pickles and chutneys (06/03)

50 mins

Coriander Ltd own two small but successful Indian restaurants in London. According to the restaurant staff, diners are always asking if it is possible to buy the home-made pickles and chutneys which are used in the restaurants. These are made from fresh fruit, vegetables and spices, and cover a range of five flavours (lemon & garlic; tomato & ginger; aubergine & tamarind; mango & lime; onion & ginger). Mr Sharma, the owner, is considering manufacturing the pickles and chutneys for retail sale, but is nervous about doing so as a previous venture to launch curry sauces was unsuccessful.

He wishes to conduct some research to assess the wider demand for these products and the best retail outlets to target, such as supermarkets, delicatessens, speciality Asian stores or more informal outlets like open-air markets. As a first step, he is considering some form of research amongst his customers. He has identified two potential routes to gathering information, either by providing diners with questionnaires which they complete during their visit to the restaurant or by using his customer database to mail out questionnaires. He realises that further research might be necessary following the questionnaire, but is unsure how it should be carried out.

You are a research executive who visits the restaurants regularly and Mr Sharma has asked you for your advice.

(a) Evaluate each of the data collection methods which Mr Sharma has identified. What are the advantages and disadvantages of each? Which, if any, would you recommend and why?
(Weighting: 33%)

(b) Mr Sharma would like to know which flavours are most popular, and where his customers would expect to buy his products. Devise two questions, one for each of these areas, which would be suitable for inclusion in a self-completion questionnaire.
(Weighting: 33%)

(c) Outline a programme of secondary research which would help Mr Sharma understand the structure of his potential market (e.g. size; profile; shopping habits). Give reasons for your choices.
(Weighting: 33%)

(Total weighting: one third of the marks for the whole exam)

58 EduWeb's new market (09/03)

50 mins

EduWeb is an educational technology company based in the USA which specialises in creating online training courses for adult learners. Their biggest market is in language training, providing beginner-level courses in most European languages. In the USA, customers can access these courses via local colleges or directly from the company.

EduWeb now wants to set up a UK arm of the company but first wants to commission research into the best ways to market their services in their new market. Before commissioning the research, the marketing department in the USA wants to find out about market research in the UK and, in particular, wants to know about the best way to gather data in what, for them, is a new market.

You have been employed as one of EduWeb's representatives in the UK and have been asked to gather information on what data collection methods are used in the UK to present to the director of marketing. You have found the information contained in the table below, published by the BMRA (British Market Research Association).

The following shows data published by BMRA (British Market Research Association) about data collection methods in UK:

	2001 Market Share	2001 vs. 2000 Year-on-Year Change	2000 Turnover * (£m)
Retail Audit	0.4%	-42.3%	£2.34
Face-to-face Quantitative	40.6%	-3.9%	£243.28
Web/Internet	0.5%	18.4%	£3.09
Telephone Quantitative	20.4%	5.1%	£122.06
Qualitative	12.8%	-7.9%	£76.75
Postal/ Self Completion	7.7%	-1.4%	£46.15
Observation/ Mystery shopping	2.8%	21.3%	£16.65
Consumer Panel	9.9%	9.4%	£59.61
Other	4.9%	7.6%	£29.51

Based on returns from members accounting for c66% of BMRA turnover, representing c50% of estimated UK industry turnover.

(a) How could you reorganise and/or rework this table to make it easier to interpret? Explain the changes you would make, giving reasons for your choices. You are not expected to recalculate any of the data. **(Weighting: 15%)**

(b) Write a short report which summarises these findings and draws conclusions about data collection methods in the UK. **(Weighting: 50%)**

(c) The table above gives an extract of data from the survey. In cases like this, it can be difficult to give a full interpretation of findings because information is missing. What other information would be useful in order to improve a report based on this data? Give reasons for the suggestions you make. **(Weighting: 35%)**

(Total weighting: one third of the marks for the whole exam)

Answer Bank

1   Tutorial question: Marketing research process

> *Tutorial note.* The question asks how you propose to conduct the research, and so you will need to make appropriate assumptions. We have assumed that the organisation has a field sales force, but does not employ a specialist market research analyst.

REPORT

To: Marketing Manager
From: Jill Riley
Date: 21 January 20X5
Subject: Identifying areas of improvement in the distribution and logistics function

This report outlines the marketing research process, giving the key stages in undertaking research and the specific research objectives and methodology to be followed.

(a) **Marketing research process - key stages**

(i)   Set the objectives of the research
(ii)   Define the research problem
(iii)   Assess the value of the research
(iv)   Construct the research proposal
(v)   Specify data collection method(s)
(vi)   Specify technique(s) of measurement
(vii)   Select the sample
(viii) Collect the data
(ix)   Analyse the result
(x)   Present the final report

The following points relating to each key stage should be borne in mind.

(i)   Research objectives need to be SMART - Specific, Measurable, Actionable, Reasonable and Timescaled.

(ii)   Some exploratory research may be necessary to clarify problem areas and further understand customer requirements.

(iii)   A cost benefit exercise will need to be carried out to ensure that undertaking the research is cost-effective.

(iv)   Proposals need to be submitted for the category of research to be undertaken and must be agreed by all parties.

(v)   Data can be primary (field research) or secondary (desk research). Collection methods will vary according to the type of research.

(vi)   At the measurement stage, all the factors under investigation will need to be converted into quantitative data to allow for analysis.

(vii)   Sample size will be dependent on time and resources but must be sufficient to be statistically significant.

(viii) Decisions as to who will undertake the research and how will it be carried out must be made.

(ix)   Statistical analysis may involve using manual techniques, computer techniques or a combination of both.

(x)   Findings will need to be presented and a formal report submitted.

(b) **Specific research objectives and method of conducting research**

   (i)   **Research objectives**

Separate objectives are needed for the two groups of customers, those using Electronic Data Interchange (EDI) and those not using it.

   (1) **Customers using EDI**

- To establish how they rate current distributive and logistics processes
- To identify areas where improvements can be made
- To establish to what extent perceived customer service levels can be improved by better distributive and logistics processes

   (2) **Customers not using EDI**

- To establish reasons for non-use of EDI
- To identify incentives to encourage non-users to invest in EDI technology
- To quantify the likely benefit in improved customer service

  (ii) **Conducting the research**

The most cost-effective way to undertake the research is likely to be a combination of in-house and external agency resource. My proposal is as follows.

   (1) Draw up a research brief internally.

   (2) Short list and then commission a specialist marketing research agency.

   (3) Ask the agency to compile questionnaires (one for EDI customers, one for non-EDI users).

   (4) Use the company's sales representatives to collect questionnaire data.

   (5) Await questionnaire analysis and presentation of findings by the agency.

The **questionnaire format** should be such that the sales team can conduct semi-structured interviews. This would facilitate the collection of quantitative data (tick box, pre-coded choices) and qualitative data (views and opinions recorded from open-ended questions). Probing questions, such as 'What other factors are there?' can also be used to clarify responses or gather additional information. They are also useful for triggering further responses. More skill is required in conducting semi-structured interviews, but these should be within the capabilities of the sales team, provided that they are given an adequate brief.

2 Tutorial question: Market research industry structure

(a) **The nature of market research**

Market research is the function that links the consumer, customer and public to the marketer through information. The information is used to identify and define marketing opportunities and problems, generate, refine, and evaluate marketing actions, monitor marketing performance and improve understanding of marketing as a process. Marketing research specifies the information required to address these issues; designs the method for collecting information; manages and implements the data collection process; analyses the results and communicates the findings and their implications (American Marketing Association).

One of the duties of the manager of an organisation is to plan resources in such a way as to minimise risk. By gathering all the available information on any given venture (s)he will be able to maximise the probability of the outcome of a project coinciding with the original plan.

The need for such information when planning projects underpins the discipline of market research.

Customer and market research

By researching the customer or the market, the resulting information can produce both qualitative and quantitative facts on the markets, segments or niches on which the organisation is focusing. Such information might be in terms of volumes, values or market share.

The research can also produce information on the location and distribution of customers and potential customers, their profiles, spending patterns and preferences.

Advertising and promotion research

Advertising research measures the success of advertising campaigns compared to their objectives. The research also investigates the available and potential media for advertising and which media is likely to prove most effective for a given message.

Advertising research also provides information on the medium that is most likely to reach the target audience for given campaigns and the messages that appeal to the target audience.

The impact effectiveness of advertising campaigns can be evaluated by test research on sample media audiences. Such research can be evaluated at all stages of an advertising campaign from its inception to its final roll out and the subsequent feedback from mass audiences.

Product research

Product research investigates new uses for new products or services. It also investigates and tests markets new products or services and researches potential users' feedback on such products.

Once the feedback on the uses of new or existing products has been collated, it can be used to refine product designs and eliminate or reduce product weaknesses.

The research can also investigate customer reaction on packaging of products or services and obtain feedback on the impact and image of the printing and packaging used.

Distribution research

As distribution is one of the essential elements of the marketing mix, it is important that the organisation must research the best distribution channels for its product or service.

Physical distribution can be researched by industry specialists with knowledge of the best sites for storage, distribution and retail outlets.

In the age of the Internet, it is becoming increasingly important to research the best way to construct and locate websites and to obtain customer feedback on the visual and informational impact of an organisation's web design.

Sales research

This form of market research investigates and measures the effectiveness and the variety of measures and techniques of selling. It uses appropriate algorithms for evaluating sales areas to ensure optimal distribution of sales and customer potential.

Sales research can also be used to provide information on appropriate and equitable methods of remuneration for the sales force.

Research on training and education methods for the sales force in terms of effectiveness of the sales effort and the customer relations aspect of the sales executive's job.

Marketing environment

All organisations need information on the environment in which they operate in terms of social, political, technological, economic and ecological matters. Techniques such as econometrics and research of market trends are used to provide information on which firms can formulate their strategic plans.

(b) **Structure of the market research industry**

Types of market researchers

Specialist agencies specialise in:

(i)   Particular markets or market sectors or regions

(ii)   Questionnaire design, or collection and analysis of qualitative information

(iii)   Conducting personal or telephone interviews and administering postal or e-mail surveys

Data analysis agencies code up, read in or input data collected.

Independent consultants undertake a variety of tasks, usually on a smaller scale.

Syndicated research agencies conduct regular research into areas that the agency knows will be required by a range of organisations and is then sold to customers for an appropriate fee.

List brokers create or acquire lists of potential consumers for the purpose of selling them on to companies who are interested. Lists may be created from publicly available sources or the electoral rolls but they will usually be organised for convenience, presented in formats that can be easily incorporated into clients' systems, and checked for accuracy.

Profilers take an organisation's database and superimpose profiling information (demographics, lifestyle and life stage information) on the basis of postcodes. This allows the organisation's database to be segmented according to the criteria that are most appropriate to that organisation. Profilers may also have access to other lists and be able to offer these to its clients.

Full service agencies offer a full/wide range of services and are able to conduct a research project from start to finish.

Adverting agencies and **Management Consultancies** also offer marketing research services.

3   Background report

> *Tutorial note.* We have answered in fairly general terms, since it would be unhelpful for your revision if we concentrated on one specific industry that is unfamiliar to you. You, however, should have picked a global industry that you know about and drawn your examples from that. There are always extra marks available for good examples.

Although we won't dwell upon the point it is worth observing that it **could be unwise** of an agency to take on a client in a global industry of which they had no previous experience. At the very least this fact should be explained to the client, who may prefer to employ a different agency. On the other hand the question does not mention a specific client so perhaps the report is being prepared for **internal purposes** initially, prior to bidding for work in the industry in question.

Information sources

Given that it is a global industry there is certain to be a good deal of secondary information about it.

(a) The *Financial Times* regularly produces supplements on major global industries (Telecoms, Aerospace, Energy and Mining, Drugs and healthcare, Retailing and leisure, etc)

(b) More detail can be obtained from various **information services** such as Reuters, Lexis Nexis, Mintel, and the Economist Intelligence Unit. Some of these offer online subscription services so their reports are quick and easy to obtain, though they may be expensive.

(c) **Statistics** on the industry are likely to be available from the **governments** of many countries. Although these tend to be highly aggregated they are certain to contain some information that will be of use for a report of this nature. For a more international perspective organisations such as the EU, the World Trade Organisation (WTO), and the Asia-Pacific Economic Co-operation Forum (APEC) may provide relevant information: the initial point of research will be the websites of these bodies.

(d) Websites will no doubt provide a wealth of information, but not all of it will be up to date or of good quality. Key sites to look at will be the sites of **institutions and professional bodies** associated with the industry, the sites of the **major corporations** in the industry and the sites of any **consumer groups** with an interest in the industry.

(e) There are likely to be many other published sources such as **trade magazines** devoted to the industry and its participants and suppliers.

Report contents

There is no set format for such a report, but it would typically contain sections on the following matters.

(a) **History**

This section need not go into a great deal of depth, but it should give an overview of how the industry has grown and any major events, for example "The industry suffered a major downturn in the early 1990s due to ..."

(b) **Economic information**

The **size** of the industry in **financial** terms and also in terms of number of **customers** and numbers **employed**. It would be most useful to include some trend information such as a five-year summary and if possible some predicted information about likely growth.

This section may also contain information about political and economic conditions and how they are likely to impact upon the industry. No doubt this will vary in different parts of the world. Information about the degree of interdependence between the industry and both national and global economies would be useful. In certain types of industry forecasts for **commodities** prices may be highly relevant.

(c) **Key players**

An **overview** would be required, for example "The aerospace industry comprises companies producing aircraft, guided missiles, space vehicles, aircraft engines, propulsion units, and related parts. Aircraft overhaul, rebuilding, and parts also are included."

Most global industries comprise a relatively small number of **major corporations** and brief descriptions of the key players in the market and their relative market shares should be provided. Factors that **differentiate** the different brands should also be mentioned. **Ownership** of participants may be relevant, for example some may be state owned because they are regarded as crucial to a particular country's economy.

Existing and potential **new entrants**, for example in developing countries like India and China, should also be considered, even if they are not currently regarded as key players.

(d) **Major products/services**

This part of the report would be at category level. For example the insurance industry might be divided into distinct categories including:

(i)   Life insurance
(ii)   Pensions
(iii)   Health insurance
(iv)   Business liability insurance
(v)   Property insurance
(vi)   Vehicle insurance

The report should include an outline of the nature and relative importance of each major category.

(e) **Distribution, sales and marketing information**

For example, the buying process, how consumer markets are segmented, current sales trends, demographic data, developing markets. Again this is likely to vary widely from country to country – for example beer production could be considered to be a global industry, but tastes are very different in different countries – and from segment to segment.

(f) **Legal and regulatory issues**

Some industries are highly regulated and subject to international standards, for example on safety issues: this can have a major impact on the way the industry operates. Some individual governments or alliances impose protectionist measures, for example the EU on agriculture or the US on steel.

(g) **Human resource issues**

This section would include information about matters such as skills shortages (for example, in technological industries), and about working conditions and relative rates of pay if that is an issue, as it is for example in footwear manufacturing.

(h) **Future developments**

This would include matters such as new technologies that were likely to affect the industry, regulatory changes that may make doing business more or less difficult, possible changes in attitudes and behaviour amongst customers, for example the impact of increasingly aged populations.

4   Choosing a market research agency

The merits of choosing an external agency

Outsourcing market research has been increasingly prevalent over recent years due to the increasing specialism of the subject. The greater amounts of data and information available to companies means that it is more effective for companies to collect information on behalf of a range of clients who can select from that information for their own needs.

Computerisation has led to increasingly sophisticated statistical analysis and the use of specialist software has led to increasingly specialised knowledge. Because of the specialism of such firms, it can often prove to be more cost effective to outsource market research to outside agencies.

Points to consider in choosing an outside agency

(a) Internal departments may not have the necessary range of skills and experience.

(b) Choosing an external agency with previous experience of a similar problem may prove to be both cheaper and more effective.

(c) Agencies may have the necessary facilities for the task (eg a dedicated call centre for telephone research).

(d) An external agency may be more objective and approach the problem with a fresh mind and no preconceptions.

(e) An external agency can give the research an 'anonymous cloak'.

Choosing the right agency

Draw up a shortlist using a range of companies of the appropriate size, with the appropriate level of experience and with the necessary skills. Such lists can be obtained from the Market Research Society and headings included are:

- Name
- Contact
- Establishment date
- Turnover
- Parent company
- Associate companies and members
- Accredited standards
- Total employees
- Personnel
- Senior contacts
- Research markets
- Research services
- Research locations
- Promotional statement

Ask questions

When a shortlist of potentially suitable firms has been drawn up and quotes have been obtained meetings need to be arranged to ask pertinent questions such as:

- Is there a Fieldwork manager?
- How many supervisors and interviewers will be allocated to the case?
- Are the workers full time, part time or contractors?
- What are the selection and training criteria and procedures for personnel used on the project?
- What are the staff turnover statistics?
- What are the quality control procedures?

■ Does the firm have the relevant experience for the project?

It will need to be ascertained that the staff who are to work on the project have appropriate qualifications and whether they have experience of the same or similar projects. Similarly it will need to be established that the interviewers are familiar with the industry, in order to provide a more informed report.

Costs

It will need to be established what basis the firm uses to calculate its costs:

■ How will the samples be constructed?
■ What will be the length of the interviews?
■ What types of respondents and interviewers will be engaged?

If a firm is constructing its cost structure in such a way that it will benefit the firm to cut quality and minimise inputs at the expense of quality of market research, then this may need to be renegotiated or taken as a pointer to choose an alternative supplier.

What should clients do and ask when researching potential agencies?

Clients should look for **evidence** to substantiate potential agencies' own marketing claims, for example they should obtain independent testimonials of their work, do a walk through test to observe the operations and where possible examine previous work. If the agency makes claims as to (say) a certain size of work force, clients should look for physical and documentary evidence of it and also look for evidence of its quality control/assurance procedures.

What should a firm expect of a research agency?

■ A statement of the general background of the management problems at hand

■ A statement of the management problem

■ A statement of the research problem and objectives and the use to which the research result will be put

■ A chance to discuss these problem statements and background

■ A range of budgets available for the project

■ The desired timing

■ An assurance that the supplier will be approached only when there is a reasonable expectation that the buyer will select it

5   Left on the shelf

Tutorial note. In part (a) you should identify a range of points from different stages (at least 4) within the research process. Better answers will provide a wider range of points or a more detailed explanation of the points they make. In part (b) try to link the suggestions made with the problems you identified in part (a). You will get extra credit for appropriate illustrations (from general knowledge or from your own experience) which justify the points made.

Our answer is a good deal longer than you could have managed in the time available. Don't be frightened by this: we do not know what particular points you raised and we wanted to cover as many as possible to help with your revision.

(a) **Factors that can limit the usefulness of research**

Reports may be of limited use for a variety of reasons, including the following.

(i) The researchers may not have understood the **brief**. It may be that the client's brief is poor, but ongoing discussions with the client should rectify this. If the researchers have not bothered to remain in communication with the client to seek confirmation of their understanding and clarify uncertain matters the resulting research is unlikely to be of much value to the client.

(ii) **Problem definition**. A 'problem' for the purposes of research can be any unexpected change in the circumstances a business deals with, including clients, competitors, the business environment, legislation etc. Something which a researcher may term 'a problem' is really the marketing manager's vision of a marketing opportunity. Generally speaking 'the problem' is a formal way of identifying the 'core need' for the research to be undertaken. If the researcher has defined the problem poorly then the research may not be of use to the client.

(iii) **Research design**. A research design is a summary description of the research methods, including the data collection, sampling and data analysis, which the researcher proposes to undertake to solve the client's research problem. If the techniques and methods proposed are poor or inappropriate for the problem, or too limited the resulting research will not produce the desired information.

(iv) The research itself may be **conducted badly,** for example focus groups may have been conducted by interviewers who lacked the necessary skills to elicit the true feelings of the participants. There may have been insufficient safeguards to prevent error. The results may be inadequately or wrongly analysed. They may be misinterpreted by the researcher.

(v) Some kind of **external bias** may have crept into the context in which the research was set: the views from a respondent in Devon, say, may not be truly reflective of respondents who could have been chosen in, say, Birmingham.

(vi) The **client may not be able to understand** the report, perhaps because it is written in marketing research jargon rather than language that the client understands, or it contains complex statistical analyses without proper explanation, or because it does not clearly identify the options available and the decisions that need to be made.

(vii) **Circumstances in the market may have changed** shortly after the report was produced, for example because of actions of competitors or the introduction of a new technology, and these may have made the research irrelevant because the client will now be pursuing options that were not even envisaged at the time the research was conducted.

(b) **Steps to ensure that a client can make full use of research findings**

Communication

Above all it is essential to remain in good communication with the client, not just at the beginning and end of the project but throughout, so that the client's needs and the decisions that need to be made can be clarified when necessary and the research can be refined and adapted in the light of findings. The researcher should be aware of who is involved at the client's organisation in the various stages of the research and know what are they looking to get out of the research. The **budget implications** of any changes

BPP
PROFESSIONAL EDUCATION

should be fully discussed, explained and agreed, especially if it becomes apparent that the original budget will not be adequate to complete the research fully.

Background research

A important step that should not be neglected is background research or **exploratory research**. For example, the researchers may think that they already understand the business and the industry it is in – they may even have been appointed as a result of previous experience in that industry – but that does not automatically mean that they understand the particular client's problems.

The researcher may have to carry out some **secondary background research** into elements of the problem to substantiate their expertise in the area of research required. For example, the researcher may have to investigate the office supplies market by visiting some office supply stores, exploring the Internet or looking at relevant trade press if undertaking research for a producer of office supplies.

Primary background research data should also be obtained directly from the client for the identification of elements in the business environment which are particularly relevant to this specific client's problem, and the researcher should look at their records such as sales figures and reports, complaint statistics and customer feedback forms. This research may also involve interviewing experts in a particular field or business area to gain insights into the dynamics and main areas of concern in any particular industrial and/or consumer market.

All of this will help the researcher to better understand the consumer, the markets, the buying process and the external economic and social environment. Proper background research, together with continuing dialogue with the customer, will ensure that the researcher fully understands the brief and has clearly defined the problem.

Research design

The researcher should select a research design which they are sure will provide **valid and accurate data**. For example the client may have requested a one-off study, thinking that that will be sufficient, but the researcher may know from previous experience that a longitudinal study will provide better results, and should not shy away from explaining this to the client.

The researcher should ensure, probably by initial testing, that the **data collection methods** chosen can be implemented properly in practice and that they will genuinely generate the type of information needed to address the client's problem and help with decision making.

(i)   **Questionnaires** should be well-designed and fully piloted before use.

(ii)   **Interviewers** should possess the appropriate skills and be well-briefed. Their work should be monitored on an ongoing basis to nip any problems in the bud.

(iii)   Potential sources of **error** should be identified in advance as far as possible, and collection methods should be refined while the research is in progress if unanticipated problems arise.

(iv)   Obviously data should be **transcribed** accurately, especially for qualitative research. **Technology** should be used where practicable – taping, videoing, and computer assisted data collection will all help.

Processing and analysis

Checks should be employed to ensure that all the data collected is processed accurately. For example, for quantitative data it may be found that the system of pre-coding used was not adequate in the light of the information collected and the coding should be revised and the information coded again before the data is processed for analysis. Qualitative data is time-consuming to analyse, and analysis methods are always somewhat subjective.

A variety of approaches should be used to ensure that important information is not missed. For example with a **deductive** approach the researcher speculates in advance about what the results will be and the analysis either proves or disproves this. With an **inductive** approach general principles are identified because they emerge from an analysis of the data.

Appropriate **software tools** should be used to aid the process such as **data mining** software to identify patterns, and **QSR** NVivo and QSR N6 (NUD*IST) to aid qualitative analysis.

It is particularly important at this stage to watch out for potential **bias** in the results, for example considering the validity of transferring the research results to other contexts.

Reporting and presentation

When drawing up the report it is advisable to return to the client and the brief and ensure once again that the researcher has a clear **understanding of the decisions** that need to be made. The report should **address those decisions directly**, not just point out the results that the researcher happens to think are 'interesting'. Positive suggestions should be made to assist the client's decision making.

Limitations in the research should be clearly identified: 'further research would be needed to test the validity of these results in such and such a market'; 'the rapid change in this industry mean that these results may not be valid in three months time' and so on.

Proper account should be taken of the **client's level of understanding** of research findings: matters that are obvious to an experienced researcher may not be obvious at all to the client. Ideally the results should be conveyed in **presentations** to interested parties initially accompanies by discussions, brainstorming, workshops and the like.

It may be helpful to supply results in **digital format** to enable the client to drill down into areas of interest, and/or as 'raw data' to enable the client to carry out further analyses of their own.

Finally, usual reporting standards of course apply: in particular the final report should have a good **executive summary** and clear **recommendations** and action points, which may include suggestions for further research that could or should be carried out. The language used should be the language of the client's industry not the jargon of marketing research.

6   Research techniques and legal issues

Tutorial note. This is a rather vague question: almost any research techniques may be used in customer relationship management, depending on how you define customer relationship management. It is also not clear how much emphasis should be given to research techniques and how much to legal issues (more recent questions have tended to be much more specific about the weighting of their different parts). To help with your revision we have focused in our answer on the Data Protection Act and included some details of recent MRS guidance that you may not be aware of.

Customer relationship management (CRM)

Customer relationship management (CRM) is a vague term that means different things in different companies, **ranging** from the activities of a **basic sales department** to a highly sophisticated **loyalty card system** such as are operated by major retailers.

A 'CRM system' is also not clearly definable – it may vary considerably in features, depending on the software supplier – but in all cases it will have at its heart a customer database.

At its most sophisticated CRM involves tracking all the customers' transactions and relating them to their geo-demographic profile. Many of the basic characteristics of individuals, such as age, income, gender, culture, nationality and where they live are called geo-demographic characteristics and make up the geo-demographic profile of each consumer.

More **sophisticated CRM systems allocate individuals to market segments** by one or all of the following.

- Life-style characteristics eg hobbies and pastimes

- The stage they are at in the family life-cycle eg newly weds, with young children, with older children etc

- Their values and attitudes eg political, sexual and social orientation – this is sometimes called pyschographics

Legal issues

In the UK the use of such data is governed by the **Data Protection Act 1998 (DPA)**, the aim of which is to ensure that individuals have access to data which is held on them, and to give them some control over the ways in which that data is used. Awareness of the DPA is essential for anyone involved in processing 'personal data', which means data that identifies a living individual person. Personal data includes such things as the individual's name, address, National Insurance number and, where the individual has been recorded (eg on video for qualitative research) his or her image and voice.

The DPA sets down a number of principles including the following.

(a) Personal data shall be processed fairly and lawfully and shall not be processed unless the individual **agrees** to the processing and it is **necessary from the individual's point of view**, for example for the performance of a contract or compliance with legal obligations.

(b) Personal data cannot be used for purposes which have not been **specified in advance**.

(c) Personal data shall be adequate, relevant and not excessive in relation to the purpose or purposes for which they are processed. In other words you cannot collect data which is not directly relevant to your research.

(d) Personal data shall be accurate and, where necessary kept up to date.

(e) Personal data processed for any purpose or purposes shall not be kept for longer than is necessary for that purpose or purposes.

(f) Personal data which is collected in the UK may be transferred to other countries, but only to those which guarantee the individual the same rights as the DPA.

The DPA defines market research as 'The application of scientific research methods to obtain objective information on people's attitudes and behaviour based usually on representative samples of the relevant populations. The process **guarantees the confidentiality** of personal information in such a way that the data can only be used for research purposes.' The research will meet the strict terms of the *MRS Code of Conduct*. This is a voluntary code of practice which governs all of the Society's members, but the DPA gives weight to the Code, lending it increased authority.

The MRS code states that 'Members shall only use the term *confidential survey research* to describe research projects which are based upon respondent anonymity and do not involve the divulgence of identities or personal details of respondents to others except for research purposes.'

Classic research projects are confidential market research where the information gathered is used **only to understand and predict attitudes and behaviour**.

In projects that **do not** meet the requirements of classic research ('Category Six' projects) the information is used to **take direct action**, such as staff training, database enhancement, list building, or direct marketing aimed at the individuals contacted.

CRM-based research and the DPA

Clearly the very idea of a 'relationship' implies personal knowledge and such research will typically fall into **Category 6,** which covers all projects where some or all of the data will be used at a personal level for purposes in addition to or instead of those defined in the 1998 Act and the MRS Code as confidential research.

In September 2003 the MRS issued their *Draft Guidelines for Collecting Data for Mixed or Non-Market Research Purposes: Category 6*. Some of the key points are summarised below.

(a) The MRS Code of Conduct only applies to confidential survey research and so Category 6 projects cannot be covered by the Code. However, the basic ethical principles upon which the Code is based remain equally valid for all projects that involve interviewing individuals, and Category 6 projects are of course still subject to the Data Protection Act 1998.

(b) MRS Interviewer Identity (IID) Cards and standard 'Thank you' leaflets must not be used. The MRS Code of Conduct must not be mentioned.

(c) Category 6 projects need to meet the same criteria as those applied to personal data used for direct marketing – that is, they should conform to the conditions within the 1998 Act covering direct marketing (eg the respondent's right to prevent the processing of their data for direct marketing purposes, and to be told at the commencement of the interview that the data will be passed to a third party for direct marketing purposes). Those undertaking Category 6 projects should also be familiar with the Direct Marketing Association (DMA) Code of Conduct and the DMA data protection guidelines.

(d) Researchers should ensure that respondents give their informed consent to **each** purpose that their data will be used for (including confidential market research, if this is one of the purposes for which the data will be used), and that they have the opportunity to opt-out of any purposes to which they object.

7   MRS Code of Conduct

Tutorial note. It is difficult to know how best to structure an answer to this question because much of the MRS Code is structured around Researcher/Respondent/Client, not around specific research roles. Most points that apply to, say, fieldworkers also apply equally to focus group moderators. More recent questions have been more carefully written by the examiner.

At the time of writing (beginning of 2005) a draft revision to the MRS Code has been issued but this is still subject to a consultation exercise, so our answer refers only to the current (1999) version. Check the MRS website for the latest details, since the new version may well have been finalised and be in force by the time take your exam.

The MRS *Code of Conduct* ('the Code') is a **voluntary code of practice** which all MRS members are **obliged to follow**. The Code also **incorporates the principles of the Data Protection Act** 1998, and the ESOMAR/ICC *Code of Marketing and Social Research Practice.*

The **aim** of the Code is to ensure that **professional standards are maintained at all stages within the research process**. In general terms it is useful to all those mentioned in the question for similar reasons. If the code is complied with fully, researchers will know that they have maintained high standards of behaviour and kept within the law, and respondents can rest assured that they have been treated fairly and lawfully and that neither their personal data nor their responses will be misused.

The Code thus provides a **framework** which gives **guidance to researchers** and **reassures respondents** that their personal data is handled professionally and in confidence. As such, it plays an important part in the assurance of quality in market research.

(a) **Fieldworkers**

Fieldwork is the **actual data collection process**, for example personal interviewing, telephone interviewing or sending out postal or email questionnaires. It also includes the **day to day control** of these operations, and the **collection and checking of the returns**.

The code gives some guidance as to how fieldworkers should behave when dealing with respondents. The **basic principle** is that of **informed consent**.

Research is founded upon **willing co-operation**: this means that the fieldworker must obtain the respondent's permission before the research begins. For interviews with children, the fieldworker should seek the permission of the parent or responsible adult.

Research should be conducted **without unwelcome intrusion or harm to respondents**: there should be no attempt by fieldworkers to intimidate potential respondents, for example by obstructing their path or phoning them up repeatedly so that they co-operate in the end simply to make the fieldworker stop bothering them and wasting their time.

The principles of the Code also make it clear that fieldworkers should **inform** respondents of the **purpose** of the research and of the likely **length of time** it will take to collect the information, and they should assure respondents that their data will be treated **confidentially**. Every interview should therefore begin with a preamble explaining these things, and the interviewer should see to it that it really does take no longer than promised. If details of identity need to be collected for the purpose of later quality checks this should be explained to the respondent and suitable assurances given that the information will not be retained for longer than necessary to complete these checks.

Fieldworkers should act **honestly** at all times (A2) and **not make false claims** about their skills and experience. For instance a fieldworker who ignored this provision may be able to persuade respondents to divulge information that they would normally only divulge to some kind of specialist such as their doctor.

Fieldworkers should **not divulge identities or personal details** to others except for research purposes (A12). This implies that they should resist the temptation to discuss their work informally outside work, or at least they should not do so in such a way that individuals are identifiable.

Fieldworkers should **not attempt to influence** a respondent's opinions or attitudes on any issue except for experimental purposes (A13(h)). Fieldworkers may have strong views of their own about certain issues, but they should keep these to themselves when conducting interviews.

Marketing research must be carried out objectively. This might affect fieldworkers in the choice of respondents, for instance, when filling a quota: they should not let personal prejudices over matters such as race or gender influence their selection of people to interview; they should not limit their selection to people that they personally find attractive.

Finally fieldworkers should **ensure the security** of research records in their possession.

(b) **Questionnaire designers**

In accordance with the above, questionnaire designers are given clear instructions by the Code about information that must be included – an **explanation of the purpose of the questionnaire** and **appropriate assurances about confidentiality**.

There are a number of specific points in the code (A13) that directly affect the work of questionnaire designers.

(i)   Confidential survey research questionnaires should **not include questions that attempt to obtain information that might be used for certain other purposes** such as credit-rating, list compilation for direct marketing, industrial espionage, or fund raising.

(ii)   Questions should **not be framed** in a way that is intended to **influence the respondent on any issue**. For example a question about voting intentions should not be worded in such a way that it portrays a particular political party in a favourable or unfavourable light. A question such as: "Would the fact that Party X will reduce your tax bill by 10% persuade you to vote for them?" should be rewritten so that it excludes mention of a specific party and that it does not describe something as a 'fact' when it may not be so.

(c) **Focus group moderators**

Many of the points made about fieldworkers apply equally to moderators and need not be repeated. In a group discussion the moderator is in a position of some trust and authority, and this could be abused if proper standards are not followed.

Objectivity demands that the discussion is conducted in such a way that **everyone gets a chance to contribute**, not just those that the moderator happens to agree with.

The requirement to ensure that respondents are not harmed or adversely affected is relevant in the sense that some group members may be personally offended or upset by others. The moderator should make every attempt to avoid the discussion taking this turn and should certainly **not deliberately provoke conflict** that may affect individuals personally.

It is common for group discussions to be **recorded on audio tape or video, or observed** from another room, and if this is the intention **respondents should be told about it**, normally at the beginning of the session.

(d) **Respondents**

Many of the key points have been indicated already: the Code is of use to respondents because if it is adhered to they will not be deceived by researchers, and so on. There is in fact a section of the Code that sets out the **rights** of respondents in detail, reinforcing all of the above.

B3 Respondents' **co-operation** in a marketing research project is entirely **voluntary** at all stages. They must not be misled when being asked for co-operation.

B4 Respondents' **anonymity must be strictly preserved**. If the respondent on request from the Researcher has given permission for data to be passed on in a form which allows that respondent to be identified personally:

(a) the Respondent must first have been told to whom the information would be supplied and the purposes for which it will be used, and also

(b) the Researcher must ensure that the information will not be used for any non-research purpose and that the recipient of the information has agreed to conform to the requirements of the Code.

B5 The Researcher must take all reasonable precautions to ensure that Respondents are in **no way directly harmed or adversely affected** as a result of their participation in a marketing research project.

B6 The Researcher must take **special care** when interviewing **children and young people**. The informed consent of the parent or responsible adult must first be obtained for interviews with children.

B7 Respondents must be **told** (normally at the beginning of the interview) if **observation** techniques or **recording equipment** are used, except where these are used in a public place. If a respondent so wishes, the record or relevant section of it must be destroyed or deleted. Respondents' anonymity must not be infringed by the use of such methods.

B8 Respondents must be enabled to **check** without difficulty the **identity** and **bona fides of the Researcher**.

8 Ethical issues

In line with most professional bodies the MRS has issued clear guidelines for its members to help them conduct their work in a way that is acceptable to general society, in other words to work in accordance with appropriate **ethical** standards.

The MRS *Code of Conduct* ('the Code') is the code of practice that all MRS members are obliged to follow. The Code incorporates the principles of the Data Protection Act 1998, and the ESOMAR/ICC *Code of Marketing and Social Research Practice*, which has worldwide approval.

The aim of the Code is to ensure that professional standards are maintained at all stages within the research process.

(a) **The respondent**

Key ethical issues relating to the respondent in market research are how the respondent is treated at the time of the interview, what undertakings the interviewer makes to the respondent, how the data is collected, what is done with it.

The most important principle is that of **informed consent**. The interviewer should make it clear to the respondent what is the purpose of the research and how the information that is collected will be used.

(i) **Transparency** means that the respondent has a clear and unambiguous understanding of the purposes of collecting the information and the extent of the uses to which it can be put.

(ii) **Consent** means that at the time that the data is collected, individuals agree to their data being collected, and have the opportunity to withhold their agreement to any subsequent use of data.

The Code specifies a number of other important principles which researchers should bear in mind when dealing with respondents:

(i) Respondents should **not be harmed or adversely affected** as a result of taking part in the research. This could involve physical harm – hopefully not because the researcher gets violent, but it could be dangerous to conduct interviews in certain circumstances, for example if the respondent is driving or operating some kind of machinery, or in a state of emotional stress or facing negative financial or professional consequences.

BPP
PROFESSIONAL EDUCATION

(ii)   If the interviewer promises **anonymity** then identifying information about the respondent should only be stored with the data collected for as long as is necessary for quality control purposes (if the researcher intends to make a second contact to check up on the accuracy and veracity of the original fieldworkers data collection).

(iii)   Data can be collected on an **attributable basis** for a market research related purpose, but only if this is done with the full consent and knowledge of the respondent.

(b) The client

Although clients are not governed by the Code certain ethical issues arise and the Code specifies that researchers should ensure that clients are aware of the existence of a code and the need to comply with it. Clients are of course subject to the provisions of Data Protection legislation, and the contract with the researcher may stipulate client compliance with the Code.

The **key ethical issues** for clients relate to the **way the relationship with the researcher is handled** and **way the research data is used**.

Regarding the **relationship**:

(i)   Unless otherwise agreed clients should not assume that they have exclusive use of the researcher's services

(ii)   Clients should not normally invite more than four agencies to tender in writing for a project. If they do so, they should disclose how many invitations to tender they are seeking.

(iii)   Clients should not disclose details of the researcher's market research proposals and cost quotations to third parties, particularly not to influence quotations from other researchers

(iv)   In the case of syndicated research where there are multiple clients, none of the clients may disclose the findings of the research to third parties without the researcher's permission

(v)   Clients may, if they wish, arrange for checks to be made (at their own expense) on the quality of the research work

Regarding the **data**, where any of the findings of a research project are published by the client, the client has a responsibility to ensure that these are not misleading. The researcher must be consulted and agree in advance the form and content of publication, and must take action to correct any misleading statements about the research and its findings.

(c) The researcher

The researcher has responsibilities both to the respondent and the client and to other agencies and the industry as a whole.

Obligations to treat **respondents** and their data in an ethical way are outlined in the first part of this answer. Additionally, the researcher has a duty as a data controller to notify the information commissioner about the extent, types and uses of the data they collect. In the UK the **Data Protection Act** sets out eight data protection principles and amongst other things these require researchers not to collect more information about a respondent (personal data) than is necessary for the task at hand, to take special care over the collection and storage of sensitive information, and to ensure that personal data is not transferred to an area which does not have legal safeguards equivalent to the Data Protection Act.

The Code contains a number of provisions relating to researchers that are intended to ensure ethical dealings between researchers and their **clients**. These include the following.

(i)   The Researcher must inform the Client if the work to be carried out for that Client is to be combined or syndicated in the same project with work for other Clients but must not disclose the identity of such clients without their permission.

(ii)   The Researcher must inform the Client as soon as possible in advance when any part of the work for that Client is to be subcontracted outside the Researcher's own organisation (including the use of any outside consultants). On request the Client must be told the identity of any such subcontractor.

(iii) The Researcher must conform to current agreed professional practice relating to the keeping of such records for an appropriate period of time after the end of the project. On request the Researcher must supply the Client with duplicate copies of such records provided that such duplicates do not breach anonymity and confidentiality requirements

(iv)   The Researcher must not disclose the identity of the Client (provided there is no legal obligation to do so) or any confidential information about the latter's business, to any third party without the Client's permission.

(v)   The Researcher must provide the Client with all appropriate technical details of any research project carried out for that Client.

Regarding **other agencies** the Code makes a number of stipulations.

(i)   MRS members shall not knowingly take advantage, without permission, of the unpublished work of a fellow member which is the property of that member.

(ii)   Members shall not place other members in a position in which they might unwittingly breach any part of this Code of Conduct. (This might otherwise be done, for example, if some of the work is sub-contracted: this provision ensures that researchers cannot 'pass the buck' for breaches of the code.)

(iii) Unless paid for by the client, a specification for a project drawn up by one research agency is the property of that agency and may not be passed on to another agency without the permission of the originating research agency.

(iv)   Researchers must not unjustifiably criticise or disparage other researchers.

Finally a variety of provisions are made in the Code about maintaining the reputation of the **market research profession**, for example that research should be carried out objectively and in accordance with established scientific principles; that it should conform to any relevant legislation; that nothing should be done that could bring discredit on the market research profession; and that conclusions are not disseminated unless they are adequately supported by the data gathered.

9   Marketing ethics and social responsibility

(a)   I would be most **concerned** about the proposal put to me by Dell Boy Enterprises as much of it appears to be in **breach of the Data Protection Act** and in **breach of many of the provisions of the MRS Code of Conduct**. There are also **concerns** about undertaking market research work for **products** that may be of **doubtful social and legal acceptability**.

Any market research work undertaken should not damage the industry goodwill, nor the trust that is necessary to maintain the integrity of the industry and its output. By taking on the proposed work in this case, I would be concerned that it might **damage** the **professionalism and professional reputation of my practice**. I would also be concerned that the results of any research may be in **breach of confidentiality** rules and laws.

(b) There appear to be several **social issues**. The first is the part that the market research would be playing in the **potential incitement of under age drinking** of alcohol for which the client wishes to target market the product. The second social issue would be the possible **social implications of the personal services and medicine sales over the Internet**. I would be rather wary and cautious of associating my professional market research company without further details and assurances of the potential moral and social issues involved.

The principal **legal issue** that would concern me would be **potential breaches of the Data Protection Act 1998**. By indicating that Dell Boy want the database procured by 'Any means possible' indicates that the client appears to be wanting to capture data and use it for a process for which it was not originally intended. Unless the subject of the market research gives specific consent, the company may not use the data.

As a market researcher, there is a legal requirement that my organisation must register annually with the Data Protection Registrar, whether the details of the research were held electronically or on hard copy. If the client were to hold any of the results of the market research on their files, I would want to ensure they were also similarly registered.

I would need to point out to the client that, under the provisions of the data protection legislation, it would be illegal to use secretly filmed interviews obtained in the process of market research as when an organisation collects information from individuals it should be honest and open about why it wants the information and it should have a legitimate reason for processing the data and for what they intend to use the information.

Likewise if the firm intends to sell the data commercially, it must indicate to whom, if anybody, they intend to give the personal data. Given the information we have, it seems Dell Boy are not intending to follow this procedure.

(c) It would appear that the **provisions of the MRS Code of Conduct have been breached** in several areas. For example:

(i) The proposed market research appears to run the risk of not being objective as the company may be using the data for purposes outside the original market research project.

(ii) The possibility of sending information to the operation in the USA may breach either national or international legislation, depending on what the term 'Personal Services' means.

(iii) The unauthorised sale of data to other organisations is clearly against the Code of Practice.

(iv) The covert obtaining and proposed unauthorised use of video data is in contravention of the Code, as subject participants should be notified of recording in advance of the event. Subsequent probable breach of subjects' anonymity is also likely to be in breach of the Code.

(v)   I would be concerned that market research of alcohol for young people could in some way involve a breach of the researcher's duty of special care when interviewing young people.

(vi)   The involvement of market researchers in potentially under age alcohol sales and 'Personal Services' are both seem to run the risk of being in breach of the Code's requirement not to bring discredit on the marketing research profession.

(vii)   By getting involved with the unauthorised video and dissemination of marketing data both in the UK and overseas, the market researchers would be running a serious risk of being in breach of the Code's requirement not to become involved in non research activities.

(viii) The client seems to intend using the proposed research for a variety of uses. Should any of it be agreed to proceed and should there be any intention to publish any of the findings, I would want to be consulted in advance of publication to agree the form and content of the publication and to ensure the correctness of the material.

(ix)   I would need to ensure that the client is aware of the existence of this Code of Practice and the need for the researchers to comply with its requirements.

10 Tutorial question: Qualitative and quantitative

(a) **Qualitative methods of marketing research**

Market research is the gathering, recording and analysing of facts about problems relating to the transfer and sales of goods and services from producer to consumer or user.

Qualitative methods tend to be used when suitable concrete statistical data is not available or when it is considered unable to provide an adequate basis for forecasting on its own. Qualitative research is useful for 'depth interviews', 'focus groups', 'repertory grid' and 'observation'. These are the techniques that involve the use of human judgement, flair and experience. Methods might also include expert opinion, the Delphi method and executive judgement.

Quantitative methods use statistical techniques based on the analysis of past numeric data. Quantitative research is useful for experimentation, sampling and surveys. The techniques used could include sampling theory, probability and the normal distribution.

(b) Data gathering can be obtained from primary data (original research commissioned by the marketing department) or secondary data (data and information that already exists in the market (external data) or within the firm's records (internal data)).

Tools used to gather the data from the above sources include the following.

Primary data

(i)   **Syndicated research** is the periodical gathering of consumer and trade information by firms such as AC Nielsen or TGI. The surveys are conducted on behalf of a number of organisations and the costs recovered from the clients of the data gathering firm.

(ii)   **Omnibus surveys** are carried out by a research firm who, in effect, sub-lets space thus allowing 'piggy backing' on a wider survey or ongoing surveys.

(iii)   **Made to measure research** can be carried out by the principal or their agent and gathers data for a carefully designed and specific purpose.

(iv)   **Experimentation** – in a controlled environment where stimuli are introduced to observe and measure the effect they have.

(v)   **Census or sample survey** – asking questions of the target market population or sample frame(s).

(vi)   **Observation** – watching participants as they undertake some activity – eg shopping flows in a supermarket.

Secondary data

(i)   **Internal – from records** such as order and sales statistics, stock records and delivery details – these sources will allow the researcher to build up a picture of historical consumption patterns.

(ii)   **External data** can be gathered from a wide range of sources such as Directories, Computer databases (eg Acorn or Prestel), Associations (eg Chartered Accountancy Institutes), Government Agencies (eg DTI), syndicated services (eg Nielsen Retail Index) and other published sources (eg Economist, ABI Inform)

(c)

	Advantages	Disadvantages
Syndicated research	Costs are shared between organisations	Too expensive for any individual or organisation to collect
Omnibus surveys	Fast turnround of results, low cost, useful for researching minority groups	Short non complex questionnaire, low control of researchers
Made to measure research	Highly suited to specific applications, useful for quantitative research, useful for in depth and psychological interviews	Relatively high cost, quality variable due to competitive nature of this type of research
Experimentation	External influences can be eliminated	Results can be subjective
Census or sample survey	Specific to a target market	Questions can be limited and highly structured
Observation	Useful for taking into account when designing store planagrams that need to take account of customer behaviour	Results can be hypothetical
Internal research from records	Inexpensive, objective, high level of control over the data	Data historic and may not be future relevant. May be insufficient or inappropriate heads of analysis
External data	Not cheap to use. Data gathered by experienced researchers	Can be much less expensive than original research. Data may only be an approximation of the required sample frame and target market

(d) An example of the preference of qualitative over quantitative methods would be in **researching of packaging** for different types of teas or coffees. In qualitative research, group interviews could be used and the respondents asked questions by a skilled interviewer. The interviewer would carefully lead discussions which would allow the group members to develop their ideas in an unstructured way. By recording the session(s) it would allow later in depth analysis, which would give an insight that would be concealed or missed by preconceived question in conventional surveys. In addition quantitative surveys would not allow the creative and spontaneous thoughts that the qualitative process described above would allow.

11 Tutorial question: ICT and marketing research

(Chosen organisation – a franchised motor car dealer in High Street, Anytown.)

REPORT

To: S Moss Head of the Marketing Team
From: A Pass
Date: 13 June 20X3
Subject: New communication technologies

Further to your request for an explanation of recent Information Communication Technologies (ICTs) and their use to improve the quality of marketing decisions, please find below the definition of terms and a discussion of their use.

Definition of terms

(a) **Internet**: the international network of computer and telecommunication systems that enables the global transmission of data and information. Effectively it is a network of networks, linked by 'gateways'.

The dealer can use the Internet as a medium to advertise, to inform of models and special offers as well as using the e-mail facilities to e-mail clients whose details are held on database with communications such as special offers, or advising customers that their vehicle is due for a service.

(b) **Intranet**: a network based on Internet protocols belonging to an organisation, usually a corporation, accessible only by the organisation's members, employees, or others with authorisation. An intranet's pages look and act just like any other web pages, but the firewall surrounding an intranet fends off unauthorised access. Like the Internet itself, intranets are used to share information. Secure intranets are much less expensive to build and manage than private networks based on proprietary protocols.

An intranet can be used to circulate information around the firm. An example may be forthcoming promotions, or details of local events such as the plan for a local motor show. It can also be used to access internal databases on items such as the availability of spare parts or servicing dates and times. This can enable more staff to add value to their information services.

(c) An **extranet** is an intranet that is partially accessible to authorised outsiders. Whereas an intranet resides behind a firewall and is accessible only to people who are members of the same company or organisation, an extranet provides various levels of accessibility to outsiders. You can access an extranet only if you have a valid username and password, and your identity determines which parts of the extranet you can view. Extranets in various guises (such as 'business exchanges') are becoming a very popular means for business partners to share information and process transactions.

This can enable dealers to become part of the information system of the supplier (Ford have long had electronic data interchange links with their business partners). If the dealer has customers who have fleets of cars, they too can become part of the secure web. Banks are a case in point, account-holding customers can now access information derived from the relevant secure part of the banks' network with the appropriate access codes. (They can only access the information and request changes, not actually change the bank's data themselves.)

(d) A **data warehouse** is a centrally stored source of data that has been extracted from various organisational databases and standardised and integrated for use throughout an organisation. Data warehouses contain a wide variety of data that present a coherent picture of business conditions at a single point in time.

This could enable the sales and service departments to pool their respective databases to give them improved customer profiles, eg the service records could be used by the sales department to identify customers with high mileage vehicles who may be an ideal target market for appropriate products.

(e) **Data mining** is a method of using databases to look for hidden patterns in a group of data. For example, data mining software can help retail companies find customers with common interests. The term is commonly misused to describe software that presents data in new ways. True data mining software doesn't just change the presentation, but actually discovers previously unknown relationships among the data.

Data mining could, for example, be used to match associated traits in buyer behaviour. For example, motorists who book in for accident repairs more than once in two years and have also revealed low mileage between annual services could be targeted to inform them of tuition in advanced driving techniques run by the garage.

12 Continuous and *ad hoc*

Tutorial note. To answer this question well you will need to think carefully about the housing market and the possible information needs of those involved in it and apply your knowledge. General comments about the different types of continuous research – tracking studies and so on – will not earn you many marks. Because we have had the opportunity to research this question our answer is rather more specific than yours could have been, unless you happen to be an expert in this market, and rather longer. We have mentioned a number of specific sources since this information may be helpful for your revision in a variety of contexts.

Continuous research is research that is repeated at regular intervals such as every week, every month or every quarter.

The business in question – a national chain of estate agents which we will assume is based in the UK and dealing in domestic property – is fortunate in the sense that a great deal of reliable continuous research is **already undertaken** into its market and into factors in its market that are of relevance, and much of this is either freely available or available at relatively little cost. For the purposes of this answer we will assume that the estate agent is solely engaged in selling and renting properties, although in reality most such organisations will have some involvement in related activities such as property development and financial services, all of which would add to the information needs.

On the other hand it will need to collate secondary data from a large variety of different sources with that from its own information systems to gain a full and accurate picture of its market. Its own information systems will need to be designed or re-organised with this in mind.

The estate agents will require **continuous information** on matters such as the following.

- Property prices and volume of sales
- Income levels
- Demographics of buyers, renters and sellers
- Advertising media effectiveness
- Competitors' activities

Property price information and sales volume should be monitored on a weekly basis; for the other items monthly or quarterly information will probably be adequate.

Property prices and volume of sales

The estate agents can continuously monitor their own records of current properties on their books, their asking prices, numbers sold per period and eventual selling prices. It will be simple and very useful to map this data to readily available demographic data such as ACORN (A Classification of Residential Neighbourhoods) which classifies postcodes into 17 distinct groups, which, in turn, contain 56 'typical' ACORN neighbourhood categories. For example a residential area just north of BPP's offices has the following ACORN profile.

W14 0BJ

Type 18: Multi-ethnic young, converted flats

(1.14% of the population live in this ACORN type)

Likely Characteristics

This type is almost exclusively a London phenomenon, with high concentrations in most inner and outer London boroughs.

Family Income :	High	Interest in current affairs :	Very high
Housing - with Mortgage :	Low	Educated - to degree :	Very high
Couples with Children :	Low	Have satellite TV :	Low

ACORN includes information such as the typical age range of residents, ethnic population, details of household composition in the area (single households, number of children etc), and typical residential patterns (owner-occupier, council tenant, second home), most popular newspapers, and entertainment preferences.

The estate agent is likely to have more detailed information of its own about the **types** of property on its books (flat or house, age, detached, semi-detached, number of bedrooms, size of garden if any, etc), whether it is **for sale or for rent**. All of this information is likely to be organised by **region**, since property prices vary hugely in different parts of the UK and comparisons between properties in London and the South East, say, and properties in other parts of the country will not be useful for day to day management purposes.

The estate agent may wish to collect price data from other estate agents for comparative purposes. This could be done simply by registering on competitors' lists as a potential buyer, but it would be an onerous task to compile all the data continuously on a national basis. In the UK there are relatively few estate agents that operate nationally, but there are many smaller chains that deal in a particular region, and many individual businesses that only deal in properties in their immediate vicinity. In view of this it will be most useful to collect data from competitors on a local basis and produce an analysis and comparison no more than once a month.

A further source of information that should be continuously monitored is the Office of the Deputy Prime Minister (www.odpm.gov.uk), which conducts a good deal of research into a number of aspects of the housing market, such as the House Price Index and the Survey of English Housing which records statistical data about the national housing stock categorised in several different ways.

Income levels

This data has a direct impact on how much people can afford to pay for properties. Monthly statistics are available from the website of the Office of National Statistics (ONS) (www.statistics.gov.uk) which publishes an Average Earnings Index. This measures how earnings in the latest month compare with those for the last base year (2000) when the index took the value of 100. The AEI is based on information obtained from the ONS's Monthly Wages and Salary Survey.

Information about levels of lending for mortgages is regularly published by banks and building societies and the estate agents simply need to monitor the financial press. Regular statistics and forecasts are also freely available from the website of the Council of Mortgage Lenders (www.cml.org.uk), whose members undertake around 98% of UK residential mortgage lending.

Demographic data

We have mentioned that ACORN is a source for demographic data, but this information is limited and it is not updated as often as the estate agents might wish. For more detailed information and clues as to the future there are a variety of government publications from the ONS that should be monitored, notably *Social Trends* (published annually), which includes an entire chapter on Housing and a wealth of other information which may be relevant, and the *Monthly Digest of Statistics* which contains a variety of economic, business and social data.

Advertising effectiveness

The estate agent will use a number of different media for advertising, in particular local newspaper advertisements but also door drops and For Sale boards outside the properties on its books, and it is likely to have a fairly elaborate website. The effectiveness of each can be tracked continuously in-house simply by asking enquirers where they saw the agency or a particular property advertised.

The best source of information on regional newspaper readership, including free newspapers, is JICREG (www.jicreg.co.uk) which has an online database that provides regularly updated circulation figures, analysed by gender, age and social grade (the ABC1 system).

Competitors activities

The activities of competitors should be kept under continual observation. This can be done by scanning their advertisements, visiting their branches and their websites if any.

Ad hoc research (one-off research projects) could include all manner of things, as the information needs arise. Here are some suggestions.

(a) Attitude research amongst different kinds of customers into perceptions of the agency as compared with its competitors

(b) Research into local issues on house prices and house buying, for instance the impact of a new road or a new shopping centre

(c) Branch location comparisons, for example the extent to which the success or otherwise of a branch is influenced by proximity to other businesses involved in house-buying such as banks, building societies and solicitors.

13 Developments in research techniques

> *Tutorial note.* You will probably be glad to know that 'history questions' like this are not common in the exam. This is the only example from recent years. Obviously you must be able to show that you know what kind of research techniques are available today, but it is questionable whether you need to know whether or not it was not possible to do that research up to a century ago ... except in the event that your market research project involves the use of data that relates to times long past.
>
> In our answer we interpret the question as one that asks you to demonstrate an understanding of why market research has become so much more relevant to modern life and (in outline only) how modern thinking and technology has expanded research possibilities.
>
> On the other hand, perhaps it is true that there is no real difference between gathering everyone in their place of birth and asking them your questions (as in the case of New Testament Joseph and Mary) compared with phoning them up to ask them your questions, wherever they happen to be. It is quicker and more convenient to phone them, but you are still just asking questions: is telephone research really a 'new technique'?

It could be argued that research with at least some of the characteristics of 'market research' has a very ancient history. Surveys such as the **Domesday Book** come to mind, as does the census that features in the New Testament story of the **Nativity**.

In both cases the intention was to **record information about people** to help with **decision making**, even though the 'decision' was a relatively simple one about how much tax could be raised by the authorities.

It could also be argued that whenever research has been conducted with people as the subject it has always aimed to discover the answer(s) to one or both of **two basic questions**, and again, there is nothing new about wishing to know the information that will be gathered as a result.

> **How many** times per period do you do X?
>
> What is your **opinion** of X (and why)?

However, the real issues are: whether it has always been **perceived** that there is a **need** to know what people do or think; **how much** representative information it is **practical** to collect; and what can be done with the information once it has been collected – how it can be **analysed and interpreted**.

In modern times the development of market research parallels social and industrial/commercial developments and the rise of the marketing concept.

(a) Originally a **'market'** was a physical place, where **buyers and sellers met up** and exchanged things, so that they both got what they needed: a sheep in exchange for three bags of corn, say.

(b) The production of goods before the industrial revolution was usually small-scale and aimed at local customers. Buyers and sellers had **direct contact**, which made it easy for sellers to know who their buyers were and find out their needs and wants. There was **no real need for marketing** in the modern sense.

(c) During the industrial revolution (18th and 19th century), production became organised into larger units. As towns grew bigger, producers and the people they sold to began to be **geographically separated**.

(d) This division was a clue to the future, but right **up until the early 20th century** it was still most important to **produce enough** of a product to satisfy strong demand. Thinking about 'customer needs' was secondary, at best, and so there was **little need for 'market research'** in anything like the modern sense.

(e) The production orientation is epitomised by the famous comment attributed to **Henry Ford** about his Model T car, which customers could buy in **"any colour, so long as it's black"**. Whether or not Ford really made the comment, the fact remains that it was **inconvenient** for his company's production process to make cars in colours other than black. Black was the quickest-drying paint and changing colours meant flushing out the production system. The **customer's behaviour and wishes were unimportant** because there was **no competition** and the customers had **no choice**.

(f) **Mass production** techniques have increased the volume and range of goods on the market. For most products and services the ability now exists to produce much more than is demanded. Meanwhile developments in transportation and communications have made it possible to reach buyers in any part of the world.

(g) Simple **mass marketing techniques** were first used in the 1950s for fast-moving consumer goods (FMCG) such as washing powder and groceries. The focus switched from **'how to produce and supply enough'** to **'how to increase demand'**. Modern marketing techniques, and marketing as a **managerial function**, grew out of this switch.

(h) Marketing techniques have grown in importance and sophistication as **competition** (that is, consumer **choice**) and **geographical separation** have increased, especially since the 1980s. From concentrating on advertising and sales, marketing methods have become wide-ranging, complex and scientific.

Modern marketing is about **identifying ever-changing customer needs** in a **global market** and continually creating new products that **satisfy those needs**. Many organisations have adopted this as the **philosophy** that drives all of their business functions. To inform the decisions that need to be made **market research** is essential.

Market research methods have **developed to meet modern information needs** with the help of modern **technology** so as to reflect all of these social, industrial and commercial changes.

(a) Developments such as **tape recording** and **video recording** date back at least to the beginning of the last century but they are now so cheap and easily available that information that could not practicably be collected before can now be gathered and analysed routinely, with ease, and in large quantities.

(b) Continual developments throughout the 20th century in understanding of human **psychology and behaviour** mean that questions are now asked that would not have been asked before and actions are observed and interpreted in ways that were not considered before.

(c) **Computers** and associated technologies make it possible to collect and analyse much larger quantities of data than was possible before, much more quickly than before, and using mathematical and statistical techniques that, although not new, would not have been feasible before, in terms of time and cost and given the volume of data that needs to be collected to obtain representative results, perhaps on a global basis.

(d) **Telecommunications** make it quick and easy to contact and keep in touch with a much larger sample of people than before, and those people may be located in much more widely geographically spread places.

14 Marketing database

Memo

To: Tom Crapper
From: B. Day
Date: 31 July 20X3

The processes for setting up and maintaining a database

Databases are usually created and maintained centrally on a computer, often with distributed access via a local area network (a series of computers linked together on one site) or via an intranet (like the Internet, but on secure links between the firm's various geographically diverse sites). Such a single corporate database is useful for several reasons.

(a) Data is common between many users

(b) It avoids data duplication found where files are kept by different users

(c) Consistency in the organisation's use of data, and in the accuracy of data accessed by different users, because all records are centrally maintained and updated

(d) Flexibility in the way in which shared data can be queried, analysed and formatted by individual users for specific purposes, without altering the store of data itself

(e) Speed of data retrieval

You ask 'What types of information would be required to set up a database?'. We already have some of the information required for a database, items such as customer name and address. However there is much more that can be so stored for marketing purposes as shown in the table below.

Element	Examples
Customer or company details	Account numbers, names, addresses and contact (telephone, fax, e-mail) details; basic 'mailing list' data, relationship to other customers. For business customers these fields might include sales contact, technical contact, parent company or subsidiaries, number of employees and so on
Professional details	Company; job title; responsibilities - especially for business-to-business marketing; industry type
Personal details	Gender, age, number of people at the same address, spouse's name, children, interests, and any other relevant data known, such as newspapers read, journals subscribed to
Transaction history	What products/services are ordered, date, how often, how much is spent (turnover), payment methods
Call/contact history	Sales or after sales service calls made, complaints/queries received, meetings at shows/exhibitions, mailings sent, etc

Element	Examples
Credit/payment history	Credit rating, amounts outstanding, aged debts
Credit transaction details	Items currently on order, dates, prices, delivery arrangements
Special account details	Membership number, loyalty or incentive points earned, discount awarded), where customer loyalty or incentive schemes are used

How are such files stored on the database?

There are two basic kinds of database.

Flat systems are easy to build and maintain, and are quite adequate for applications such as mailing lists, or membership databases. Spreadsheet software might be used for this purpose.

Relational systems (Microsoft Access is a basic example) are harder to construct because the data items are linked and structured in various ways. Marketing analysis databases have some kind of structure to enable researchers to retrieve different sets of information, as required, from the same basic data.

(a) **Fields** are the labels given to types of data. A simple customer database, for example, might include fields such as: *Title, First name, Last name, Address fields*, and *other contact* details.

(b) **Records** are the collection of fields relevant to one entry. So all the above data fields for a particular customer make up one customer record.

(c) **Tables** are collections of records that describe similar data, eg all the customer records in a given sales area may be stored in a table.

(d) **Databases** are collections of all the tables relating to a particular set of information.

Once entered the database management system (DBMS) will allow you to:

- Find particular records, using search criteria such as account number, name or postcode.

- Sort records alphabetically, numerically or by date, in ascending or descending order.

- Interrogate records, based on a set of criteria, from one or more linked tables.

- Calculate statistical information such as purchase orders or payment histories.

- Format selected data for a variety of uses, as reports, forms, mailing labels, charts and diagrams.

Data will be captured in a variety of ways.

- Manual input
- Scanned in from paper documents
- Captured by EPOS/EFTPOS systems
- Imported in various formats from other systems
- Purchased from another organisation

Computer input data integrity checks

The integrity of new data can be verified by various methods when it is initially entered into a system. For example, computerised forms for data entry can contain a variety of elements that help to avoid human error and bad data.

Pre-defined responses such as the ones below require the user to select the appropriate option.

(a) Radio buttons force the user to choose one and only one of a number of options eg

Reason for studying

○ Gain qualification required for present employment

◉ Gain qualification required for future employment

○ Gain optional qualification for present employment

○ Gain optional qualification for future employment

○ General interest

(b) Check boxes allow more than one choice, but still from a limited range of options

Please check ALL that apply:

☑ Check this box if you want

☐ You may check this one as well

☐ You may leave some blank

☐ You may check them all if you like

☑ Some can start out checked

☑ You may uncheck some if you like

(c) Lists/menus operate in a similar way to either radio buttons or check boxes, but the selectable option or options drop down instead of being written out (this saves space on screen).

Manual data integrity checks

To ensure manually input data is correct, validation takes place via pre-programmed tests and rules by the data entry program to ensure that data input is reasonable.

(a) Format checks test the data in each input area against rules governing whether it should be numeric, alphabetic or a combination of the two and whether it should have a minimum or maximum number of characters.

(b) Range checks test that the data is within an appropriate range.

(c) Existence checks compare the input data with some other piece of data in the system, to see if it is reasonable.

(d) Completeness checks ensure that all required data items have been entered.

Duplication

You query the problem of duplication within a database. Software should be able to compare a common field such as postcode and either delete duplicates automatically or generate a report for further investigation. This may be more problematic in business-to-business marketing, where several different businesses may operate out of the same location, or the same business may operate out of multiple locations.

In conclusion, you can see that modern database software and procedures eliminate duplication, and have wide ranging integrity checks to minimise errors in the data they contain.

15 Data mining

(a) Data Mining is the **exploration** and **analysis**, by **automatic** or **semiautomatic means**, of **large quantities of data** using **statistical analysis tools** and various types of **artificial intelligence techniques** such as neural networks in order to **discover meaningful patterns and rules**. The **goal** of data mining is to allow a company to **improve its marketing, sales and customer support operations through better understanding of its customers**. (Berry & Linoff, 1997 (adapted)).

Firms such as Barclaycard (via their data input processes), Tesco and Sainsbury (via their EPOS swipe loyalty cards) have built up large volumes of data, not just on customers and their accounts, but also on their spending and payment patterns and product profiles.

The **cost of computing power and storage** has **fallen** dramatically over the last two decades and especially so over the last few years. This has **enabled large volumes** of data to be **stored**. Also as the **relational database** has become commonplace, this has enabled **data** to be **manipulated** to turn it into **information**, then **knowledge**, then a **state of commercial wisdom**.

The **information-rich industries** such as telecommunications, insurance and financial services are operating in a highly competitive market and in order to build in **competitive advantage** (increasingly in service industries in the UK) and to offer their products for mass customisation, they are using **data mining to tailor their product offerings** to provide benefits that most closely **match the needs of differing consumers**.

Examples of relationships or patterns that data mining might uncover could be:

Relationship/ Discovery	Comment
Classification or cluster	These terms refer to the identification of patterns within the database between a range of data items. For example, data mining may find that young people between the ages of 18 and 22 with low credit scores are more likely to purchase mobile phones for the first time (the undergraduate population away from home for the first time). This group could then be targeted when marketing material is produced/distributed.
Association	One event can be linked or correlated to another. For example, it has been found that DIY customers who buy paint also buy brushes (but not the other way round).
Forecasting	Trends are identified within the data that can be extrapolated into the future.

(b) **Most data mining models are either**:

- **Predictive**: using known observations to predict future events (for example, predicting the probability that a recipient will opt out of an e-mail list).

- **Descriptive**: interrogating the database to identify patterns and relationships (for example, profiling the audience of a particular advertising campaign).

Some of the key statistical techniques used in data mining

Neural networks: non-linear predictive models or formulas that adjust inputs and weightings through 'training'

Decision-trees: paths are followed towards a solution or result, branching at decision points which are governed by rules (is gender male? Yes/No) giving a complex picture of possible outcomes

Classification techniques: assigning people to predetermined classes based on their profile data (in complex combinations)

Clustering: identifying occurrences in the database with similar characteristics and grouping them into clusters

(c) Data can be mined to **identify** which products or promotions should be **offered to attract particular customers** to the business and which products or services should be **linked** in **promotional offers** (for example, Boots the Chemist (who have their own 'Advantage' loyalty Card) have linked offers of their own brand sun tan products to their own brand travel insurance).

Data mining can be used for **market research purposes**. For example, Tesco might wish to test customer reaction to a new brand of curry sauce. It could use its loyalty card data to identify large users of Indian cooking products and their shopping characteristics. Data mining can also be used to identify which customers are the most profitable and worth retaining.

Loyalty cards get customers to increase their spend in one store. Most retailers who have launched a loyalty scheme experience a 1-4% sales uplift. Given that, for example, Tesco's UK sales are over £20bn per year, that small percentage represents a significant consolidation.

Via data mining, retailers **scrutinise the shopper as an individual**. For example, the 'Nectar' card asks how many people live in your house, the ages of those under 18, the number of cars you have and your total household mileage. The Clubcard form puts its questions about dietary preferences and who you live with; such information means that retailers' marketing communications are addressed to someone who they know doesn't buy their product, but looks as if they could.

Retailers use loyalty card knowledge to find new markets, plan new range rollouts and manage fresh food - and in the process **save operational costs and advertising, direct mail and market research costs**. Having discovered their individual customers they sell the analysis on to their manufacturers, in the knowledge of which products are winners and losers.

16 Data fusion

> *Tutorial note.* In part (a) you should outline a minimum of three potential problems or describe two potential problems in detail. There should be some reference to the effect of each problem on the resultant research. Better answers will provide more detailed descriptions of the problems and/or deeper awareness of the potential effects.
>
> In part (b) you should address each of the problems that you discussed in part (a). Examples should demonstrate that you recognise how to apply each 'solution' The best answers will provide a convincing solution and illustration for each problem mentioned.

(a) **Potential problems when using data fusion in research**

Data fusion (also called 'statistical matching') is the process whereby two or more different data sources are combined to provide further information about consumers or markets. For example, a company can fuse its own survey results with external data such as BMRB's Target Group Index, a survey carried out at regular intervals which combines product usage with media exposure.

Problems that the researcher may face include the following.

(i) **Incompatible technologies**. For example, data stored in a Microsoft Access database may not be compatible with data in a database written in an old Cobol program and stored on a proprietary mainframe computer. Many large organisations, such as banks and insurance companies have vast amounts of data stored in so-called legacy systems that may have been in use since the 1960s. In the worst case it will not be possible to fuse the data for new research purposes at all.

(ii) **Incompatible field formats and entries**. Something as innocuous as a space or a punctuation mark can cause problems: for example, one database may store postcodes in the form EC1V 0JR and another, without the space, as EC1V0JR. This would cause problems in extracting the first part of the postcode. One source may abbreviate a title as 'Rev', while the other has 'Rev.', so that identical categories would be treated as distinct Other examples include differences in field length, and inconsistencies between numeric, alphabetic and alpha-numeric fields.

(iii) It may not be possible to find a **common link** between the datasets to be fused. For the data to be transferred from the 'donor' survey to the 'recipient' survey there must be a number of questions or categories that gives rise to variables common to both surveys. The most obvious examples of linking variables are postcode, age, gender, and income bracket, and while most surveys would include questions on all of these if one of them did not include, say, male/female information because it was not felt to be relevant to the original research, then that could limit the value of fusing the data. It may not be valid to assume that respondents would have given the same answers irrespective of whether they were male or female.

(iv) Similar variables in two datasets may not have been **measured** in the same way, leading to difficulty in comparing findings. Different **category boundaries** may be used in each survey. For example, one survey may have asked respondents to tick a box to identify their age group (0-18; 19-30; 31-40 etc.) whereas the other may have different 'age' categories (0-21; 22-35; 36-45 etc.). The research client may be particularly interested in, say, the distinction between respondents in their twenties as opposed to those in their thirties, but the fused data would not give valid information.

(v) Identical variables may exist in both surveys but they may not be **computer coded** in the same way, so that a computer analysis would not recognise that they represented the same data. The results in the fused data would be at best incomplete and at worst entirely invalid.

(vi) When fusing data from two countries difficulties could arise because of **language differences** (for example would 'M' for Monsieur be recognised as the same thing as 'Mr'; 'Oui/Non' as 'Yes/No'?) and **country conventions**, such as different formats for postcodes. Again results would be incomplete and invalid.

(vii) Researchers need to be aware that there are **legal and ethical** restrictions on what they can do with data. A data fusion exercise may give rise to information that could be abused and which the respondent did not agree to provide.

(b) **Steps to minimise these problems**

The **first step** is to **recognise that the problem exists**. The issue should be considered at a very early stage in any new research design. If the new data collected can potentially be fused with existing data the collection methods should be such that the new data will be capable of being fused from the outset. For example, variables that are common to both the existing data and the new data should be measured in the same way by the new collection method.

Alternatively, and probably preferably, it should be **measured in a way that makes it possible to fuse the data and also analyse it in a different way**. For example, if the age categories wanted by the client are 0-18; 19-30; 31-40, but the existing data has categories 0-21; 22-35; 36-45, then this problem can be resolved to some extent by asking respondents to give their exact year of birth in the new data.

If both sets of data already exist there are still options to make the process easier, and because data fusion is potentially so valuable **new techniques** to aid the process are constantly being developed.

(i) A wide variety of **middleware** now exists to enable different software applications to talk to each other and data from different software packages and platforms to be combined. Typically these will use XML to impose common data standards.

(ii) **Data from one set can be recoded to match the other set**. This needs to be done with great care because there is considerable potential for error.

(iii) Data from both sets can be '**cleansed**' to remove incompatibilities such as different styles of field entries. Again, great care is needed to avoid errors.

(iv) It may be possible to **manipulate** the existing data and **re-analyse** it. The extent to which this can be done accurately will depend how much of the original raw data is still available. If any extrapolation is involved this should be made clear to the users of the fused data.

Regarding the **legal and ethical issues** the researcher will need to ensure that any new research will comply with the relevant provisions of data protection legislation and with the MRS Code of Conduct. Respondents must be informed of how the information to be collected may be used and they must give their consent. This may make it more difficult to collect the new data, since respondents are increasingly wary of potential marketing abuses. The best the researcher can do is be open and honest.

17 Proposal document

(a) **The role and importance of the proposal document**

The proposal will set out the **objectives, methods, analysis, time scales** and **costs** of a research project. It is a competitive **'tender'** document written by the researcher or research agency in **response to a client brief** and designed to win the contract to carry out the research. This means that it needs to include evidence that the researcher is a suitable choice for the job.

(i) It will refine the original brief and demonstrate that the researcher understands the client's business in general and the client's research problem in particular.

(ii) It will show that the researcher has the ability both to design an appropriate research project (explaining why the proposed approach is suitable) and has the expertise, human and technical resources and management skills needed to complete the research.

(iii) It will include information that enables comparisons with other tenders, for example over cost.

(iv) It will indicate what the client can expect to be delivered at the end of the research.

Although it is produced at the beginning of the project the proposal has a continuing role and it will be referred to throughout as a source of direction for the research team. It may well be the basis of, or form an actual part of, the contract between the researcher and the client and therefore it will help to avoid disputes or confusion at a later stage.

(b) **Key sections**

The level of detail of a proposal will vary depending on the type and size of client, the scale of the work involved and the likely rewards to be gained by the researcher both for this project and in the event that future research is commissioned. Sometimes a proposal may just cover the basics in one or two pages.

Key sections of a detailed proposal are as follows.

Introduction (if not already provided)

An introduction may be included to tell the client a little bit about the researcher and why they are suitable for the job. In most cases, if the researcher has been invited to tender for work, this information will already have been provided as part of the researcher's marketing literature: a general corporate brochure would suffice so long as it is relevant and up to date.

Background

This initial section of a proposal is informed by the context of the problem as outlined in the brief. It indicates that the researcher has fully grasped relevant information about the company and the problem, and its context. It is likely to include a brief description of the client's business, size of market, market growth, key players, client market share and so on.

Research objectives

This section identifies information and analysis that the research will provide for the company. It establishes clearly the aims of the research project and connects these with the problem at hand. For example, a research objective might be to establish the characteristics (age, size, type of material etc) of the 'ladies glove' market in Belgium and Germany because the research 'problem' is a glove manufacturer's need to expand abroad.

Research design and methodologies

The research design provides an overview of what research methods will be used to obtain the relevant data, why those methods have been chosen, and how they will meet the objectives.

Examples of research designs include: time series or longitudinal analysis; experiments or audits; qualitative and quantitative ad hoc studies. Depending on the brief the research may be **exploratory**, with the aim of gaining more insight into the problem, or it may be **descriptive** to enable the client to assess the size of an opportunity. A **multi-method approach** may be proposed, for example a quantitative survey to measure awareness of an advertising campaign followed by qualitative research to gain a better understanding of responses to the advertising.

The **population of interest** will be clearly identified together with an explanation of how it is proposed to draw a sample. For example, the client may wish to know how many respondents will be interviewed in a telephone survey.

Many alternatives exist, for example mystery shopping or observation; focus groups or in-depth interviews; postal questionnaires or face to face responses. Whichever method or methods are chosen they need to be appropriate for both the research problem and the sample population.

An explanation of **data collection methods** should be included in the proposal because the client then has a clear idea of the quality of research that is being undertaken. Where research has to be undertaken in a hurry, the methods used (eg convenience samples and telephone surveys) do not provide as rigorous or reliable data as when more time and care can be taken. The client needs to be aware of this.

Data analysis procedures

Although this is not always included, most clients, especially those who are knowledgeable about research techniques and analysis, will want a résumé of how the data will be processed. They may want input to the data specifications that are written, and they may want to know how the researcher will ensure that there are no errors inputting or coding the data as well as how valid, reliable and generalisable the results will be. They may also be interested in the project management tools (if any) being used and will almost certainly be interested in hearing about any analysis packages or models being used which may affect data output.

Outputs/Deliverables

This section makes it clear what the client will get, and in what format, at the end of the project and perhaps at various interim stages. Deliverables may include presentations and reports, databases for the client's own future use (subject to data protection and ethical issues), detailed statistical appendices.

Personnel/Relevant experience

It is usual to include a list of personnel to be involved in the research project and to impress the client with their qualifications and experience, ie their suitability for carrying through the project successfully. The proposal should at least indicate who the project manager is and who will be in charge of the fieldwork. More detail in this section could include short CVs for the analysts and other researchers, indicating number of years they have worked in the industry and their professional accreditations.

Relevant previous experience, both of individuals and of the researcher's organisation as a whole, should be set out. This may be a crucial factor in obtaining the work.

Time schedule

A time schedule is useful to help the client envisage the progress of the research and to ensure that it fits in with their own plans and expectations. Such a schedule can include information on how deadlines will be met and whether and when up-dates and interim reports will be provided. Explaining the exigencies of time to clients in the proposal is important as, if **clients** are not familiar with the research process and how long things take, they are likely to **underestimate the time** needed to complete research and thus put undue pressure on the research agency. This can result in insufficient time being allocated to analysis and interpretation of the data, which means that less is absorbed from the data than might be.

If a client needs research results very quickly researchers should suggest what **can** reasonably be done in the time available but also make it clear what are the implications for the quality and usefulness of the research of a short time frame.

Costs

This section of the proposal should include total costs including major breakdowns for expenses and materials (out of pocket costs) and executive or staff costs etc. The client will be looking for value-for-money.

It is becoming increasingly popular to offer various **costing options** by breaking down the project into smaller parts. Therefore, there may be one cost estimate for any exploratory research, one for a quantitative survey (if there is one) and one for a second level of data analysis. For international research projects, it is not uncommon for clients to want to see what the differing fieldwork costs are for the different countries involved, as these can vary hugely. This information will allow the client to choose between a variety of options, depending on their budget.

Terms and conditions of business

This section will include information on matters such as payment terms (for instance advance and interim payments for long projects); ownership of methodologies, data and final reports; adherence to the MRS Code of Conduct.

18 Research proposal

Tutorial note It is important that you are thoroughly familiar with the headings for a research proposal and the contents of each section and the rationale behind them. This is not dissimilar to the previous question, though it is slightly more 'applied' and you need to see matters from the perspective of the client.

(a) **Expected features of the report**

Background – I would want to read about the background to the case by outlining the researchers' perceptions of our organisation, the relevant product/service range, the reason for undertaking the proposed research, the markets and the environment in which we operate.

Statement of objectives – The proposal should provide a clearly defined statement of the objectives for the survey. What these might be would depend on the agreement reached in this regard at the briefing.

Description of how the research will be done – This will include sampling methodology, description of the proposed fieldwork research methods, nature of the questionnaire and its design/format, how the data would be handled, what tables would be produced and any cross tabulations and how any interview tapes will be processed/transcribed.

Timings – A full schedule of start and finish dates for each phase of the research. The proposal should show when the results will be made available to the client. The timings should be realistic and achievable.

Reporting and presentation procedures – The proposal should indicate whether or not a written report is included in the costs. Where a large report is required, it may be necessary/understood that an additional charge may be made for this. Where multiple copies are required, this should be indicated. Where a verbal presentation is required this will be indicated in the proposal and the costings should take account of this.

Costs – The proposal should give an appropriate table of costs, showing how these are computed and derived. Where there are optional elements in the proposal, these should be clearly shown as should contingency costs where extra work turns out to be needed.

Supporting evidence and CVs – This section of the report gives the opportunity for the tendering company to sell its strong points. It is the point where the commissioning company can satisfy itself that the market research company has the necessary expertise. This section of the proposal can contain the CVs of key personnel, illustrating/highlighting their particular and relevant skills.

I would expect to see any references from previous clients included in this section of the report.

Contract details – I would want to examine the tendering company's proposed terms of the contract at this stage.

(b) **The proposal should provide answers to the following questions.**

- Why was the sample selection procedure chosen?
- What was the methodology and rationale for the sample sizes?
- Why were the proposed interview techniques and durations chosen?
- Were the proposed questions/question types suitable?
- Were the report/presentations suitable for the proposed research?
- Were the timings and costs suitable/reasonable/competitive?

19 Type of research

To: Managing Director
From: Marketing Manager
Subject: Market research for overseas market development
Date: 8 December 20X8

The following report highlights the type of marketing research that will have to be undertaken when considering entry to new overseas markets. The report is structured in the following sections.

- The research objectives
- Type of research and justification
- Conducting the research
- Benefits to be gained

(a) **The research objectives**

Research objectives must be specific, measurable, appropriate, realisable and timescaled (ie **SMART**). For the initial overseas market development activity the following objectives are recommended.

(i)   To gain comparable data on the countries' economic, political and legal backgrounds

(ii) To identify the annual market size and growth rates for management training programmes within the selected countries

(iii) To produce a picture of the management training market structure within the selected countries

(iv) To produce a competitive analysis of management training within each of the selected countries, detailing market shares and competitive strengths

At later stages of the project more specific objectives would be needed to ascertain further details on competitors, requirements for training course content and structure, pricing and promotion.

(b) **Types of research**

The research into overseas markets utilises the same research methods as other projects. These can be listed as follows.

(i)   **Secondary (or desk) research**

This is information **produced for another purpose** which can be applied to the problem at hand.

Secondary research on overseas markets can be conducted in the UK. The UK government offer a range of free assistance within this area. For example, The Export Market Information Centre in London houses a wide range of foreign statistical publications, trade directories and market reports. Other services include the Export Intelligence Service which provides information on tariff rates and import regulations. Other secondary sources include HMSO Economic surveys, CBI overseas reports and a wealth of other information.

(ii)   **Primary (or field) research**

As with domestic based projects, overseas primary research can be devised to produce either quantitative or qualitative data using the same marketing research techniques. Projects would be constructed using a standard primary marketing research process. It is recommended that any projects of this type are conducted through research agencies based in the target country.

It is recommended that **both secondary and primary research techniques** are used to identify the most attractive overseas markets and to devise appropriate entry strategies. Initially secondary research should be used to provide a comparative analysis around a larger sample of selected overseas markets. This information would be used to select a short-list of countries which would then be chosen for further examination. This examination would consist of more detailed secondary research together with primary research. This process is outlined in further detail in the section below.

(c)   **Conducting the research**

After the initial sample of target overseas markets has been selected, comparable secondary research would be gathered from UK based sources. This research would be used to build a comparable picture of each of the markets in terms of economic trends, legal background, market structures, sizes and trends and so on. This initial stage would then be used to **shortlist attractive markets** for further examination.

The shortlisted markets would then be **investigated in further detail**. Initially, further secondary research would be conducted, utilising a wider range of the information services offered by UK based facilities and export specialists. Further detail would also be sought on market competitors by gaining their marketing materials, pricelists, course materials and so on.

Finally, **primary market research projects** should be devised for the shortlisted markets. These projects would be designed to fill important information gaps left by the previous stages of research. It is envisaged that information may still be required on issues such as training features, communication messages and media types, pricing and so on. For this stage we would have to produce SMART objectives and agency briefs for local research companies to conduct the projects. Projects should be conducted with identical sample makeups and research design so as to produce comparable data.

(d)   **Benefits**

This type of approach to overseas markets has many advantages. By systematically comparing markets for their potential it is possible to start the overseas market project with a larger number of possibilities. The markets shortlisted from the initial stage have already been objectively selected for their attractiveness before the detailed market research process begins.

The detailed research will then allow the company to address many **market entry issues**. Information can be supplied to devise market segmentation strategy and to plan the marketing details for the market entry; details such as course content and timings, venues, pricing and promotion.

In short, all of the research objectives can be addressed in order to maximise the chance of success in the new market and to minimise the risk associated with the venture.

20 Research plan

> *Tutorial note.* In answering this question it is important to explain:
>
> - Possible ways of conducting the research
> - Whether it could be done in-house or externally
> - Budgetary constraints

Market research for new product launch

The following report outlines the market research plan to be conducted prior to the launch of our new magazine aimed at teenage females.

Research conducted last year revealed the UK female teenage market as a viable new market for our magazine publications. The secondary research carried out at this time has defined a demographic and psychographic profile of our target market.

The following plan has been developed for **pre-launch research** into the market to define the most successful product characteristics, pricing and advertising support. As a wealth of secondary research has already been gathered, this plan will focus entirely on primary sources of information.

The plan is structured to cover each stage in the standard research process. Sections therefore cover the following areas:

- Define the research objectives
- Ascertain the best methods for obtaining the information
- Collect the data
- Process the data
- Make recommendations
- Implement the recommendations

Research objectives

Research objectives must be devised to be specific, measurable, actionable, reasonable and timescaled (ie **SMART**). Suggested objectives for the research are as follows.

(a) To investigate attitudes to magazine content and layout styles amongst the target group, to discover the most appropriate product mix

(b) To investigate attitudes to advertising message and content amongst the target group to discover the most appropriate advertising mix

(c) To quantify media consumption of the target group

(d) To investigate attitudes to magazine pricing amongst the target group

Methods for obtaining information

There are two appropriate primary research methods which could be used to obtain qualitative data of this type. These methods are discussed in the sections below.

Focus groups

This is a research method which should be given consideration. In this method, a group of six to ten respondents from the target group is engaged in a group discussion with a moderator. Typically, the sessions are recorded or videoed through a two way mirror for later analysis. This format of research allows props to be used, such as advertising visuals and magazine layouts.

Hall tests

The usual format of this method is to recruit respondents from the target group on the street and to invite then to a nearby research room to view material and test their reactions. This could also be combined with a short interview. This method, would allow props to be used and appropriate qualitative data could be obtained.

The recommendation is to use focus groups for this research for the following reasons.

(a) It is a more cost-effective way of gathering respondent data, leading to a larger number of respondents being involved within the budget.

(b) The recording of focus groups allows more in depth analysis of the discussion.

(c) The target group is more likely to 'open up' in a group.

(d) There are potential legal and/or moral implications surrounding street recruitment of this target group.

Collect the data

The first issue to consider is that of sampling. Although we have defined demographic and psychographic profiles of the target group, it is recommended that we address geographic considerations for the sample. Previous research projects have used specific city locations in the North, Midlands and South East of the UK to mirror the UK population. It is suggested that this research uses the same locations.

Respondents will be recruited through snowballing techniques which could be achieved through schools and colleges within the target areas. We must also consider the legal and moral implications of respondent recruitment. We will need to gain parental permission and possibly parental accompaniment for the respondents.

Process the data

Discussions will be captured on video. Transcripts of discussions will be produced and qualitative analysis techniques applied to the results.

Recommendations

The results will be written into a report format and a presentation given to company directors and marketing management.

Resource/costs/timing issues

We do not have the in-house expertise to conduct a research project of this type. A research brief will be written and submitted to two external marketing research companies. Previous experience would suggest that the budget of £30,000 will finance recruitment, data collection, analysis and reporting of 15 focus groups. The likely timescale for this project is two months from the award of the contract.

21 Tutorial question: Random and judgement sampling

(a) Conducting marketing research around a whole population (ie a census) is often impractical, hence the value of sampling. Sampling allows a researcher to obtain data from a **representative section** of the population from which valid conclusions about the **whole population** can be drawn. There are two basic types of sampling methods available, **probability** and **non-probability**. Here I will define random sampling, sometimes referred to as probability sampling and judgement sampling which is often called non-probability sampling.

A **random sample** is a sample which is constructed so that each unit of the population has an equal chance of being included. Quasi random sampling techniques include stratified and systematic sampling where the chance of being selected is not equal, but is still greater than zero. The idea of a true random sample is to remove **all subjective bias** arising from the choice of respondents to be included. The sample is therefore generated completely randomly from a sampling frame. One method of generating a random sample is to allocate a number to each member of the sample frame and generate the sample by a 'lottery' method or by random tables.

A **judgement sample**, on the other hand, is a non-probability sample and is not randomly compiled. This type of sample, often referred to as expert choice is compiled using human judgement. The most commonly used example of judgement sampling is **quota sampling**, where a sample is compiled to reflect chosen criteria within the population, for example age or sex. Unlike random sampling, an individual unit of the population does not have an equal chance of selection for the sample. Judgement sampling has often been described as **convenience sampling** as although such samples are typically easier to compile than random samples they are not believed to be as reliable. This is because they are dependent on human judgement and not on the application of probability theory. The representativeness of the sample is therefore subject to some doubt as it has been compiled using subjective judgement rather than objective criteria.

(b) If research were to be conducted within an organisation, the **choice of sampling technique** would depend primarily on the organisation's size. If the organisation were small with few staff it would be possible to conduct a census. In larger organisations, this would be costly and time consuming and therefore inadvisable. In this case, a random sampling method could be used. Although a simple random sample may be appropriate, within most larger organisations it may be advisable to use stratified random sampling as it is unlikely that every employee should be given an equal chance of being selected for the sample. Constructing a stratified random sample would allow criteria such as employee age, sex and department to be taken into account.

This type of sample would be compiled as follows. Firstly calculating the exact make-up of the population. If it were decided to stratify the sample by age, sex and department, then the % size of these subgroups would be calculated. Then, a record for each employee within the company would be allocated into its appropriate subgroup. The sample would be compiled by randomly selecting records from each of the subgroups ensuring, of course, that the sample was representative of the population.

(i) The **reliability of the research findings** depends on a number of factors. However, one of the main factors is the sample size. As a general rule as **sample size increases so the sampling error decreases** and the degree of confidence improves. If we know the degree of confidence we require, it is possible to calculate statistically the numbers required to achieve this. However, to complicate the issue, this does not just depend upon numbers alone. The basic characteristics of the population and the type of information which is required from the survey can also affect the degree of confidence from a given sample size. As an extreme example, if the population is totally homogeneous then a sample of one would produce reliable findings.

(ii) Of course, the bigger the sample size, the more work the researchers have to do in collecting and data inputting the results. This will increase the time and the cost of the research. The **cost of reducing the sampling error** is high as this varies inversely with the square root of the sample size. Therefore, if we were contemplating a sample of 100, but decided we wanted to halve the sampling error we would have to increase the sample size to 400.

22 Tutorial question: Sample size determination

Ideally, **statistical calculations** will be carried out to help determine the size of the sample required in a survey, as samples that are too small can produce misleading data and ones that are too large can waste resources.

Although it is true to say that the larger the **sample** the less the **sampling error**, the level of error decreases at a rate equal to the square root of the increase in sample size. In other words, to halve the sampling error, the sample will need to be four times the size. This is clearly expensive as the costs of interviewing and analysis will increase proportionately. It should be noted that statistical means of calculating the sample size can really only be applied to random samples (ie where everybody in the 'population' has an equal and non-zero chance of being picked).

There are, however, other ways of deciding upon the size of the sample.

(a) **Budget available**. Frequently this is the most important factor. In an ideal world, the appropriate size of sample would be calculated and the research costed accordingly. However, in most cases, the budget is already allocated and therefore the sample is the size that can be afforded. To achieve a larger sample, it might be possible to look at alternative cheaper means of data collection: interviewing in the high street rather than door-to-door or by telephone rather than in the street. However, the method of data collection should not be altered if this is going to lead to incorrect or inadequate data. It would be better to recommend that the research is not done at all in that case.

(b) **Rule of thumb or gut feeling**. Frequently managers commissioning research will demand a sample of 300 or 500. It may be based on past experience or other similar research or it may not be based on any sound reasoning at all, except that it sounds about right.

(c) **Number of sub-groups**. To mean anything, each major sub-group should contain at least 50 members and each minor sub-group at least 20.

If, for example, the sample is to be based on smokers and non-smokers and then age within those two categories, there would have to be at least 20 non-smokers and 20 smokers under 25, at least 20 of each between the age of 25 and 34 and so on. If there were five age bands, the minimum sample size would be $2 \times 5 \times 20$, ie 200 respondents.

23 Sample selection

> *Tutorial note*. Questions 23, 24 and 26 are essentially the same question, though each has a slight variation and the topic of the research is different in each case. More recent questions on sampling have tended to focus on specific issues, rather than asking for an overview of the entire process.

Sampling is the selection of a fraction of the total number of units in the population of interest to decision-makers for the purpose of being able to draw general conclusions about the entire population of interest. A **sampling plan** sets out how this fraction is to be chosen.

Typically the development of a sampling plan has five stages.

(1) Define the population of interest
(2) Identify a sampling frame
(3) Choose the sampling method
(4) Decide on sample size
(5) Produce sampling instructions

Population of interest

The population of interest in this case is **'lower income groups'**. The researcher will need to discuss with the client exactly what is meant by this. Does the client have a specific figure in mind (for instance, any amount less than the national average, according to government statistics), or does this mean people who fall into socio-economic categories C2 (skilled manual workers), D (unskilled/semi-skilled manual workers) and E (low waged/unwaged), or perhaps just DEs? Is it important to the research project to differentiate between individual and household income, between men and women, or between different age groups? Are regional differences relevant?

In this case it is likely that the client will be more interested in **individual income** and it will be most straightforward to sample those in the DE socio-economic category rather than setting a precise figure, since the latter would make it more difficult to identify respondents who fit the criteria exactly. The client would probably want to survey a national sample in gender and age proportions equal to the average for that group.

Sampling frame

A sampling frame is a **list** of **all** members in a population of interest from which a sample can be drawn. Such a list should include all members of the defined population and should be accurate and up-to-date. No population member should be listed more than once. It should be easily available and in a suitable format. Unfortunately, there are few occasions in practice when such a comprehensive list exists.

The **electoral register** and the **Postcode Address File (PAF)** are the most commonly used sample frames for researchers interested in drawing samples of the general population.

In this case the PAF is probably the most appropriate sampling frame. This could be used in conjunction with ACORN data which will identify postcode areas that have a high proportion of DEs. There is some room for error, since there will be some high income people who choose to live in areas dominated by lower income groups, but the incidence of such cases is likely to be small enough to make the risk tolerable. Such cases can be eliminated when the data is analysed, if not earlier.

Sampling method

The selection of a particular sampling method will depend on: the objectives of the research; the financial resources available; the time available; and the nature of the problem under investigation. There are two main methods.

(a) **Probability sampling**, which is an objective procedure in which the probability of selection is known in advance for each population unit. This is most suitable for conclusive (explanatory) research, in other words where there is a need to obtain measurements of known precision. Probability or random sampling allows for the calculation of statistical measures of sampling error – the degree of error and/or bias which may be present in the sample as compared to the population of interest. However, probability sampling is only feasible if a suitable sampling frame exists, as it does in this case. It can be costly and time-consuming, depending on how the data is collected.

(b) **Non-probability sampling**, which is a subjective procedure in which the probability of selection is unknown beforehand. Here, there is a degree of researcher-influence. This method is most suitable for exploratory research, where the researcher can make inferences about the population without highly accurate measurement. In spite of this if the non-sampling error (sample design error, measurement error, non-response errors and response errors) is likely to be higher than the sampling error the results from non-probability sampling may be just as representative as they would have been from probability sampling.

The research in this case aims to 'identify trends' and (although it depends precisely what this means) it seems likely on the face of it that a non-probability method such as **quota sampling** will give satisfactory results at a good deal less expense. This method identifies the total number of units to sample and the specific characteristics of sections of the sample, but it does not select each individual unit.

(a) The population of interest is divided into segments (cells) via certain control characteristics such as age, gender and geographical region.

(b) The number of units to be selected is determined by the expert judgement of the researcher.

(c) Interviewers are instructed to fill quotas assigned to the cells. Unlike probability sampling, the interviewer is given some freedom in selecting the sample units.

Sample size

Two general rules apply when deciding on a sample size.

(a) The larger the sample, the more accurately it will reflect the population

(b) The more homogeneous (similar) the population, the greater likelihood that the sample will reflect the population

The statistical determination of sample size is based on calculating the **standard error (SE)** of the mean, in other words the difference between the sample average and the population average. A measure of the difference between each case and the sample mean is required to estimate the SE, and this is called the standard deviation or 's'.

The larger the sample the smaller the standard error, and this means that the client will be asked to specify the level of accuracy required (eg 90%) and the sample size can be determined from that.

(a) In this case the sample mean must be within 10% of the population mean, in other words the SE is 0.1

(b) The standard deviation is estimated based on the homogeneity of the sample. Let's say the sample is considered to be very homogeneous so the standard deviation is small, say 4.

(c) The sample size is calculated as $s^2/SE^2 = 16/0.01 = 1,600$.

If 95% accuracy were required the sample size would be $4^2/0.05^2 = 6,400$.

Sampling instructions

Interviewers should be given a **clear, unambiguous plan** which leaves no opportunity for the process to suffer from bias or interference. Such bias or interference are not necessarily conscious or deliberate (such as choosing people to interview who look pleasant and amenable), although they can be.

The aim of the instructions is to **minimise sampling and non-sampling error** (these terms are explained above). The instructions would include the definition of the population of interest, details of the sampling frame, the sampling method to be used, the sample size required, pitfalls to avoid when questioning respondents, and what to do in the case of non-response.

In this case interviews would probably be best conducted on a door-to-door basis within the postcode regions identified. Telephone interviewing is a possibility, and would be a good deal cheaper, but the level of telephone ownership is likely to be lower amongst lower income groups and the subject of the research (financial services) may be one that some people are reluctant to discuss over the telephone.

If time and/or costs are limited

Various methods can be used to cut costs or time, such as **reducing the sample size** and **restricting the amount of data** that is collected. As already indicated, **telephone interviewing** would be cheaper, though less reliable, than face-to-face methods.

If there are severe limitations it may be more cost-effective to survey financial institutions about uptake of certain services rather than approaching individuals. (If the client itself is a financial institution it can examine its own records, of course, although these may not be representative.) It will not be possible to collect data about why particular services are used by the group in question, but it should be possible to identify trends in a broad sense.

24 Sampling plan

> *Tutorial note.* Although similar in many respects to the previous question, in this case you are asked to discuss continuous research and the population of interest is a much smaller one.

Continuous research is research that is repeated at regular intervals such as every week, every month or every quarter. In this case a mail order Office Supplies company wants to monitor customers' likes, dislikes and purchases on a continuous basis.

One approach would be to send a questionnaire to customers whenever fulfilling an order, as part of the invoice or delivery documentation. This has a number of possible **drawbacks**, however.

(a) Customers would quickly become fatigued by the questionnaire and would not bother to respond after the first occasion, unless given some additional incentive such as a discount.

(b) The person dealing with the invoice or the delivery may not be the person who places the order.

(c) Dissatisfied customers are the least likely to respond, yet their views are the ones the company most urgently needs to know about.

A sampling approach, whereby a representative selection of customers is surveyed each period, but not the same customers each time, is likely to produce better results.

Sampling is the selection of a fraction of the total number of units in the population of interest to decision-makers for the purpose of being able to draw general conclusions about the entire population of interest. A **sampling plan** sets out how this fraction is to be chosen.

Typically the development of a sampling plan has **five stages**.

(1) Define the population of interest
(2) Identify a sampling frame
(3) Choose the sampling method
(4) Decide on sample size
(5) Produce sampling instructions

Population of interest

The population of interest in this case consists of the **customers of the Office Supplies company**. These are likely to be predominantly businesses.

It should be possible to analyse the customer database of the company and identify distinct groups, based on actual knowledge of the customer (this is likely to be obtained when setting up customer accounts and setting credit limits) and on volume of orders/amount spent. This will help to obtain a clearer definition of the target population.

Sampling frame

A sampling frame is a **list** of **all** members in a population of interest from which a sample can be drawn. Such a list should include all members of the defined population and should be accurate and up-to-date. No population member should be listed more than once. It should be easily available and in a suitable format. Unfortunately, there are few occasions in practice when such a comprehensive list exists.

In this case the quality of the sampling frame is directly dependent upon the quality of the customer database, which may well be out-of-date to some extent (it may include many lapsed customers) and may well contain duplicates, especially for larger customers, several of whose branches may place separate orders. A list derived from the database should be cleansed as far as possible to eliminate these problems: for example, customers who have not placed an order in the last year, say, could be excluded.

It should be observed that the company's own database will only contain information about existing customers, not potential new ones. That does not appear to be a problem in this case.

Sampling method

There are two main methods.

(a) **Probability sampling**, which is an objective procedure in which the probability of selection is known in advance for each population unit. This is most suitable for conclusive (explanatory) research, in other words where there is a need to obtain measurements of known precision. Probability or random sampling allows for the calculation of statistical measures of sampling error – the degree of error and/or bias which may be present in the sample as compared to the population of interest. However, probability sampling is only feasible if a suitable sampling frame exists. It can be costly and time-consuming, depending on how the data is collected.

(b) **Non-probability sampling**, which is a subjective procedure in which the probability of selection is unknown beforehand. Here, there is a degree of researcher-influence. This method is most suitable for exploratory research, where the researcher can make inferences about the population without highly accurate measurement. In spite of this if the non-sampling error (sample design error, measurement error, non-response errors and response errors) is likely to be higher than the sampling error the results from non-probability sampling may be just as representative as they would have been from probability sampling.

The selection of a particular sampling method will depend on: the objectives of the research; the financial resources available; the time available; and the nature of the problem under investigation.

In this case a probability method is feasible and the most appropriate technique, given the assumptions we have made about the Office Supplies business, would be **disproportionate stratified random sampling**. This is a procedure in which the chosen sample is forced to contain units from each of the segments, or strata, of the population. The population of interest (customers) is divided into strata (groups) on the basis of the desired population characteristics, in this case perhaps size of business, volume of orders, type of products purchased and so on. Units are then selected from each population stratum according to how varied or important the units within the stratum are.

Given that this is continuous research and it is not desirable to survey the same customer over and over again the method would be further refined by restricting the population of interest to customers who had not already been surveyed in, say, the previous nine months.

Sample size

Two general rules apply when deciding on a sample size.

(a) The larger the sample, the more accurately it will reflect the population.

(b) The more homogeneous (similar) the population, the greater likelihood that the sample will reflect the population. As already noted, it should be possible to analyse the customer database and determine the relative proportions of different types of customer.

The statistical determination of sample size is based on calculating the **standard error (SE)** of the mean, in other words the difference between the sample average and the population average. A measure of the difference between each case and the sample mean is required to estimate the SE, and this is called the standard deviation or 's'.

The larger the sample the smaller the standard error, and this means that the client will be asked to specify the level of accuracy required (eg 95%) and the sample size can be determined from that.

Sampling instructions

The aim of the instructions is to **minimise sampling and non-sampling error** (these terms are explained above). The instructions would include the definition of the population of interest, details of the sampling frame, the sampling method to be used, the sample size required, pitfalls to avoid when questioning respondents, and what to do in the case of non-response.

A survey such as this could be conducted in a variety of ways.

(a) Questionnaires could be sent out to the selected sample by post when fulfilling the order, as mentioned above. This has the problem of possible non-response.

(b) Selected orders could be followed up by a telephone call once they had been completed. This method is likely to yield more satisfactory results.

25 Sampling frame

> *Tutorial note.* Part (a) could be answered very briefly, but we have assumed that the examiner wanted you to demonstrate that you know what a sampling frame is and to outline the different types of probability sampling and the relative importance of a complete and up-to-date sampling frame.

(a) **Sampling frame**

Sampling is carried out because it is often impractical to conduct a survey amongst all members of a population of interest: to do so would take too long, and be too costly.

A sampling frame is a **list** of **all** members in a population of interest from which a sample can be drawn. A sampling frame is **essential for random (probability) sampling**, but not necessarily so for non-probability methods. In probability sampling each element of the population of interest has a known (non-zero) chance of being selected. Provided certain conditions apply random selection from a complete, accurate and up-to-date sampling frame will produce a sample that is representative of the population as a whole.

■   The sample size must be at least 100.
■   The population should be homogeneous.
■   Non-response must be zero.

If these conditions apply it is then possible to use statistical techniques to draw conclusions about the population as a whole.

The sampling frame may be a list of names and telephone numbers (for example a telephone directory), a list of addresses and postcodes, or a map showing local housing. It should have the following **properties**.

(i)   It should include all members of the defined population.

(ii)   It should be up-to-date.

(iii)   No population member should be listed more than once.

(iv)   The list should contain accurate information about each individual that could be used for satisfying the sample.

(v)   It should be easily available and in a suitable format for use (for example, a computerised list is more useful than an hand-written one – the latter could of course be input into a computer, but not without risk of error)

Unfortunately, there are few occasions in practice when such a comprehensive list exists. If the researcher wanted to interview every household in a particular town the telephone directory might seem to be a good starting point, but this would not take account of people who had moved or had died since the directory was last compiled, it would not include households that were ex-directory, it would not include households where the residents preferred to use mobile phones (for example, student houses), and of course it would not include households that did not have a telephone.

The sample is therefore likely to have a **sampling frame error**. The amount of error can be reduced by compiling the sampling frame from a number of different sources and cleansing the resulting data so that it is as complete and accurate as possible, but it may not be possible to eliminate the risk of error completely and this must be taken into account in subsequent analysis of results.

In spite of the difficulties it will almost always be more efficient to attempt to establish some kind of sampling frame to avoid the wasted effort of surveying respondents who do not fit the characteristics of the target population.

The main types of probability sampling are as follows.

(i)   **Simple random sampling**. This is a procedure in which every possible unit within a population has a known and equal probability of being chosen for the sample. Each item in the population will be allocated a number and a sample of the required size will be selected based on random numbers generated by computer.

(ii)   **Systematic sampling**. With this method the population size is divided by the sample size and every n^{th} item is selected from a random starting point. For example, if the population is 5,000 and the sample size is 250 then every 20th (5,000/250) item in the list would be selected.

(iii) **Stratified random sampling**. This method may be used when the population of interest is not homogeneous. For example it may known in advance that people in one age group will have significantly different views to those in other age groups, and in this case a simple random sample may not be truly representative of the whole. To avoid the potential error the population will be first be divided into its different strata and then random samples are taken from within each stratum.

(iv) **Cluster sampling**. This approach is suitable when the sampling frame is not adequate to permit any of the previous approaches. A sampling frame is not developed for the whole population but only for 'clusters' such as postcode regions or electoral wards.

(v) **Multi-stage sampling**. This approach uses a combination of all the above methods: stratified and cluster sampling would be used to restrict the sample to a convenient geographical region while remaining representative, and then simple random sampling would be used to select the final targets.

The first three approaches require a complete sampling frame, but this is less important for the other two.

(b) **Manufacturer of airline seating**

Given the nature of the product it is likely that the number of purchasers worldwide will be fairly small – thousands rather than millions – mostly comprising airlines and aircraft manufacturers. There may possibly be other organisations that use airline seats for other purposes, for example for training facilities, for research or testing purposes, or for rides in adventure theme parks.

The manufacturer's **own database** of existing customers will provide a starting point for the compilation of a sampling frame, and an analysis of this should reveal both conventional customers and give further clues as to the type of customers to look for that do not fall into the airline or aircraft manufacturer categories. The current database is not enough on its own, however, because it will only include existing and previous customers, not potential new customers nor those who buy their airline seating from competitors.

Some or all of the following **measures** may therefore be required **to complete the sampling frame**.

(i) Professional bodies relating to airlines and aircraft manufacturers may be able to provide subscription lists.

(ii) It is likely that airline seating has to conform to certain safety standards, so it may be possible to obtain a list of users of airline seating from safety bodies.

(iii) It may be possible to buy the customer lists of competitors.

(iv) A web search for business exchanges that deal in aviation supplies may bring further potential customers to light.

26 Voting behaviour and sampling plan

Tutorial note. This is a very general question about sampling, covering the entire process, and the main difficulty, assuming you know the subject well, is likely to be resisting the temptation to write everything you know on each individual stage and then running out of time.

Stages in developing a sampling plan

Sampling is the selection of a fraction of the total number of units in the population of interest to decision-makers for the purpose of being able to draw general conclusions about the entire population of interest. A **sampling plan** sets out how this fraction is to be chosen.

Typically the development of a sampling plan has **five stages**.

(1) Define the population of interest
(2) Identify a sampling frame
(3) Choose the sampling method
(4) Decide on sample size
(5) Produce sampling instructions

Stage 1: Define the population of interest

The objective here is to specify the characteristics of the population under investigation. The population of interest is often specified in terms of characteristics such as demographics, geographical location, product or service usage and awareness of the matter under research.

In this instance, however, the population of interest includes everybody in the nation who has the single characteristic that they are eligible to vote. Although this seems straightforward it is likely that not everyone who is eligible to vote is actually registered to vote. (Some countries such as Australia impose fines on eligible voters who do not register, but this practice is by no means universal.) Presumably one aspect of voting behaviour that may be of interest is **not voting** and therefore eligible but unregistered voters may need to be considered. A decision would have to be made depending on the precise nature of the research and whether results were likely to be distorted if non-registered eligible people were excluded.

Stage 2: Identify a sampling frame

A sampling frame is a **list** of **all** members in a population of interest from which a sample can be drawn. Such a list should have the following **properties**.

(a) It should include all members of the defined population.

(b) It should be up-to-date.

(c) No population member should be listed more than once.

(d) The list should contain accurate information about each individual that could be used for satisfying the sample.

(e) It should be easily available and in a suitable format for use (for example, a computerised list is more useful than an hand-written one – the latter could of course be input into a computer, but not without risk of error).

Unfortunately, there are few occasions in practice when such a comprehensive list exists.

The **electoral register and the Postcode Address File (PAF)** are the most commonly used sample frames for researchers interested in drawing samples of the general population.

The **electoral register** is clearly **appropriate** in this case, subject to the concerns raised above about non-registered eligible voters (in other words, about completeness). The electoral register contains not only name and sex but also addresses, including postcodes, so allowing for geo-demographic segmentation. It is usually compiled annually (in October in the UK), so it is reasonably up-to-date, except that it does not take account of deaths since it was last compiled or changes of circumstances that may make a person ineligible to vote such as imprisonment. It also lacks detailed age information and contains no income information: these factors may be relevant, depending on the nature of the research.

Stage 3: Choose the sampling method

The selection of a particular sampling method will depend on: the objectives of the research; the financial resources available; the time available; and the nature of the problem under investigation. There are two main methods.

(a) **Probability sampling**, which is an objective procedure in which the probability of selection is known in advance for each population unit. This is most suitable for conclusive (explanatory) research, in other words where there is a need to obtain measurements of known precision. Probability or random sampling allows for the calculation of statistical measures of sampling error – the degree of error and/or bias which may be present in the sample as compared to the population of interest. However, probability sampling is only feasible if a suitable sampling frame exists, as it does in this case. It can be costly and time-consuming, depending on how the data is collected.

(b) **Non-probability sampling**, which is a subjective procedure in which the probability of selection is unknown beforehand. Here, there is a degree of researcher-influence. This method is most suitable for exploratory research, where the researcher can make inferences about the population without highly accurate measurement. In spite of this if the non-sampling error (sample design error, measurement error, non-response errors and response errors) is likely to be higher than the sampling error the results from non-probability sampling may be just as representative as they would have been from probability sampling.

In this case some kind of probability sampling is likely to be required since the government in question would typically want results of known precision.

A technique that is often used in this sort of survey is **multistage cluster sampling**. Cluster sampling is a probability sampling procedure in which 'clusters' (groups) of population units are selected at random and then all or some of the chosen cluster are studied. Each cluster represents an area of population. If using the electoral register as the sampling frame, the researcher will randomly select a number of electoral districts (the cluster sample), and within each electoral district a number of electoral wards (one-stage cluster sampling). If the researcher then selects a number of streets within each electoral ward, and then a number of houses in each street, this would be multistage cluster sampling. At each stage the selected sample units should represent the whole population, rather than a segment of it.

Although this approach means that the standard error will be higher than it would be if random sampling were used, the advantage of this approach is its cost-effectiveness.

Stage 4: Decide on sample size

Two general rules apply when deciding on a sample size.

(a) The larger the sample, the more accurately it will reflect the population

(b) The more homogeneous (similar) the population, the greater likelihood that the sample will reflect the population

The statistical determination of sample size is based on calculating the **standard error (SE)** of the mean, in other words the difference between the sample average and the population average. A measure of the difference between each case and the sample mean is required to estimate the SE, and this is called the standard deviation or 's'.

The larger the sample the smaller the standard error, and this means that the client will be asked to specify the level of accuracy required (eg 90%) and the sample size can be determined from that.

(a)   In this case the sample mean must be within 10% of the population mean, in other words the SE is 0.1

(b)   The standard deviation is estimated based on the homogeneity of the sample. Let's say the sample is considered to be very homogeneous so the standard deviation is small, say 4.

(c)   The sample size is calculated as $s^2/SE^2 = 16/0.01 = 1,600$.

If 95% accuracy were required the sample size would be $4^2/0.05^2 = 6,400$.

Stage 5: Produce sampling instructions

The fieldworkers should be given a **clear, unambiguous plan** which leaves no opportunity for the process to suffer from bias or interference. Such bias or interference are not necessarily conscious or deliberate (such as choosing people to interview who look pleasant and amenable), although they can be.

The aim of the instructions is to **minimise sampling and non-sampling error** (these terms are explained above). The instructions would include the definition of the population of interest, details of the sampling frame, the sampling method to be used, the sample size required, pitfalls to avoid when questioning respondents, and what to do in the case of non-response.

Typically in the case in the question interviews would be conducted by telephone from a central location and this method is easier to monitor and control than face-to-face interviewing.

27 Quota sampling

Tutorial note. In part (a) you should demonstrate that you understand the principles of quota sampling, and ideally make clear and distinct comparisons between quota and random sampling. In part (b) you should discuss a minimum of two limitations and give convincing suggestions for overcoming each limitation. Ideally, you should acknowledge that certain factors need to be considered in order to decide if quota sampling will be detrimental to meeting the research objectives, such as the nature of the research.

(a)   **Reasons for growth in the use of quota sampling**

Quota sampling identifies the total number of units to sample and the specific characteristics of sections of the sample, but it does not select each individual unit.

(i)   The population of interest is divided into segments (cells) via certain control characteristics such as age, gender, level of education.

(ii)   The number of units to be selected is determined by the expert judgement of the researcher.

(iii)   Interviewers are instructed to fill quotas assigned to the cells. Unlike probability sampling, the interviewer is given some freedom in selecting the sample units.

The use of this method has grown because it has the following advantages.

BPP
PROFESSIONAL EDUCATION

(i)   It is not dependent on tracking down a specific individual to interview, which may often be difficult. **Interviewers have some flexibility** in choosing the respondents, so long as they match the defined characteristics of the population of interest. This makes the whole process quicker and more cost-effective.

(ii)   The large amount of **geo-demographic information** that is now available to researchers means that they can concentrate their work on areas that are likely to produce the appropriate number of respondents to obtain a representative sample of the population of interest.

(iii)   There are cases where quota sampling can yield **more reliable data** than simple random sampling. For example, the population may include certain **low-incidence groups** that would not otherwise be adequately surveyed for reliable analysis, or the markets may be such that a small proportion of the population account for a **disproportionately large** sales volume.

(iv)   It is a useful method where **no satisfactory sampling frame** exists, as is often the case. The quota can be based precisely on the characteristics desirable in a sample frame if there were one, and it is likely to produce equally good results.

(v)   It can be used for either **quantitative or qualitative** research.

Quota sampling is similar in some ways to stratified random sampling, a probability-based sampling procedure in which the chosen sample is forced to contain units from each of the segments, or strata, of the population. In both cases, the population is divided into homogeneous strata on the basis of some appropriate population characteristics.

In quota sampling, however, although each control characteristic has to be relevant to the survey, there is no requirement to have any data available about the frequency of characteristics in the population before conducting the survey. For stratified random sampling purposes, the characteristics serve as the basis for stratification.

(b) **Limitations of quota sampling**

Quota sampling is obviously **not a suitable method** if the research objectives require results that are backed up by **statistical theory** based on probabilities, especially if the client's needs will only tolerate a very small amount of error. Likewise, if the research concerns a topic where **little is known** in advance about the characteristics of the target population it will be very difficult to construct a quota sample that will be representative. On the other hand, for some research projects the target population may be **very clearly defined** – a product aimed at airline pilots, for example – in which case it will be quicker and easier to contact specific individuals, not linger in an airport and wait for people in uniform to pass by.

Perhaps the main limitation of quota sampling is that it is highly **dependent on the performance of interviewers**. They will need clear instruction and will require training, particularly in screening respondents.

The integrity of interviewers is highly important: the researcher needs assurance that the results are not made up by the interviewer. For example, if an interview is interrupted for some reason, or if the respondent refuses to answer some questions, it may be tempting for the interviewer to fill in the missing answers themselves.

This risk can probably not be eliminated completely, but some checks and controls can be used.

(i)   It may become apparent that some interviewers are not doing their job properly if analysis shows that their results are significantly different from those expected, especially if this happens regularly. Conversely, results that are regularly exactly what was expected may be suspect: this may be too good to be true.

(ii)   Interviewers could be asked to tape record their interviews, but of course this means that someone else will have to go through the tapes, adding to the time and cost.

(iii)   Respondents could be asked to agree to a second contact from the researcher to verify that the interview was conducted properly. Only a small sample of the interviewer's sample would actually need to be contacted, so this may not be too onerous a control.

(iv)   Interviewers can be made aware that their work will be checked, and hopefully this will discourage them from falsifying results.

(v)   It may be possible to employ 'mystery respondents' who will be able to spot whether the interviews are being conducted properly. Of course, this is extremely hit and miss because it depends on the mystery respondent being selected by the interviewer.

A second limitation is that no matter how well interviewers perform the sample may still **not be entirely representative** of the population of interest. For example, a station may have a lot of passers-by but the characteristics of people using it will vary considerably at different times of day, ranging from commuters in the mornings and evenings, followed by school children later in the morning and mid-afternoon, then followed by, say, retired persons and young mothers in the middle of the day.

Such problems can be overcome by insisting that the time and location of interviews is suitably varied. The quota itself can be refined to ensure that it includes 'hard to reach' groups such as people who are at work or people who are housebound. This will help to limit bias in the sample.

A third problem is that the quota controls may not be based on the most **up-to-date** information. For example, the quota may have been designed on the basis that 60% of the target population are male and 40% female, and therefore interviewers would be instructed to fill their quota with respondents in these proportions. If the actual spread of genders in the target population has changed then the research results will be inaccurate.

The researcher needs to take full account of the research objectives and ensure that the quota controls are fully relevant.

Finally, a quota sample may only be representative of the population in the particular respects that were specified in devising the quota, not in other respects. Unlike probability-based methods it is not possible to estimate the **degree of representativeness**.

28 Qualitative research and data collection

Tutorial note. This question gives you the opportunity to show off your knowledge of qualitative research techniques in general and apply it to a specific case. The example of the development of a toy is a fairly classic one, so hopefully you had a lot of ideas about how this might be researched. Given that children are involved, don't forget to mention the ethical issues, though you only need do so briefly.

Qualitative research is the collection and analysis of non-numeric, aural, written and visual data to gain understanding of a research problem. Qualitative research aims to uncover prevailing trends in **thought and opinion**.

Qualitative research provides an insight for the client into the characteristics of the user of the product (and non-user where these are interviewed): their attitudes and feelings; the way they think about themselves; how they express themselves and the type of language they use. As importantly, qualitative research can tell the client how to communicate with the audience.

Consequently qualitative research is often used at the **exploratory stage** of a new research project when no prior research studies or surveys of a similar nature can be referred to.

Qualitative data does not have statistical validity and so the results cannot, with known levels of confidence, be applied to the whole population under investigation. The analysis and interpretation, therefore, provide findings that are not technically 'conclusive'. For example, as a result of a qualitative study, we may be able to say that there are a known number of features which consumers consider when buying a brand, but we cannot say how many people in the population consider which features important. Qualitative data does, however, tend to provide a useful and sound basis for further decision making. Usually, it is followed by a quantitative survey.

Children's dolls

The **buyer** in this case is typically an **adult** (parent or relative) whereas the **user** is the **child**. Both groups will need to be researched. Qualitative research is generally carried out on relatively small samples using unstructured or semi-structured techniques, such as individual in depth interviews, group discussions and observation.

One issue that will need to be considered when designing the research is how the respondents will be **recruited**. Although schools may seem an obvious target this would not normally be acceptable for commercial research. It is more likely that the participants will be recruited in street interviews, for example outside a toy shop. The **venue** is also important: individual homes are a possibility, since this will be most comfortable and convenient for participants, but this is less likely to be practical if the researcher intends to engage in passive observation techniques.

In this case **individual in-depth interviews** are **not** a particularly appropriate technique for either group: they are time-consuming and costly and the issues under discussion are not of the nature that favours individual interviews (intimate personal matters).

Group discussions for both adults and children, and observation in the case of children hold far more promise. In general participants are encouraged to exchange experiences and beliefs about a product under the guidance of a trained moderator. This means that the participants prompt each other and may even query or challenge each other so real discussion and debate ensue, and so provide more data and richer data than if interviewed alone. Group discussions can also reveal how ideas about the product are influenced by other members of the group.

(a) Discussions amongst groups of, say, 8 to 12 **adults** will be cost-effective and will help to establish what is and is not regarded as acceptable amongst buyers. Key issues are likely to be the safety, durability and cost of the products and accessories. Themes that may emerge include the desirability or otherwise of products that promote certain attitudes towards war, fashion, sex, and racial and social stereotypes.

(b) Discussions involving a mix of **children and adults** are also likely to be very revealing, to study the extent to which the opinions of each are influenced by the other, and the impact of 'pester-power'.

(c) Research with **children** alone is more difficult. Children tend to have less regard for social etiquette, will be far more honest, and will often be hugely creative, but they may not be able to articulate their ideas and feelings in the way that an adult would. Considerable skill is needed by the researcher both in gathering data and in interpreting the research findings in ways that are useful to the manufacturer.

Moderators will need to have suitable training in child psychology, and be able to establish a rapport with children so that they are taken seriously but not regarded as threatening. Considerable care is needed with group dynamics because acceptance by peers is highly important to most children.

Typically mini groups (3-5 respondents) are used when interviewing children, but it can be difficult to recruit respondents and/or to arrange repeated sessions, particularly if the researcher wishes to bring the same group back together. A revealing alternative or additional method might be 'friendship pairs' – a brother and sister, perhaps.

Stimulus material should be used in all cases including existing products from various manufacturers and new prototypes developed by the manufacturer in question, perhaps in response to an initial round of research. The researcher may have to accept that children will want to take away the stimulus material if it is especially popular, or perhaps come to some arrangement with parents about free products when fully developed, and with children about immediate rewards for taking part. The researcher may also develop TV advertisements mixed in with normal children's TV programming to study the impact of these on product preferences.

Passive **observation** (where the researcher observes objectively the behaviours of children, using CCTV or one-way mirrors) offers a number of opportunities for research in this case: children can be left to play with products, either alone or in a group, in the way they would in real life, assuming the setting can be made as naturalistic as possible.

It must be borne in mind that observation only measures behaviour, it does not explain the reasons behind it. For example, one child may decide to play with a particular doll solely because another child in the group is also playing with it.

As a final point it is worth mentioning the principle of informed consent is especially important when dealing with children. The permission of parents or another responsible adult must be obtained and a clear explanation must be given of the purpose of the research and the intended use of all research data, including video footage and audio tapes.

29 Data collection and analysis

> *Tutorial note.* Modern technology is a very broad term. In our answer we interpret it to mean developments that have come about from the 1990s onwards, largely as a result of the convergence of computing and communication technologies.

Data collection

Thanks to modern technology a vast amount of data that is of value for research purposes is now collected automatically, often as a by-product of another process.

(a) Items such as **pressure mats** that sound a buzzer in smaller shops or **sliding doors** in larger ones have the practical purpose of either alerting staff to the fact that there is someone in the shop or simply of letting customers in and out, but if linked to a computer they also collect information about number and movements of customers. The same applies to ticket scanners in car parks, stations, and leisure facilities like sports venues.

(b) **CCTV** in shops has the practical purpose of guarding against shoplifting and other breaches of security, but CCTV footage also records data about customer behaviour – what route they take around a shop, how long they dwell over particular purchasing decisions, how they respond to in-store promotions and so on.

(c) **EPOS** systems (**barcode** scanners and tills) are primarily intended to speed up and avoid error in the check-out process, to allow customers to complete transactions, and to manage stocks. In addition, however, they collect precise and detailed information about **how many** of **what products** are being bought at **what times**. If linked to a **loyalty scheme** we can add **'and by whom'** since this allows the purchase data to be combined with demographic data.

Modern developments have also given rise to technologies used specifically for research.

(a) **Scanners** and **optical mark readers** or optical character recognition devices eliminate the need for manual entry of data onto a computer system.

(b) Hand-held computers, often with touch sensitive screens, are now frequently used in place of clipboard and pen to record responses to questionnaires. This is known as **computer-assisted personal interviewing (CAPI)**. Again the advantage is that there is no need for subsequent manual entry of data, speeding up the process and reducing the chance of error, because there are no transcription errors and computerised data validation techniques can be employed.

(c) The **telephone** on its own may not be regarded as an example of modern technology, but its use for research purposes has grown considerably as telephone ownership and usage has increased. This has allowed researchers to reach respondents in widely geographically dispersed areas at relatively little expense in terms of cost and time, compared with face-to-face interviews or postal questionnaires.

(d) There are even greater possibilities when the telephone is combined with computer technology. **CATI (computer-assisted telephone interviewing)** is now the norm in developed countries. This allows direct data entry and validation, with the advantages mentioned above, and it also provides much greater control over the interviewing process, because it can be done centrally and it can be monitored (and adapted if necessary) in real time.

(i) All interviewers can be briefed simultaneously and start work straight away.

(ii) Short lead times and fast response rates make it possible for surveys to take place immediately after topical events.

(iii) Complete standardisation is ensured, since everything the interviewer says is scripted and no deviation or ad-libbing is allowed.

(iv) There are no routing problems or decisions for the interviewer to make about what questions should or should be asked next – these decisions are made by computer on the basis of responses so far.

(e) The **Internet** allows researchers to collect information at any time (to suit the respondent) from anywhere in the world that has access to the web. This has similar advantages to CATI (direct data entry, short lead times, standardisation, computer-controlled routing).

Data analysis

Even such commonplace components of modern computing as word processing packages and spreadsheets have made a considerable difference to the way in which data can be analysed, because they allow it to be searched at great speed and sorted, resorted, re-organised and summarised at will.

Moving up a level, databases and database query languages allow more sophisticated analyses of data.

(a) A **data warehouse** is a centrally stored source of data that has been extracted from various organisational databases and standardised and integrated for use throughout an organisation. Data warehouses contain a wide variety of data that present a coherent picture of business conditions at a single point in time.

This could enable the sales and service departments to pool their respective databases to give them improved customer profiles, eg the service records could be used by the sales department to identify customers with high mileage vehicles who may be an ideal target market for appropriate products.

(b) **Data mining** is a method of using databases to look for hidden patterns in a group of data. For example, data mining software can help retail companies find customers with common interests. Data mining software not only changes way data is presented, but also discovers previously unknown relationships among the data using **neural networking** techniques that impose a mathematical structure on interconnected elements, supposedly like the neural pathways in the brain.

A common technique in the analysis of research results is **cross tabulation,** whereby responses to questions are tabulated against responses to other questions (for example: "How many ice creams do you eat in a week?" by "What age are you?"). At one time tasks like this were performed manually by cutting and pasting all the relevant parts of the transcripts into sections, like a collage or by writing on large "analysis sheets" and then noting down the findings for each interview or group undertaken under the different topic guide headings.

Naturally a number of software products have now been developed with market research analysis specifically in mind. Well-known examples include **QSR** NVivo and QSR N6 (NUD*IST). These allow the researcher to input the data into a base file and then allocate chunks of the data to relevant sections which the researcher identifies as they work through the data. The program then provides a 'tree' diagram, which shows how the data has been allocated. There are a number of other more sophisticated techniques that the program will allow. For example, it is possible to identify and show links between different data sections with common themes and also to include pictorial and other documentation in the overall project file.

For quantitative data one of the more widely used packages, especially among in-house researchers and independent research consultants, is **SPSS**. It provides tools for producing a range of different tables and charts which the researcher requests on screen, in one window, and the results are processed and presented more or less immediately in another window. It offers a very comprehensive range of uni-variate, bivariate and multi-variate statistics.

30 The Internet and data collection

Tutorial note. Our answer makes some use of the relatively recently issued MRS *Internet Research Guidelines* (December 2003). Be sure to obtain a copy from the MRS website if you are not already aware of this document. Of course, the very fact that the MRS has issued guidelines could be seen to contradict the assertion made in the question, but a case can be made for it.

Our answer disagrees with the question's proposition, but you may have chosen an area of applied research that led you to different conclusions. It could indeed be argued that there is little information that can currently be collected via the Internet that cannot be collected by other means, apart from information about Internet-usage behaviour itself (eg click-throughs). An Internet questionnaire, for example, is still just a questionnaire, essentially the same as a well-written and well-administered paper-based questionnaire delivered by post, except that the process is a bit quicker.

Our answer takes a longer term view, however.

The MRS *Internet Research Guidelines* (December 2003) usefully define **Internet research** as follows.

'Research in which a respondent – either on a single occasion or as part of a panel – is involved in any of the below.

■ Completing a questionnaire online via the Internet regardless of access route.

■ Downloading a questionnaire from a server on the Internet and returning it by email.

■ Receiving the questionnaire incorporated into an email and returning it in the same way.

■ Participating in an online qualitative interview or discussion.

■ Taking part in a measurement system which tracks web usage using specialist software installed on the user's computer.'

Applied research is generally aimed at solving a specific pragmatic problem, gaining a better understanding of the market place, determining why a strategy or tactic failed, or reducing the level of uncertainty in management decision making (ie it has a direct commercial application).

For our example we will take a company that provides health insurance to the business market. We will suppose that the company has noticed an increased incidence of claims from business people whose work entails a lot of travel and it wishes to investigate this phenomenon in more depth. Part of the research will entail asking subjects to keep a diary of what they eat each day, how long they have worked, what travelling they have done, and how healthy or otherwise they feel. Respondents will have a choice of completing a daily paper-based diary (which has been sent by post) or submitting information via the Internet.

Data collection via the Internet has a number of advantages over, and certain differences as compared with, conventional techniques.

(a) **Greater response rate/greater convenience**

The **costs** of asking people to complete a web questionnaire are considerably smaller than, say, a postal questionnaire. Potentially a much larger number of people can be contacted at little cost. Those people may be anywhere in the world, so (allowing for language differences) a wider geographical spread can be reached. The data is submitted in electronic form so it **does not need to be keyed in and validated** again.

Specific respondents who are **difficult to reach by other means**, such as business people who travel a great deal, as in our example of applied research, can also be contacted much more easily. In our example they could be **sent a reminder** by email if they do not submit a diary return on a particular day and, arguably, they are much more likely to keep up their online diaries and **remember** accurate details.

There is already a good deal of evidence that people are more willing to respond to computerised questionnaires than to postal ones. This may simply be because they do not have to remember to keep the pre-paid envelope and remember to post it the next day, they just have to click on a **Submit button**. In our example they can fill in their questionnaire when prompted by an email reminder while checking other email: they do not have to search through their luggage for the papers, find a pen, keep everything in order, and so on.

A well-designed web questionnaire should also be **easier and quicker** to complete, since there should be no need for the respondent to follow complex **routing** instructions such as "If X applies please skip to question 23". If previous answers have indicated that questions 17 to 22 (say) are not relevant, the web-server simply will not present them.

(b)   **Response mechanisms**

The question refers to the long term, and in the long term (the next three to five years, say, given the current pace of development) **all kinds of devices** are likely to include electronic components and could be **Internet-enabled**. This means that data could be collected from them and sent to interested parties. Assuming adequate safeguards can be put in place to protect personal data, this would entail little or no effort on behalf of the respondent apart from giving permission for the transfer of the data.

In the case of our travelling businessperson this could mean that data collected by the EPOS system in the restaurant that he or she ate in about what was ordered could be transferred (with appropriate permission) to the data-collecting organisation.

Internet-enabled fridges are already a reality and these include touch screens and barcode readers. In the connected world of the near future it is likely to be possible for a fridge to examine its own contents and dial up the local supermarket to order replacements for any items that are about to pass their sell-by dates. This has implications for the researcher, too, since it provides previously unavailable information about product usage as opposed to product purchase.

Our travelling businessperson may be required (for billing purposes) to scan items consumed from the hotel room mini-bar using the fridge's barcode reader, but (as always, given permission) this information could also be transmitted to the medical insurance company.

A **toilet** is in development that will monitor human waste and spot health and dietary problems. Following input from a user, the Internet toilet could 'talk' to the Internet fridge and order more fruit and fresh vegetables and fewer burgers and chips, say — or call Alcoholics Anonymous!

In our example of applied research, a hotel toilet could perhaps be permitted to transmit information to the medical insurance company.

In conclusion, it is probably true that the data that **could** be collected, **in theory**, will not change as a result of Internet technology. However, the data that **will be collectible by**

practical means and then be available in a readily analysable form is likely to increase continuously for the foreseeable future, and the uses to which it can be put will only be restricted by the imagination of researchers.

31 Panels

> *Tutorial note.* No indication is given of the weighting of the separate parts of this question. We have assumed that part (a) is only worth about 20%, since it asks for a brief description. The balance of your answer may have been different (surely a major 'role' of a panel is to be 'useful' to researchers, after all), but don't worry too much so long as you got similar points to the ones made in our answer somewhere into your own.

(a) **The roles of panels**

In the marketing research process panels are a **means of collecting data as part of a longitudinal research study**. Data is collected from the same pool of individuals (or households, or organisations) over time, either continuously (every day) or at regular intervals. Panels typically generate quantitative data but they can also be used for qualitative research.

The panel is intended to be representative of a particular population such as owners of a particular make of car or all households in Birmingham.

Some of the best-known consumer panels (FMCGs) are products from Taylor Nelson Sofres such as Superpanel (UK), Europanel and Worldpanel, and ACNielsen's Homescan. Some omnibus surveys such as BMRB's Access Online are also panel-based. (An omnibus survey is one that contains questions for more than one client: clients with relatively short questionnaires can thus get their research conducted to high standards without bearing the cost of setting up an entire survey themselves.)

Another form of panel is the **retail panel** which is made up of a sample of retail outlets. These are used to collect retail audit information such as prices, promotions, amount of stock held, number of brands covered and so on.

(b) **Usefulness to researchers**

The results of panel research provide the researcher with a **picture of changing habits**.

Panels provide quantitative data that can be used to produce grossed-up measurements of the whole population of interest, based on samples of individuals or households, where the data is standardised and consistent over time. They combine both accurate absolute measurements of such parameters as consumer expenditure and product consumption with the ability to analyse micro behaviour and change over time.

The data collected from panels is usually, but not exclusively, **behavioural** (What? How many? How much?) rather than attitudinal. It may be used for various purposes.

- To monitor **long term trends** such as brand share
- To measure reaction to **short-term changes** such as a money-off promotion
- To measure the effect of *ad hoc* developments such as a new TV advertisement.

Panel data is very expensive. To reduce the cost to the client, much panel data is syndicated, as with the examples cited. Alternatively, clients purchase only that part of the report that is relevant to their market and products.

Running panels

The choice of data collection method is critical in terms of the quality of data and should avoid tedium for the panellist. **Traditionally, diaries** have been the most common form of data collection, where panel shoppers record their purchases in a diary and return it periodically to the research agency. This is still done in certain countries where more advanced technology is not available, but in **developed countries electronic methods** of recording and transmitting data are more likely to be used. With Superpanel, for example, data is collected twice weekly via electronic terminals in the panel member's home, with purchases being recorded via home-scanning technology.

Plainly this is a quick, convenient and highly accurate, method of recording data for products such as FMCGs. The **barcode** gives a unique identification of products down to brand, size, flavour and offer.

If the subject matter of the panel research is not a bar-coded product or products, however, other approaches are required. Alternative methods are **postal questionnaires, telephone interviews** and **Internet-based questionnaires**. Some researchers argue that interviewer-based panels provide greater accuracy of data recording, greater continuity of panel membership and increased quality control via the use of a trained field force.

Panel research can only meet its objectives of accurately reflecting population consumption and other behavioural trends if the data is measured consistently over long periods of time. Clients need to know that the researcher's methodology and controls are appropriate and complete.

Once in place, therefore, panels are rarely changed. So, in designing the sample, the provider needs to have an extremely accurate understanding of the population of interest. It is common practice when setting up such a service to have, for example, three panels of identical composition. These will be rotated to minimise respondent 'fatigue' . So, if the service operates on a monthly basis, for example, any given panel member will participate only every third month.

Maintenance of a stable panel is the top priority. A good panel aims for 80%+ in terms of continuity. In some cases members may willingly co-operate because they perceive the research to be valuable, as may be the case in an academic or scientific survey. In less altruistic cases, though, incentives for members are often crucial. Research agencies tend to be very secretive about what they give their members – usually it amounts to points or voucher accumulation, to keep them interested. Good communication always helps. Agencies may distributes a newsletter to make panel members feel part of a team, or even set up an online community for them, if this would not distort the research.

Panel **replacement**, for example because of illness or boredom, is an ongoing concern. Ideally, the newcomer should really be a clone of the 'drop-out' in every way, but this may not be easy to achieve.

Another problem is the degree of **bias** that creeps in over time when people are consciously recording their behaviour. Their raised level of awareness of the activities being tracked means that a certain distortion of their typical behaviour may occur over time. This is something that needs to be assessed. In some cases it may not be very important, but in others it may be important enough that the selection of new respondents for each wave of *ad hoc* or 'repeat continuous' studies may be the preferred method.

32 Focus groups v in-depth interviews

> *Tutorial note.* This was a very popular question when it came up, but the average mark was relatively low. Weak answers tended to mention few suitable uses for groups or depth interviews and explanations were either limited or unclear or both. Examples used tended not be relevant. The strongest answers covered a comprehensive range of advantages and disadvantages and gave interesting and relevant examples.

The term **group discussion**, also known as a **focus group**, is largely self-explanatory. Typically, a group of 8 to 10 respondents is specially recruited, on certain basic criteria, for example male drivers in the Nottingham area, and brought together to discuss topics raised by the researcher. In the course of the discussion they are encouraged to exchange experiences and beliefs about a product category (brand, packaging, advertisement) under the guidance of a trained moderator.

An **in depth interview** ('depths') is normally on a one-to-one basis (a respondent and an interviewer) but there may be occasions when 'paired interviews' are used (for example, husband and wife or mother and child plus the interviewer).

Focus groups are **recommended** in the following circumstances.

(a)   Group discussions offer good **value for money** in terms of cost per respondent and a project consisting of groups can usually be carried out in a **shorter period of time** than one with a similar-sized sample consisting of individual interviews – and the need to obtain information quickly can be a determining factor. In-depths can be time-consuming, and therefore expensive in terms of cost per respondent, both in terms of getting to and conducting the interview and in terms of analysing the tapes.

(b)   If the researcher wants to find out about a relatively **wide range of attitudes and opinions**. The process highlights differences between consumers, thus making it possible to understand the range of attitudes and opinions, in a relatively short time. The **social and cultural influences** on attitudes and behaviour are also highlighted.

(c)   Group discussions are a good vehicle for **creativity** and interactivity. Respondents feel "safety in numbers" and therefore appear to relax. The supportive environment encourages emotional involvement and the expression of insight. Spontaneity of response is encouraged, and one person's experiences or feelings tend to spark off another's. One-to-ones provide far less opportunity in this respect because responses can be very rational and considered, not mirroring the range of emotions that may affect the true opinion or purchase decision.

(d)   **Stimulus materials** (pictures, products etc) and **projective techniques** (eg sentence completion) are likely to be more successful because in a group respondents will not feel so much pressure to come up with views and answers or feel they are being tested.

(e)   Where the **product** culture belongs in the **social arena** (for example beer, or fashion), or will be advertised in the public media, then group discussions are usually the more appropriate method.

(f)   Focus groups are more appropriate for certain groups, such as **children** (though the group would be a smaller one). Interactive methods can be used to counteract the more limited concentration span that children tend to have, and children are likely to find what they regard as a 'play' session more enjoyable than an interview.

In-depth interviews are more **appropriate** in the following cases.

(a) When the topic is of a **sensitive or intimate nature**: something that people would not normally be prepared to discuss with strangers. Topics in Western Europe that might be considered sensitive could include sexual practices, some bodily ailments and remedies, personal finance, religion and political issues. In an in-depth interview rapport can be established with the moderator and respondent are more likely to talk openly and freely. The interview may be conducted via telephone to increase anonymity (and also cut down on costs).

(b) When the research requires detailed information on **individual attitudes and behaviour**, uninfluenced by others. In a group a strong personality (or perceived expert) may overawe the other members who either withdraw or simply agree with him or her. In-depths are orientated to penetrate the superficial or 'public' face of the respondent, for example to find out the person's true opinion about an issue rather than their publicly stated opinion, which is possibly a socially acceptable opinion.

(c) When the research is concerned with **minority views**, especially if others might not find those views socially acceptable. Group members may feel insecure at voicing opinions that appear to be different from the majority, or if they do express their views conflict could arise that might be difficult to control.

(d) When **individual longitudinal data** is needed, such as the decision making involved in a particular purchase process or views on technical subjects (for instance, if someone has to look up their old gas bills).

(e) Research into products that are privately used or consumed and advertising that will be experienced in private rather than public media (for example, magazines compared with television or cinema) are more appropriate for the one-to-one rather than the group environment.

(f) In some circumstances group discussions are ruled out by the nature of the research. For example, in business research respondents may be uncomfortable about saying too much in front of possible competitors.

(g) On a more practical level, one-to-ones may be the only option if the required sample characteristics make it **difficult to gather together** a group, for example the very rich, wheelchair users, key professionals or opinion-leaders.

(h) Equally if a sample for research is very **heterogeneous** (diverse), it may prove too **costly** to bring people together into group discussions, and individual interviews may be the only cost-effective approach.

33 In-home interviews

Tutorial note. In part (a) you can mentions benefits that apply specifically to in-home interviewing and also more general benefits of any kind of face-to-face interviewing methods. In part (b) you should mention a range of alternatives, giving reasons why they might be used in preference to in-home interviews. Good answers will not just list the benefits of the different methodologies but will constantly focus on the alternatives in relation to in-home interviewing. Note that the parts of the question have equal weighting, so you should write about the same amount for each. As often, our answer is probably longer than you could have managed in the time available: this is to give you some ideas to help with your revision.

(a) **In-home interviewing**

In-home surveys are used when it is useful to speak to people in their own homes rather than at some central location, hall or store.

Benefits

There are many benefits in conducting an in-home survey.

(i) If they are by appointment it is more likely that they will go ahead, so the incidence of **non-response** and **not filling quotas** is **reduced**. Appointments may be made by telephone (either cold calling or otherwise), as a follow-up to an on-street interview or a completed postal questionnaire, or by knocking on doors.

(ii) It is **more reliable** than some other methods if **geographical location** is **important**, for example if sampling on the basis of ACORN information. Cold calling may be important for random sampling where the interviewer has to adopt an alternative strategy if they get a non-response from the sample unit selected. This usually involves picking the nth house in the same street or similar technique to replace the non-respondent when a return visit also produces non-response.

(iii) Respondents are likely to be more relaxed in their own surroundings, which should lead to **fuller** and **more open answers** and more opportunity to probe and prompt and explore topics in-depth. This may be especially important if intimate personal topics need to be discussed.

(iv) The respondent normally enjoys the experience, although this depends on the skill of the interviewer. This may make it easier to build up a rapport and recruit people for follow-ups such as participation in focus groups or panels.

(v) If appropriate, other family members can also be involved.

(vi) They are more **suitable** than other methods if the interview is likely to be a **lengthy** or **complex** one. Having invited the interviewer in it is difficult for the respondent to stop the interview if it over-runs, though obviously this should not be abused.

(vii) Like all face-to-face (F2F) methods, the answers are likely to be collected more **accurately** than they might be with a self-administered questionnaire, thanks to the skill and training of the interviewer.

(viii) They are useful when **demonstrating and testing products**, especially those that it is not practical to demonstrate on street, either because of the nature of the product or the complexity of the stimulus material. When there is some of the 'test'

product available, an in-home survey comes into its own, especially when the product is one that is used specifically in the house such as toiletries or cleaning products. It is more practical than it would be on-street to conduct exercises such as sorting and ranking prompt cards and other concept stimuli. Videos or DVDs can perhaps be shown using the respondent's equipment.

(ix) Respondents (and therefore interviewers) have **access to information** that it may not be easy to recall in other types of interview, such as the contents of food cupboards, medicine cabinets, the last CD they bought, who supplies their gas and electricity, weekly spend on such and such, and so on. More information and more reliable information can be collected.

(x) It is easier than with some other methods for the interviewer to use **electronic methods** of data recording such as a laptop or handheld computer.

(xi) For some kinds of business research an 'in-office' may have all of the above benefits.

Drawbacks

(i) There is little control over disruptive external influences such as telephone calls, other members of the family, especially young children, or other visitors.

(ii) Not all home interviewing is carried out by appointment. Some is still carried out using cold calling, in other words approaching members of the public without first making an appointment. This may be done door-to-door in person, or by telephone. This is arduous for the interviewer and in some areas, potentially **dangerous**.

(iii) Certain organisations, notably some that sell home-improvement products, have behaved in ways that give in-home experiences a bad reputation amongst consumers, for example those that engage in pressure selling, refuse to leave without a signature, or worse in some well-publicised cases. This may make respondents reluctant to let any interviewers, no matter how legitimate, into their homes.

(iv) In many households there is **nobody home** during most of the day because parents are at work and children are at school. This may vary according to socio-economic group and could distort results if a balanced socio-economic mix is required. Interviews may have to take place in the **evening**, when people may be less receptive because they are tired or have other things that they would rather be doing.

(v) Language may be a problem if the respondent's native **language** is not the same as the interviewer's. To some extent the target areas can be researched, with this in mind, in advance, but it is likely to be **difficult and expensive** to recruit bi-lingual or multi-lingual interviewers. In any case, geographical area is not always a good indicator of ethnic background.

(vi) **No supervision** is possible at the time of the interview and this means that it is more difficult to assess **quality**. A follow up call is possible, but there will be a limit to how much time respondents are prepared to give up.

(vii) Respondents may sometimes be **unduly influenced** (positively or negatively) by factors such as the interviewer's appearance or manner of speaking, whether the interviewer attempts to influence them or not.

(viii) It is relatively **expensive** compared with some other methods, and it is more **time-consuming** by its very nature.

(b) **Alternatives to in-home interviewing**

There is no method that offers quite the same set of benefits as in-home interviewing because everybody's home is unique and the home environment offers the researcher unique opportunities that cannot be replicated elsewhere.

Hall tests

A hall test allows the researcher to **set up something that looks like an average home** in the local area. This may help people to **feel a little more relaxed** than they would if interviewed in an office or similar, **but** it will also **create unnecessary distractions** in the form of furniture and fittings and décor that are not familiar.

On the other hand hall tests in a home-like setting offer the **same benefits as in-home interviews in terms of product demonstration and presentation of stimulus material**. This may be an appropriate method if the demonstration is the most important aspect of the research, and if the interview does not need to be a particularly long one. (In some cases an in street interview may be adequate, if the demonstration material is not complex or unwieldy and the interview can be quite short.)

If **cost** is an issue hall tests may be much preferable to in-homes since a much larger volume of respondents can be seen in a much shorter time, especially if the selection criteria are not so specific that precise postcodes need to be targeted.

Telephone interviewing

This has the **benefit** that **respondents are in their homes**, even if the interviewer is not, and therefore they are likely to feel reasonably **relaxed** and **in control** of the situation. If that is an important aspect of the research then it is probably better not to use mobile phone numbers. **Land-lines** are also a better choice to ensure that a particular geographical area is covered.

As with in-home interviews, respondents have **access to their own things** which may help recall, although most people are reluctant to leave another person hanging on for too long while they go and note down, say, the contents of their food cupboard.

Telephone interviewing **might be a suitable alternative to in-homes** if respondents do not need to be able to see and touch stimulus material, if body language is not a major issue, if the interview does not need to be excessively lengthy, and if the research topic is not the sort of thing that people might be reluctant to discuss over the phone. It may be safer than in-homes where there is perceived to be some danger in visiting the homes that are to be targeted.

Again, if **cost** is a concern, telephone interviewing is much cheaper and quicker than other kinds of F2F interviewing. If **control and quality** are issues telephone interviewing offers much greater opportunity for central co-ordination and monitoring. Data can be entered directly into the researcher's systems and also verified and validated directly through computer checks, so there is no risk of loss through transmission errors (as there may be with in-homes), and less risk of interviewer error in recording data.

Achieving a response may be more **difficult** than with an in-home, since it will rarely be possible to arrange an appointment to make a call, and there is no guarantee that the target will be in and that the phone line will be free.

Postal questionnaires

Postal questionnaires can be **targeted geographically** just as effectively as in-homes. Once again they are likely to be completed when respondents are actually in their homes, though the researcher has no way of controlling or verifying that.

Stimulus material can be provided, although this is far **more expensive than with F2F methods** such as in-homes, because material has to be prepared and sent to every respondent, not just to interviewers. In **other respects** postal questionnaires are **cheaper than in-homes**: there is no need to recruit and brief interviewers and allow for travelling time and expenses.

A postal questionnaire may be **appropriate** if interviewer assistance or interpretation is not felt to be essential to ensure the quality or accuracy of the data. The researcher must also be willing to wait longer for responses to be returned and be prepared to accept a considerable amount of non-response.

Internet

This method is similar to a postal questionnaire except that **data entry is done by the respondent** (which has obvious **cost advantages**).

It could be preferable to a postal questionnaire if the stimulus material is interactive (DVDs can provide a certain amount of interactivity, but production and distribution costs are considerably higher than they would be with an Internet application). An interactive presentation goes some of the way to replacing an interviewer, since respondents can be helped and guided to some extent.

For questionnaires that require complex routing an online version is possibly preferable to both an interviewer-run exercise and certainly to a postal one, since the routing can be handled seamlessly by computer.

Response rates with Internet based questionnaires tend to be slightly higher than for postal questionnaires, though nowhere matching in-homes.

The main issue with this approach is achieving a representative sample, since Internet access is by no means universal, and is heavily biased towards certain socio-economic groups. That may not be a problem if the researcher wishes to target people who are already known to have Internet access.

34 Observation and interviewing

> *Tutorial note.* In part (b) the examiner expected candidates to identify at least one method of using observation to collect each type of data and describe it in some detail, or preferably to identify a number of methods. Be sure to explain why each method might be used.

(a) **Observation and interviewing**

Observation is a form of research that involves monitoring and recording the behaviours of consumers, shoppers, product and service users etc. and seeking to understand these behaviours. Participants are not asked any questions.

In market research the term observation is used to refer not only to visual observation (watching people or recording them on camera), but also to electronic monitoring of various kinds, such as recording of EPOS data or of click-throughs on a website.

(i) Observation only provides data about **how** somebody behaved, on one occasion. It cannot explain for certain **why** they behaved in that way (although it may be possible to infer an explanation, depending on the context), nor does it confirm that they would behave in that way in the same context on every other occasion.

(ii) If the individuals **are not aware** that they are being observed, or at least **not conscious** of it, it is likely (though not certain) that they will behave in the way they 'normally' behave, so observation provides complete and objective evidence of behaviour without having to rely on memory and selective accounts of behaviour. Not telling people that they are being observed, however, raises certain **ethical issues**.

(iii) If individuals **are aware** that they are being observed their behaviour may be different to their normal behaviour, either because they are deliberately 'acting up' to the observer, or because their own perception of what they normally do is not what they really normally do.

(iv) Thanks to CCTV and video observation need not be done in real time, but it does require human analysis (conversion to words and figures) at some point if it is to provide useful information. This may be very time consuming for the researcher.

Subject to the above observation is a useful research technique in a variety of circumstances.

(i) When **complete** data is needed on behaviour, especially if that behaviour only takes place in a real context.

(ii) When the respondent is **unlikely to remember** or cannot easily **articulate** the information that the researcher needs. This may be especially true of young children.

(iii) As a **preliminary** to other kinds of research, such as an interview or focus group.

(iv) As a **follow up** to other kinds of research, for example observing behaviour after respondents have been given some information or shown some stimulus material.

(v) When the context is **new** or **unfamiliar** either to the researcher or to participants or both. For instance, if a station were to install a new high-tech type of ticket barrier it would be useful to observe how commuters dealt with it.

Interviewing involves asking the research participants questions about what they do (or have done), or what they think, and recording the responses. Interviewing is **essential** in many cases.

(i) When the information required cannot be obtained by observation at all, or not reliably ("Where did you go on holiday last year?", "What is your income bracket?"). This will very often be the case.

(ii) When the information required is an attitude, especially if it is an attitude to something abstract (a government policy, say) or something that is not physically present.

(iii) When the research requires a demographically mixed sample of people that are not likely to gather together in a place where they can be observed.

As mentioned, it may be easier to gather observational data, since behaviour can be recorded automatically, but it still needs to be analysed and converted into a useable form. With an interview there is no need to convert the data and the analysis can be done to some extent at the time the data is collected. This means that interviewing is generally quicker and more cost-effective.

By its very nature interviewing also includes observation, of course, although it must be remembered that respondents are aware that they are being observed. Depending on the research objectives the interviewer may or may not record observational data such as body language in response to stimulus material, tone of voice and so on.

(b) **Using observation techniques**

There are **two basic forms** of observation:

(i)   **Simple** (or **passive**) observation involves merely monitoring and recording people and their activity.

(ii) **Participant** (or **active**) observation includes some involvement of the researcher in the activity that is being observed.

Observation can be **both a qualitative and quantitative** technique. For example, using CCTV a researcher can both **count** the number of people behaving in a particular way (eg entering or exiting the store) (quantitative data) and can also **describe** the many different behaviours displayed by people when shopping eg browsing, reading labels, travelling around the aisles etc.(qualitative data).

Here are some specific examples of how observation can be used to collect each type of data.

(i)   **Quantitative data**

EPOS systems use a combination of barcode scanners and card readers to monitor and record purchasing activity and, in conjunction with a loyalty card scheme, this can then be mapped to demographic data to build up a fuller picture for the purposes of measuring the success of current promotions and planning future ones. The information can also be used by the store in question to determine what shelves need to be fully stocked at particular times of day and answer other stock management questions.

Web servers can be set up to log information automatically about overall volumes of traffic and about web pages visited by individuals, including information about what type of operating system and browser was being used, screen resolution, how long was spent on each page, what link the user followed to get to a page (for example, search terms used) and so on. This is of use both to marketers and to website designers.

Mystery shopping is a data collection technique that uses observation to record actual behaviour. The actual behaviour recorded is usually that of shop assistants, and the Mystery Shopping Research programme is part of a CRM (Customer Relationship Management) system, which generates feedback and information about helpfulness and friendliness of staff, particularly in the service sector. It is used mostly in the retail environment but can also be used to monitor staff performance at the interface with the client in public sector services. Essentially, this technique is used to gauge customer satisfaction. Qualitative information may also be recorded as part of the process.

A specialised form of electronic observation is an **eye movement camera**. This can be set up to track an individual's eye movement around an advertisement to determine what is looked at, for how long and in what order. They are useful when judging the success of promotional materials such as posters or in-store displays.

(ii)   **Qualitative data**

Qualitative observation data collection is usually a passive process whereby the researcher does not interact with the observed subjects. Observation may include commentary about body language as well as straightforward behavioural activity. As a passive process it contributes to the rigour of the research process because the observed activity is not influenced by the researcher, ie it is non-reactive. The researcher does, however, have to be objective when interpreting ambiguous behaviour.

Focus group discussions are often recorded in sound and video and this can provide the researcher and the client with valuable information about group dynamics, how people influence each other, how they are influenced by scripted comments by the moderator, and so on.

Qualitative observation can also involve other aspects of consumer interaction, eg **accompanied shopping**. In this case the researcher is observing the individual's behaviour, but also prompting them from their **interview guide**. This type of data collection is useful because the researcher can record behaviour and then ask questions about attitudes and opinions, thereby matching certain opinions to certain behaviours.

35 Individual interviews

> *Tutorial note.* You should make clear comparisons between the two types of interview. You may choose to organise your ideas either by 'differences' (as in our answer) or by focusing on first one type of interview then the other. Credit would be given for the range of points identified and clear and convincing examples that clearly Illustrate the points made.

(a)   **Qualitative v quantitative individual interviews**

Qualitative interviews	Quantitative interviews
Respondents are likely to be pre-recruited as a separate process to the actual interview.	Respondents may be recruited by the interviewer, especially for in-street interviews.
The number of interviews conducted will be relatively small. One interviewer may do all the interviews.	Information will be gathered from a relatively large number of people. There are likely to be several interviewers, so consistency of approach is important.
There is an interviewer guide as to topics to cover, but there is relatively little predefined structure. There is scope to expand upon topics and explore issues in as much depth as necessary. They have been called 'guided conversations'.	They are standardised, in other words the questions are worded in the same way in each interview and asked in the same order.

Qualitative interviews	Quantitative interviews
They are concerned with 'why's?' and 'how's?' and aim to get below the surface. The participants will discuss experiences, ways of doing things, motivation, attitudes, knowledge, ways of interpreting things, meanings attached to things.	They discuss factual matters: how many, what, where, when. Questions are usually structured (closed) rather than open-ended.
The interviewer has more freedom to react to the respondent and adapt the interview accordingly. The interviewer can change the way questions are asked (prompt) and the order of asking them, and can probe – add follow-up questions.	If prompting or probing is needed (for example, if the respondent says 'other' or 'don't know', and the interviewer judges that this really means that they can't remember or don't understand the question) the interviewer should follow specified procedures
They typically take place in the respondent's home, workplace, or in a comfortable central location, perhaps with viewing facilities (a one-way mirror). It may sometimes be possible to conduct the interview by phone or even on-line, depending on the research topic.	They may take place in a wide variety of settings – in street, in hall tests, on the doorstep or in-home, in office, or remotely by telephone.
They will typically last from about 45 minutes to two hours.	They will typically last no more than 30 minutes and will often be much shorter still, especially if in street.
They may be observed and are often recorded on audio or video tape. The interviewer may make handwritten notes, but not so as to disrupt the flow of the discussion.	Data is most likely to be recorded by devices such as handheld computers, although clipboards are still used. Face to face interviews are not usually audio or video recorded, but are more likely to be subject to back-checking and other quality control procedures. Telephone interviews may be recorded or monitored by a supervisor.
Projective and enabling techniques may be used such as word association, visualisation, sentence completion and so on.	Projective and enabling techniques are not relevant, but stimulus materials will often be used.
The interviewer needs strong listening skills including the ability to 'hear' what the respondent is avoiding saying, as well as what he or she is actually saying. Observation skills are also important, to detect and record body language.	Obviously the interviewer needs to listen to the answers and may have to ask for confirmation if an answer is given that is not consistent with other information, but 'higher' listening skills are not required. Observational data is unlikely to be collected.

(b) **Generating accurate and relevant data**

As a first step the organiser of the interviews should ensure that he or she understands the **research brief** and any work that has been done so far, such as **background research**.

The next step is to draw up an **interview guide** that contains topics or questions that match the research objectives and to recruit interviewers. The level of detail of the guide will depend on the experience of the interviewers and their knowledge of the project and research topic, and on the amount of 'open-endedness' required. Exploratory research is likely to be less structured than descriptive research, for example.

The research design should contain details about the size and characteristics of the sample required and so the next step is to ensure that an **appropriate sample** of respondents is recruited. The ease of difficulty of this will depend on the desired characteristics of the sample: young non-working mothers may be easier to recruit than business executives, but crèche facilities may have to be made available. Incentives or participation fees may help to ensure that the recruits turn up at the appointed time and may make them more co-operative.

Interview times will depend to some extent on when the recruits are available. The **venue** or venues should be convenient for respondents and should be appropriate for the nature of the research. The respondent should feel comfortable and relaxed, and in-home (or in-office) interviews are possibly the best way to achieve this, unless the research requires the use of complex equipment or viewing facilities.

The next step is to **brief the interviewers** on the project and the interview guide.

The researcher should of course ensure that interviewers are conversant with the **MRS Code of Conduct** and alert them to any particular ethical issues that may arise because of the nature of the research project. The introduction to the interview is likely to be pre-scripted to include information about the research, the likely length of the interview, respondents' rights, the way the information collected will be used, whether or not it is being recorded, all in accordance with the MRS Code.

The briefing may also include instruction on operating any **equipment** to be used such as recording equipment or equipment to display stimulus materials. Instructions may also be issued on matters that the interviewer should record personally, for instance about what the respondent is doing whilst speaking (**body language**, facial expressions, tone of voice and so on).

When conducting qualitative interviews the interviewer should follow the general outline of topics and questions, but the specific wording of questions and probes, and the order in which they are asked will depend upon the respondents' answers. **Prompting** and **probing** are likely to be important ways of uncovering hidden issues, and while the researcher will rely on the skills of well-trained interviewers, with highly developed **listening skills**, it may be necessary to issue some guidance about the line between prompting and leading the respondent, and about the depth of probing required. The interviewer must always keep in mind the issues that the researcher wants to know about and will need to exercise judgement about the relevance of issues that the respondent is willing to talk about.

36 Multinational quantitative surveys

Tutorial note. You are asked to discuss 'issues' that will determine whether or not the research results are sound and this gives you plenty of scope to draw from any or every part of the research process.

Please note that, to help with your revision, this is a much longer answer than you could have produced in the time available. It tries to cover as many 'issues' as possible and it includes a number of international examples that you may find useful.

A multinational survey is more complex than a domestic survey because of logistical considerations in conducting and controlling the research, because of different marketing research practices, because of differences in language and culture, and possibly because of different legislation concerning privacy and data protection.

Choosing a supplier

For a multinational survey it may be necessary to use more than one agency to conduct the research and this makes the management of the project more **complex**. There are **four basic options** available to client organisations. No one option is certain to lead to sounder results: costs and project specific factors must be taken into account, for instance whether data collection requires a particular kind of expertise, involves complex or unfamiliar techniques and so on.

(a) Appoint **one agency** that is local to the client organisation to do the project in **all of the countries**. This perhaps allows maximum quality control over the interviewing and the project schedule, while keeping costs down (if only because it reduces the workload placed on the management of the client organisation). It may be particularly suitable if the agency in question has some proprietary research technique that the client wishes to use. However, a local agency may lack detailed knowledge of the markets and the marketing research practices of the countries to be surveyed. It will need access to interviewers with all of the required languages, and that may not be easy to achieve. The country in which the client is based may not have a well-developed market research industry, so a suitable local supplier may not be available.

(b) Appoint a **multinational agency** to undertake the research (or several multinational firms, eg a European firm to handle the interviewing in Europe, an Asian firm to supply the Asian interviewing, etc). Such firms would use their own subsidiaries in each of the countries being researched. There should be no learning curve because the subsidiaries will already be used to the parent organisation's standards and methods of working. There should be consistency in quality control and the individual researchers should be more familiar with the cultures and customs. As they are geographically closer, so logistical problem and time zone differences are minimised. The cost tends to be somewhat less than using a single local firm. The choice of this option depends somewhat on the countries being researched, as the agency or agencies may not have subsidiaries in the less developed markets of the world.

(c) Appoint **one agency as project manager** responsible for briefing and selecting a consortium of research agencies, and managing the quality of the work. The principal advantage of using this one-stop approach is the convenience of dealing with a single source. The day-to-day management is the responsibility of the project-managing agency. In certain cases the project management agency may use overseas affiliates that it has dealt with before. The downside to this approach is a loss of feeling for the individual countries and control over the interviewing being done. This option also costs significantly more than going directly to local suppliers in each of the countries involved. Another possible drawback is that some marketing research agencies may be good at undertaking research but less good at managing and co-ordinating the research of other agencies.

(d) Appoint **different agencies** in each of the countries that are being researched. This ensures that the researchers have local knowledge of the country being researched, the marketing research practices of the country and the local language. The input received from the local suppliers on issues such as translation and cultural etiquette is invaluable. This approach yields the greatest control and, possibly, the lowest costs (because there is no middleman to pay). The initial selection process will probably be more complex because the client organisation will have to shortlist, brief and select a separate agency in each country. If the client has branches in each of the countries in question there may be some advantage in using that branch's 'usual' local research supplier. Nevertheless, it is more time consuming and sometimes frustrating to manage a number of suppliers from different cultures in different time zones and the related costs may outweigh the benefits of cutting out the middleman or satisfying local branches' desire for autonomy. Inconsistent data collection and data output is another problem inherent with this approach.

Timing

Multinational research projects **take longer** to conduct than domestic projects. Questionnaire translations, taking more time at the outset of the project, account for a large portion of the increase in project length. Additionally, translating and coding of open-ended questions at the back-end also takes considerably longer than for a domestic project. International shipping may also add to the time scale if samples of physical products or other non-digital stimulus materials are involved. Aside from transport it may be necessary to satisfy customs requirements. Obviously, whenever it is possible, electronic means of transferring data and documents should be used.

Communication problems, and time zone differences can add to the time necessary to finalise questionnaire and resolve difficulties in the field.

Cost

Multinational research projects typically cost **significantly more** than domestic projects on a similar scale. Reasons contributing to the higher cost include the cost of translations, costs of shipping if necessary and of long distance telephone charges, and the fact that interviewers in some countries tend to be more highly educated and are generally paid more than in other countries.

For international research projects, it is not uncommon for clients to want to see what the differing fieldwork costs are for the different countries involved, as these can vary hugely. Some countries, such as India, are relatively inexpensive for research, whereas others such as Brazil are more expensive. These comparative estimates give the client the option of undertaking research in those countries which offer best value for money. As is always the case with costs, a detailed explanation of what is driving the quotation and why costs are as they are (eg a breakdown of co-ordination costs in large projects) can help a great deal in allowing the client to make an informed decision.

Differences in language and culture

Local customs can affect everything from the wording of questions to how interviewing is conducted. Whenever possible, research should be conducted in the native **language** of the respondent. However, many **business-to-business** projects are conducted in **English** because it expedites both fieldwork and analysis. Although it is possible to conduct valid and reliable research in English, some nuances may get lost during the translations.

It is particularly important to understand **local customs and lifestyles** when deciding on the method of **interviewing**. For example, telephone interviewing is less accepted in Japan, where most surveys are conducted face-to-face. People in Mediterranean and Arabic countries tend to be reluctant to divulge personal details over the telephone whereas people in the US and northern Europe are more open about this. In many European countries, there are no shopping malls so interviewing must be done on a pre-recruited basis. In some countries even if phone interviewing is accepted, phone interviews are unreliable because in-home penetration of phones is low, particularly in many of the developing countries in Africa and Asia. This is likely to mean that telephone samples in these countries will be biased towards particular types of consumer.

Other considerations include the business hours, including the length of midday breaks, and seasonal holidays. The quality and reliability of postal and telephone services are also issues which must be dealt with. In some countries, incentives are required, while in other countries they are perceived as insulting.

For a multinational survey **questionnaire wording** may need to be changed for each country not only due to language differences but also as a result of cultural and environmental factors. Direct translation of a questionnaire may not communicate the same meaning to different nationalities of respondents. The questionnaire must be adapted to the individual environments in which it will be used and should not be biased in terms of any one culture.

(a) In many Asian cultures people are unwilling to give negative ratings. This means that the researcher will need to design and interpret **scaling questions** very differently from one country to another.

(b) **Purchasing behaviour** may be different. For instance, in developed western countries certain assumptions are typically made about the role and position of women, family members and retailers, but these may not apply elsewhere. Methods of **barter** and **negotiation** may be very different from one country to another.

(c) Depending on the countries involved the researcher may have to take account of different rates of **literacy** and anticipate in advance any possible difficulties with open-ended questions, complex wording or terminology.

In general, therefore, the co-ordinating researcher should not be excessively prescriptive about questions, because this prevents local initiative and may result in loss of data. So long as a researchers in individual countries are competent and understand what information is ultimately required some discretion should be allowed.

Analysis and presentation of findings

Open-ended questions in multinational studies can be highly problematic to analyse. Researchers will typically try to get a local fieldwork or data processing agency to carry out the coding locally. This way, only the code frame needs to be translated, not all of the answers.

The researcher may, however, provide some ideas in advance to each country of the "headings" they would like the coders to use. Unless consistent headings are used, the answers may come in very different packages, making it difficult to compare across countries. Some latitude must be allowed for country differences, so there may be a 'Miscellaneous' heading. However, imposing some rigour on the code frame of open-ended questions can be hugely helpful in multi-national studies.

For **online projects** the problem may be somewhat simplified because web programming languages are not subject to national differences (JavaScript, ASP, PHP, Perl and so on are all based on English). The researcher can design the survey instrument in a base language, but it is only what the user sees on screen that needs to be translated: the underlying processing of responses will be the same whatever the language. The data can then be collected, ready-coded, in one central data file, or separately by country, as required.

The fact that the survey in question is a **quantitative** one makes the task more difficult since the client may well wish the data derived from different countries to be amalgamated in such a way that it gives meaningful global quantitative results. The client's needs for the presentation of the final report should be built into the project at an early stage. Possible issues include the following.

- Should the results be comparable on a country by country basis?

- Should all data be aggregated where possible?

- Should results be available for each country in isolation?

- Should the results be weighted to reflect the relative size of the population of interest in each country?

Personal privacy and data protection

The researcher must have a clear understanding of, and adhere to, the privacy and data protection regimes in any country that will participate in the research.

Unless adequate data protection safeguards are in place, personal data cannot be transferred to countries outside the European Economic Area (the EU (including the ten new members) together with Liechtenstein, Norway and Iceland). In countries with weak data protection provision, transfer of data can take place but only where adequate safeguards are provided for contractual integrity and respondents provide unambiguous informed consent.

Some countries have special arrangements in place. Notably, the US has the 'Safe Harbor' agreement and by signing up to this US companies can ensure that EU organisations and legislators know that their company provides 'adequate' privacy protection, as defined by the EU Directive on the matter.

37 Hall tests and placement tests

> *Tutorial note.* This is a straightforward question that can be answered from book knowledge. You may have struggled to find enough to write to fill 50 minutes.

Both hall tests and placement tests involve showing respondents something new and then asking for their comments, but otherwise there are significant differences.

Hall tests

As the name suggests, hall tests involve **interviewing** people **large rooms** such as church halls, hotel reception rooms and so on. Often nowadays there may be facilities set aside for this purpose in shopping centres. In the US they are more likely to be called '**Mall Tests**'. Sometimes they may be carried out in a natural place of a particular product consumption or usage: for example, a new brand of alcohol may be tested in pubs or restaurants.

The hall test is most appropriate for a situation with **test materials** that can be **evaluated** quickly such as a new pack design or advertisement. They are most commonly used for

quantitative research, but they can include observation and qualitative techniques alongside a structured questionnaire. They may include usage of a product and an interview during which a respondent is asked to give his or her opinions about a product and evaluate it, as well as make a future usage and purchase declaration. An individual test usually lasts about **20 minutes**, although the simplest versions may only involve tasting a product and evaluating it on a scale.

Respondents can be recruited in advance to come along at a certain time, but in the typical hall test, interviewers approach potential respondents on the street in the vicinity of the hall, and invite them inside to be interviewed. The **key difference between this and the ordinary street interview** is that **respondents are normally shown something that would be difficult or impractical outside**.

Hall tests are equally good for collecting behavioural, attitudinal and predictive data and can be considered for each of these types of research.

Hall tests are particularly suitable for situations which require **elaborate preparations** (such as a simulated in-store display) or **test materials** (such as a new pack design, product ingredients or advertisement). **Once they are set up**, however, the strength of hall tests lies in the fact that they are **economical** and **quick**. Provided the location has a decent volume of pedestrian flow, a high throughput can be obtained in a short period of time.

Nevertheless it is important to be aware of the **constraints** before deciding to use hall tests, especially as these relate to accuracy and depth of information.

(a)   Samples drawn from the street during the day are bound to contain biases depending on time and location. For example, a survey conducted on a weekday morning will not include people who work office hours.

(b)   Not everyone is willing to give up 20 minutes, particularly if it is during a lunch hour.

(c)   They may not be suitable when a wider geographic representation is needed (typically hall tests may only take place in two to four different locations through the country).

Another possible use of hall tests is as a follow up to initial focus groups. Hall tests might be used with larger numbers to confirm or disprove theories emerging from the initial research.

Placement tests

With some products, however, it is **difficult for consumers to form an immediate opinion** based on a short trial in unfamiliar surroundings, that are not like their own normal surroundings. These include products such as domestic appliances, cars, some items of office equipment such as photocopiers or ergonomic furniture. These are better **tested over time** in the **place where they will be used**, in other words at home, in the office or on the road. Some products are only intended to work over a period of time, such as anti-ageing creams or exercise machines. In other words by no means all products are appropriate for testing in halls.

Home testing may be appropriate where the respondent might be reluctant to express an opinion unless the whole family have a chance to try the item. For example, most families have favourite brands of regularly consumed items like butter, instant coffee and so on.

Testing of products in the place where they will be used is called **'(product) placement testing'**. These type of tests are also known as **'home use tests'** or **'extended use tests'**.

In **placement testing**, respondents who match the target population are often recruited via omnibus surveys or street interviews. There may be an **initial interview** with the respondent to determine product awareness, obtain a preliminary assessment and perhaps carry out a price test ("how much would you be willing to pay for this?"). If appropriate the researcher may carry out an **in-depth interview** on the usage of particular products. During the interview a product is handed out to the respondent to test in their own home or in their office. Additionally, he or she is instructed how to fill in the **self-completion questionnaire**. Information about their experiences with and attitudes towards the products are then collected by either a questionnaire (self-completed or interviewer administered) or by a **self-completion diary**. The diary involves completing information on specific question areas about the product on a daily or weekly basis, or at an appropriate time (eg after the first usage, after the second, after the end of the test). The information is then sent back to the researcher by post or by electronic means, or it may be collected in a final interview, the results of which can be compared with the initial interview.

Products may be tested in this way for only a few days (for example, for a food item, although the days should include days on which there are the biggest chances for a product to be tested – alcohol should be left for at least a whole weekend), or for perhaps three weeks for a new electrical product, or for much longer, maybe six or twelve months for a new car or other complex equipment. There is a **risk** that **competitors** will **see** the product during the test, especially if it is something like a car. This risk must be weighed against the risk of launching a product that customers do not like.

Placement tests **can be expensive**, especially for more complex items like cars, since the manufacturer will need to produce enough products in their supposedly finished format for testing purposes, and testing will wear those products out somewhat or consume them completely. It will often be necessary to **recruit more respondents than are actually required** by sampling theory, to take account of people who drop out of the test before it is complete, perhaps because they do not like the product and are not prepared to give it a chance, or because they get bored with filling out the diary.

38 Errors in quantitative surveys

> *Tutorial note.* Don't make the mistake of thinking that this question is only to do with statistics and sampling error, although that should be mentioned. Don't forget about errors at the initial design stage or error in the analysis or interpretation stage. Strong answers to this question will consider a wide range of errors at all stages in the research process and suggest a range of solutions or steps for overcoming or addressing these.
>
> It is likely that you will be able to draw on personal experience, and even though you are not specifically asked for examples they will always gain credit if they are relevant and valid. (This is not the place to have a moan about the errors that your boss or your colleagues have made though, nor to mock the sins of competitors!)
>
> See also **question 5**, our answer to which contains many points relevant to this question.

(a)   Errors may occur at every stage of the research process.

Communication errors

Communication problems are most likely to arise at the beginning and end of the process.

(i)   At the outset, the client may **not define the problem clearly**, and/or not make it clear what information is needed to make decisions about the problem. The researcher may **misunderstand the client's brief** and could make many invalid assumptions if confirmation and clarification is not sought.

(ii) At the conclusion, the researcher may not **report the results** in a way that helps the client to understand what action should be taken. (Given that this is a quantitative study the results are likely to include important statistical analyses, but the relevance and validity of these must be explained in layman's terms.) The client may make incorrect decisions because they **do not understand the results** of the research, in spite of all reasonable efforts by the researcher, or may **ignore** them completely or at least ignore results that don't happen to suit their plans.

Design and execution errors

Errors may occur at every stage.

(i) **Data collection** methods may have been inappropriate. For example, group discussions may have been used when one-to-one interviews would have been more appropriate for the research topic. Postal questionnaires may have been used when on-street or telephone interviews would have been preferable because some kind of interviewer involvement was desirable. This may only be realised in retrospect – the real error is **not pre-testing** the chosen method to ensure that it will deliver the required information.

(ii) Even if the right method is chosen it may be poorly executed. **Questionnaires** in particular can be highly problematic: they may be badly worded, they may be unintentionally biased, they may miss out crucial questions, they may be difficult to fill in because of bad graphic design or typographical errors, or complex routing, they could be wrongly pre-coded, and so on.

(iii) **Fieldworkers** may make various mistakes in collecting data or may even falsify the data. **Respondents** may deliberately give false information.

(iv) **Sampling** problems may include the following.

    (1) **Errors in selecting sample members**, for example wrongly including respondents as examples of homeowners simply because they happen to have a certain postcode where the properties are predominantly owner-occupied, without making other checks to ensure that the chosen respondents are truly representative of the population of interest.

    (2) **Sampling error** is a **statistical** term meaning the difference between the sample statistics (mean, standard deviation etc) and the actual population parameters. Provided the sample is large enough and is a probability-based one (and provided there are no other problems such as erroneously selected members) statistical sampling error can be estimated and taken account of in reporting results. If it is not a valid probability-based sample, it is not possible to estimate the difference between the sample statistics and the actual population parameters.

(v) **Non-sampling error** means **any** of the errors mentioned in this answer besides sampling error, although the term is sometimes used more specifically to refer to **response errors** and **non-response errors**.

    (1) **Response errors** arise because of errors made by fieldworkers (bias in selecting people to interview, incorrect recording of answers, accidentally or deliberately), or because respondents give the wrong answer (again, accidentally or deliberately).

    (2) **Non-response error** occurs when some of the respondents do not respond: if corrective measures are not taken this will invalidate any conclusions drawn

from a statistical analysis of results from a sample that was selected on a probability basis.

(vi) **Data entry** has numerous possibilities for error, especially if manually collected data has to be transcribed, but also if there is a fault in the programming of computer verification and validation procedures.

(vii) **Data analysis** is equally subject to human error. Only certain types of data can be effectively analysed by computer, and even then errors may be made if the underlying programming is faulty or inadequate. If analysis is based on the researcher's **judgement** it can only ever be as good as the researcher's judgement, and that may be faulty in absolute terms or in relation to the client's particular problem.

(viii) Even if there are no data entry or analysis errors the researcher's **interpretation** of the results, as **reported** to the client, may be wrong due to various factors including sheer **incompetence**, **accidental** error, and **misunderstanding** of the client's problem and final information needs.

Finally, although it may not be an error in the original research process, it is worth pointing out that research results may only be valid for a **limited period of time**: it may be erroneous to use outdated research results to make current decisions.

(b) **Steps to minimise errors**

Communication errors should be minimised by establishing a **good relationship** with the client and maintaining regular and honest communication throughout the process. Neither party should make assumptions without checking with the other; both parties should speak up if they are unclear on any matter.

Design problems can be minimised by doing as much **pre-testing** or **piloting** of the proposed approach as possible, within the constraints of cost and time. A small amount of initial cost and time may save a vast amount of wasted effort at later stages.

It is particularly important to pilot **questionnaires**, because even the very best questionnaire designers cannot anticipate every possible problem that may arise with the wording of questions without trying them out on an actual sample of the target population.

Steps to minimise **sampling error** include the following.

(i) The researcher's information about the target population should be as **up to date** and **complete** as possible. The sampling frame should be constructed on the same principles.

(ii) The sampling **technique should be appropriate** for the research in question and early results should be closely monitored to ensure that respondents sampled are genuinely representative.

(iii) The **larger the sample size** the smaller the error, although this must always be within the constraints of time, cost and practicality.

(iv) If sampling relies upon selection by interviewers the interviewers should be **thoroughly briefed** to ensure that they understand how to operate the process. Again, this can be **monitored** as the research progresses.

Response errors can be minimised by careful recruitment of fieldworkers and proper training and briefing. CATI and CAPI methods have some built in controls and these should be used if possible. Various other quality control procedures can be used, such as calling back a sample of respondents and checking the reasonableness of results from different interviewers.

Non-response errors may be reduced in various ways.

(i) Pre-notification often improves response rates for postal and email questionnaires.

(ii) Incentives can improve response rates.

(iii) Perseverance may be required on the part of the researcher and fieldworkers, in other words if chosen sample members cannot be reached at the first attempt further attempts (call backs) should be made rather than just eliminating that person from the sample.

As regards **data entry**, errors can be minimised by planning in advance as far as possible (pre-coding) and the use of **technology** preferably at the data collection stage. Computerised **verification and validation** checks should be in place, but they should be thoroughly tested first to ensure that good information is not eliminated by a badly designed check.

Computerised analysis tools should help to reduce error at the analysis stage, but only if they are programmed and set up properly by the researcher. Results should also be subject to **reasonableness checks** by experienced and well-briefed researchers.

Finally it is important to maintain good **administration**, to guard against basic problems such as files being lost or overwritten.

39 Postal surveys

> *Tutorial note.* A strong answer would offer a comprehensive list of advantages and disadvantages, with clear explanations or evaluation and relevant examples, and a range of suggestions for overcoming the disadvantages. Do not forget the issue of the representativeness of the sample.

(a) **The usefulness of postal surveys**

A postal survey is conducted by sending out self-completion questionnaires to a mailing list. They can be useful in particular situations.

(i) Where consumers are **used to communicating by post** (such as members of a book club), particularly if it can be done as part of another regular process such as placing an order or paying a bill.

(ii) When a relatively **large sample size** with a **wide geographical spread** is required **cost effectively**. (Conversely they may also be a practical way of securing data from very restricted groups such as visitors to a particular theatre.) Hard to reach people such as those without a telephone, people who travel a great deal and people who are housebound can be targeted more effectively.

(iii) For quite lengthy questionnaires they may be preferable to other methods of data collection, because respondents can fill them in at whatever place and time is most **convenient** for them. They can take the time to give proper consideration to questions that require some thought.

(iv) They are more practical and reliable than other methods if the questions require respondents to **check documents** or other information that they keep at home (for example, "What is the current mileage on your car?").

Self-completion is an advantage in the sense that it eliminates the possibility of **interviewer bias**, but it also has several possible **disadvantages**.

(i)   The respondent **cannot be guided** through the more complex questions and may give an inaccurate or incomplete response.

(ii)   There is no **control over the order** in which the questionnaire is completed. Deliberate design techniques such as funnelling – moving from the general to the particular – may be defeated by the respondent.

(iii)   There is **no guarantee** that the questionnaire was really **filled in by the person it was sent to**. Another member of the family may have completed it, or it may have been completed by several people, individually or in group discussion. That may not have been what the researcher required.

(iv)   Questionnaires need to be **highly structured**, and typically aimed at gathering **quantitative** information. The method is therefore quite **unsuitable** for certain types of research such as **exploratory** research which is typically loosely structured and employs prompting and probing techniques.

There are a number of other disadvantages to this method.

(i)   As stated in the question, **response rates are typically low** and this is likely to affect the **representativeness** of the results. Responses are more likely from those who have particularly strong positive or negative feelings about the subject of the research and the completed sample may therefore be significantly **biased** towards extreme views.

(ii)   **Design** must be done very carefully and is likely to be more far **time-consuming** than it would be if an interviewer were administering the questionnaire, guiding the respondents through the questionnaire and motivating them to complete it.

(iii)   **Time** is also needed to print and despatch questionnaires.

(iv)   Added to this, respondents **rarely respond to time scale**, so this can be a significant constraint.

(v)   Because of the activities of direct marketers postal questionnaires may be perceived as **junk mail** by recipients and be thrown away without even being opened.

(b) **Overcoming the disadvantages**

The disadvantage of lack of guidance by interviewers cannot be overcome: if this is a very important issue another method should be used to collect the data.

A number of methods may be used to increase the volume and speed of **responses**.

(i)   The **mailing list** should be thoroughly **checked for accuracy**, audited for **duplicates** (a duplicate questionnaire is likely to annoy someone who might otherwise have responded) and against direct marketing databases such as the **Mailing Preference Service** and the **Bereavement Register** that indicate addresses that should not be targeted and from which no response can be expected.

(ii)   The **envelope** should make it clear that its contents are not junk mail, and the questionnaire itself should begin with very clear assurances about **confidentiality**.

(iii)   **Pre-paid response envelopes** should always be included.

(iv)   Many researchers include a **pen**.

(v)   **Pre-notification** can help with response rates. This means informing the participants in some way (by telephone, post or email) that they will be receiving a questionnaire in the post in the next few days. The sample are then looking out for the questionnaire and are less likely to regard it as junk mail.

(vi)   **Reminders** may be sent, either in the form of a follow-up telephone call, or sending the questionnaire a second time.

(vii)   **Incentives** can help to improve response rates, such as the chance to enter a free draw, tokens, or a reward for the first so many responses received (to encourage respondents to send back the questionnaire quickly). In some types of survey the researchers offer to **share the results** with respondents, and this may be valuable and useful information for them if they have a keen interest in the topic.

(viii)   Response rates tend to be better if the **completion process is not too arduous**, ie if there is a limited number of questions, if the questionnaire is attractively designed and looks easy to read and follow through and if it is as interesting to complete as possible.

(ix)   People are more likely to complete a questionnaire if it is on a topic that they are **interested** in, so the survey should be **targeted** accordingly. Many general purpose questionnaires include questions about the respondent's 'other' interests, and this information helps to identify likely targets for more specific research.

(x)   Alternative response methods may be used, for example some participants may be more willing to complete an on-line version of the questionnaire. This has the additional advantage that data entry is done by the respondent rather than the researcher.

(xi)   It may be helpful to run a second survey amongst **non-responders** only.

There may be some people who buck the trend and regularly fill in any questionnaires they are sent, because they enjoy doing so. Researchers may consider recruiting these rarities to a **panel** for the purpose of **continuous research**.

40 Tutorial question: Research techniques

Tutorial note. We have placed this question at the end of the batch of questions on data collection because it is rather more 'applied' than the others: you are given a mini context to write about rather than talking in general terms about the techniques mentioned. This makes it good initial practice for a case study style question.

It is assumed in the context of this question that shopping mall tests refer to mall intercept surveys and not hall tests. A good answer will describe the techniques, comment on their relevance to the context, and *evaluate* the usefulness of each in the light of the context.

REPORT

To: Marketing Director, Airdirect
From: John Smith, Consultant
Date: 10 September 20X5
Subject: Alternative marketing research techniques

Three alternative marketing research techniques and their appropriateness to achieving the stated objectives will be briefly discussed, but firstly we need to identify respondents.

Respondents will need to be drawn from **two segments** - business users and holiday travellers. These can be further sub-divided into existing users or non-users of the airline. If tour operators need to be canvassed, some form of depth interviews would need to be conducted.

(a) **Shopping mall tests**

Shopping mall tests or **intercept** surveys are carried out in shopping centres or malls in busy town centre areas. They are a form of **face-to-face** interview. The interviewer takes up a suitable position and makes approaches to potential respondents. Interviews are normally fairly brief, lasting no more than ten minutes. As soon as one interview is completed, the interviewer will seek a new respondent, thereby maximising the number of interviews achieved within a given time.

There are a number of **benefits** of this type of **face-to-face interviewing**.

(i)   Response rates are relatively high.

(ii) Initial questions can be asked in order to check the suitability of the respondent.

(iii) Use of a structured questionnaire will ensure that questions are asked in the correct order.

(iv) Targets can be set (percentage split between male and female respondents, for example).

(v)   The interviewer can check that questions have been understood.

(vi) Respondents can be prompted to answer questions fully.

Clearly shopping mall tests would be **inappropriate** to target business users. They would also seem not entirely appropriate for holiday trippers since most people select a package holiday from a tour operator and book through a travel agent. Few travellers purchase 'flight only' tickets, enabling them to fly with a preferred airline. Also, the short questionnaire format of intercept surveys does not lend itself to obtaining the qualitative data (views and opinions) which are being sought.

(b) **Focus groups**

These are groups of individuals (normally 6-10) who are selected to discuss a particular topic in some depth. The members are chosen using strict criteria so as to be representative of the target market. Focus groups are conducted at a suitable location (often a local hotel). A trained moderator guides the discussion and controls any dominant personalities. Focus groups sessions are often **recorded** for later analysis.

Focus groups are suitable for obtaining **qualitative** data, particularly at an early stage of the research. **Benefits** include the following.

(i)   Group interaction stimulates discussions and views.

(ii) Differences between consumers and their influences are highlighted.

(iii) A cheaper and fuller analysis is obtained than with depth interviews.

Focus groups would seem to be very appropriate for carrying out the airline research. The key **target groups** of business users and holiday makers can be selected and group sessions can comprise customers, non-customers or a pre-determined mix. The **in-depth discussion** generated should provide the necessary qualitative data.

There are a number of **disadvantages** to focus groups, however.

(i)   The sample size will necessarily be limited, which may lead to managers forming premature conclusions.

(ii) The quality of discussion will depend to a large extent on the skill of the moderator.

(iii) Recruiting representative samples of people may be problematical; in the case of business users, these need to be the decision makers who book or influence the choice of airline reservation.

(iv)   Analysis and interpretation can be difficult.

(c)   **Postal questionnaires**

These are questionnaires which are sent to respondents for self-completion. They are often pre-coded to facilitate subsequent analysis. Postal questionnaires are often of a 'tick-box' format for ease of completion. For this reason they lend themselves to **quantitative research** (obtaining facts and figures). However, some qualitative information can be sought. Postal questionnaires have a low **response rate** (10% would be considered a good rate of return) and therefore costs can be high if a large sample is needed. However, response rates can be increased by good, clear questionnaire design, the inclusion of a well-composed covering letter, and, in some cases, by pre-testing. Benefits include speed of response and suitability for computer processing.

This technique is worthy of consideration but may not generate the qualitative data sought. Also, some form of **incentive**, such as a prize draw for a free flight might be necessary to boost the level of response. Questionnaires sent by fax might generate a higher response amongst business users. Holidaymakers would need to be accessed via a suitable **commercial database**.

Other questionnaire distribution techniques could be considered (such as asking passengers to complete questionnaires during the flight).

41 Questionnaire design

> *Tutorial note.* In part (a) you should identify that an appropriately designed questionnaire is key to meeting research objectives. For each factor highlighted, you should provide a rationale for its inclusion. Likewise in part (b). You may have suggested a different ordering of the stages or may have grouped stages together differently. You may also have suggested additional rationales. Rest assured that credit would be given for clearly explained and justified stages.

(a)   **Factors to consider before beginning the design**

The following factors should be considered.

Research objectives. Clearly this will influence the entire process. A **quantitative** study will have mainly closed questions of the **dichotomous** (Yes/No; Male/Female) or **multiple choice** variety. If the research aims to measure attitudes Likert scale questions may be used. Exploratory research may require the use of very open-ended questions with blank spaces.

Population of interest. The characteristics of the target audience will help to determine the type of questions, their complexity and the extent to which technical language can be used or plain English is required. A survey of qualified medical practitioners, for example, is likely to be worded very differently and include very different questions to a survey of patients, even if the ultimate subject of the research is the same.

Data collection method. Questionnaires may be administered in several ways: they may be self-completed (postal or Internet-based) or administered by an interviewer. Interviews may take place over the telephone, in-street, in hall tests, in-home. Besides question wording these factors will also influence other matters.

(i)   The **length** of the questionnaire – in street questionnaires need to be short, but postal ones may be very lengthy

(ii)   The need for and type of interviewer **instructions** over and above instructions that might be given in a self-completion questionnaire – interviewers might be given alternatives for question routing or notes about acceptable and unacceptable prompting

(iii)   The use and nature of any **stimulus materials** in conjunction with the questionnaire – in-street stimulus materials need to be wieldy enough to handle while standing up and holding a clipboard or computer in the other hand; on-line materials may be highly elaborate interactive movies

Data recording. The basic options are pen and paper or computer capture (CATI, CAPI), though for control purposes there may also be some audio recording (for instance, for quality control of telephone interviews) or video recording (possibly used for hall tests, to capture additional behavioural information such as body language). This will influence the types of response formats used (see part (b) for more detail), and whether computer programmers need to be involved in the design process. There should be very early liaison with data analysts to ensure that proposed data capture methods will provide them with data in a useable form.

Time and budget constraints. The time and money available for the project will have a direct impact on the length of the questionnaire and the complexity of information collected. If time and money are tight it will be much quicker and cheaper to collect and analyse the data if the questionnaire consists of a relatively small number of simple questions.

Data analysis. The processing methods and resources available, together with time constraints, must be taken into account. For example, it may be desirable to use some open ended questions to collect richer data, but transcribing, coding and analysing free-form written responses is very time-consuming.

(b) **Key stages in the process of effective questionnaire design**

There are no definitive rules about the stages that should be followed, and the order of work may well vary from project to project. Nevertheless the following stages are likely to occur in the design of any questionnaire.

Stage 1 consists of the initial considerations discussed in part (a).

Stage 2 might be to draw up an **overall outline** of the questionnaire, subdivided as appropriate into different **topics and themes**. Reference should be made once again to the research objectives to ensure that all aspects are covered and all information required will be included (and that irrelevant information is **not** included). The result is likely to indicate the questionnaire **content** – what needs to be asked, rather than how to ask it – and the minimum number of questions that need to be asked.

Stage 3 would be a first draft of the **wording the questions** in a way that is likely to elicit the information required from the target audience. Key issues at this stage include: avoiding vagueness and ambiguity; suiting the language to the target audience (taking care over jargon, abbreviations, technical terms, possibly 'loaded' terms); sub-dividing content to avoid double-barrelled questions; not making assumptions; avoiding leading the respondent.

This stage also includes decisions about **response format.** The basic options are:

-   **Dichotomous** questions such as Yes/No questions
-   **Pre-coded** questions such as multiple choice questions or scales
-   **Open ended** questions where the answer needs to be recorded **verbatim**.

Response format is influenced by the level of detail required, particularly in the case of scales, the format of which (nominal, ordinal, interval or ratio) determines statistical tests that can be carried out at the analysis stage.

Decisions will need to be made about the inclusion of options such as 'Other' and 'Don't know', which respondents may wish to choose but which provide no useful information.

At **Stage 4** the designer will make sure that the questions are in a **logical order** (bearing in mind the logic of respondents). As a rule of thumb it is usual to put simple, non-challenging questions first and more difficult or sensitive questions later. Typically a questionnaire will try to maintain the interest of the respondent, so a balance of different types of question is desirable. Care must be taken when re-ordering questions that an early question does not cross refer to one that has not yet been asked. The wording may need to be changed in some cases.

At **Stage 5** the initial **layout** of the questionnaire would be designed, bearing in mind factors such as ease of use for respondents and/or interviewers and also for data entry (will it be scanned?) and analysis, legibility, adequate space for answers, printing costs, collation of pages. The **instructions** for interviewers or respondents including routing instructions may be drafted at this stage.

At **Stage 6** the draft questionnaire should be **tested** on a small sample of respondents to ensure that it is easy for the target audience to complete and that it does indeed give rise to the information required. Testing should bring to light any problems with question wording, with the layout of the questionnaire, and any routing problems: these must be nipped in the bud to avoid large amounts of wasted time and money once the questionnaire goes live.

Stage 7, finally, would involve revising the draft in the light of testing, incorporating any necessary changes. Stages 4 and 5 may need to be repeated, to ensure that the impact of a change in one part of the questionnaire is taken full account of in other parts.

42 Quality of a questionnaire

> *Tutorial note.* Although it is nice to get your teeth into something practical, this is a very poor quality question and a very insubstantial one for 50 minutes work. In part (b) you may well have found that you repeated points made in part (a). To keep yourself busy you may have suggested other questions that would address the research objectives, and the examiner has indicated that you would not be penalised for this.

(a) **Strengths and weaknesses**

Strengths

The wording of the questions is simple and easy to understand. The interviewer should be able to read them straight off the page.

The questions are in the correct logical order: 'why do you buy organic milk?' is not relevant to someone who does not buy it, so that is rightly the second of the two questions.

Question 6 does not simply ask 'how often?' (which could elicit answers like 'regularly' or 'occasionally' but includes a range of options that provide a means for respondents to understand what 'often' means and more detailed information for the researcher to analyse.

Likewise question 7 does not simply ask 'why?' (which on its own could elicit a huge range of answers ranging from 'don't know' to a lengthy diatribe on the evils of non-organic farming), but prompts respondents with possible reasons.

Weaknesses

Obviously we do not know what has been omitted, given that this is only an extract. On face value the weaknesses are as follows.

If the answer to question 6 is 'Never' then question 7 need not be asked, but this is not explained on the questionnaire.

It is not clear whether the 'every week' option in question 6 means 'once every week' (as the wording of options (b) and (c) seem to imply) or more often than that. No option is included for other purchase frequencies such as 'every day', 'twice a week' and so on.

In question 7 the range of options seems rather limited. There is no opportunity for respondents to give 'other' reasons, or for the interviewer to record what they might be.

Option 7(b) could be misinterpreted: organic milk is no doubt healthier than many other things, but the questionnaire should make it clear that it means 'healthier than non-organic milk' (if this is what it means). Likewise option 7(c) is ambiguous and the statement is possibly not valid: 'other milk' could include coconut milk, soya milk and so on.

Finally, it is not clear in question 7 whether the respondent can choose more than one answer.

(b) **Amendments to the questionnaire**

These are nearly all implied in the answer to part (a).

The questions should be **prefaced** by **clear instructions for the interviewers**. These might include an explanation of what organic milk is, in case respondents do not understand that, or instructions to ask these questions when standing in the supermarket's dairy products section so that the product in question can be demonstrated if necessary.

It should also be **made clear** to the interviewer whether the **questions** and **possible answers** should be **read out as shown**, or whether the answers (particularly to question 7) should only be offered to the respondent if prompting is needed.

If not explained at the beginning of the questionnaire there should be instructions as to **how to mark the option(s)** selected by the respondent: should the interviewer ring the letter, or underline the answer, or make a mark on a separate sheet? Tick boxes would be clearer, both for interviewers when collecting the data and for data entry staff later.

As already stated, **routing instructions** are needed at the end of question 6.

The possible **responses** for **question 6** should include a **wider range**, perhaps as follows.

(a)   Never
(b)   More than once a day
(c)   Once a day
(d)   2 to 6 days each week
(e)   Once a week
(f)   Once a month
(g)   Less than once a month

Note that 'Never' is placed first, because if this is the answer there is no need to waste time reading out the other options. Vertical rather than horizontal layout is likely to be easier for the interviewer to follow and easier for subsequent data entry and analysis.

For **question 7** the questionnaire needs to include an **'other' option** at the very least, and space should be provided for the interviewer to record the other reason or reasons. Initial sampling is likely to turn up a number of other reasons that recur and these should be incorporated into a revised questionnaire as soon as possible. One very obvious reason that has been omitted is 'because all the other types of milk are sold out'!

The **ambiguities** in the wording of options 7(b) and 7(c) should be removed, as indicated in the answer to part (a). There should be instructions as to how many options may be chosen, or the question should be reworded along the lines of 'What **one** of the following is your main reason for buying organic milk?'

For subsequent data entry and analysis it would be useful if the answers were **pre-coded**.

43 Tutorial question: Discussion guide and questionnaire design

(a) **Introduction** (10 minutes)

- Welcome and explain the nature of the group discussions.
- Explain the research project, and its objectives.
- Describe the format of the session.
- Group introductions, giving name(s) and limited personal details in order to relax the group and for participants to get to know each other.
- Request reasons for attending the club.

Access to the club prior to entering the main dance/music/bar arena

(20 minutes)

- Ask about good experiences of queue management prior to entry to the premises
- Ask for good examples of politeness and helpfulness of the door security staff.
- Ask for good examples of efficiency, politeness and helpfulness of the ticket/entry kiosk staff.
- What is valued most/least about the cloakroom facilities?

Main dance and bar arena (40 minutes)

The bar (20 minutes)

What enhances/spoils the bar experience?

Raise matters such as:

- Range/variety of drinks
- Speed of service
- Friendliness of bar staff
- Décor/ambience
- Range of cocktails on offer

The dance floor (20 minutes)

- Expectations of type of music
- Volume of music and quality of sound equipment
- Location of dance floor
- Ease of access to bars and rest room facilities

- Décor/Ambience/Lighting
- Provide examples of good experiences and bad experiences.
- Do the experiences vary according to the nights of the week?

Rest-room (lavatory etc) facilities   (10 minutes)

- Importance of the rest-room
- What is valued most and least about the rest-room?
- What other facilities would be valued in the rest-room?

Overall value for money   (10 minutes)

- What do the respondents perceive as being value for money?
- What are the main factors that influence the overall level of satisfaction of the club?

Summary   (10 minutes)

- Are there any other matters that the respondents wish to raise?

Thank the respondents for their participation and hand out free club entry vouchers as thanks for attendance/participation.

(b)   **XYZ Club Questionnaire**

As someone who has visited XYZ club, we wish to find out your opinion on the range of services we offer, to help us improve our services. We shall be grateful if you will take a little time to complete this questionnaire.

Have you visited XYZ night-club in the last 28 days?   ☐ **Yes** ☐ **No**

What is your gender?   ☐ **Male**   ☐ **Female**

What is your age? (tick one box)

18-20 years ☐

21-23 years ☐

24-27 years ☐

28-30 years ☐

> 31 years   ☐

How did you find out about XYZ nightclub?

Local Newspaper Advertisements ☐
Handbill / Flyer received in street ☐
Word of mouth   ☐
Other   ☐

For how long have you been visiting XYZ nightclub? (tick one box)

Less than 1 month   ☐

1 to 3 months   ☐

4 to 6 months   ☐

6 to 12 months   ☐

More than 12 months   ☐

Your welcome to the club

Thinking about your entry to the club and the welcome you received, how do you rate your welcome?

Very unwelcoming	Unwelcoming	Neither welcoming nor unwelcoming	Welcoming	Very welcoming
☐	☐	☐	☐	☐

The bar

How do you rate the selection of drinks on offer at the bar? (please circle one alternative)

Poor selection   1   2   3   4   5   Excellent selection

Music

How do you rate the selection of the music played at the club? Please circle the alternative that best describes your opinion.

Excellent   1   2   3   4   5   Poor

Club facilities

Consider your attitude to the following club facilities and for each of the following statements tell me whether you strongly agree, agree, neither agree nor disagree, disagree or strongly disagree by placing a tick in the appropriate box for each statement.

	Strongly agree	Agree	Neither agree nor disagree	Disagree	Strongly disagree
The rest room facilities are good					
The general club atmosphere is good					
The club experience is good value for money					
The dance floor is about the right size					

Your opinion

Finally, what improvements would you like to see XYZ club make to the services it provides?

_____

_____

_____

End

Thank you for taking the time to complete this questionnaire

> *Tutorial note* – If you are required to design a questionnaire, you must be careful to avoid some of the following pitfalls and ensure that the following points are considered.
>
> ■ Lack of objectivity
>
> ■ There should be a reason for every question
>
> ■ The questions should be clear and concise
>
> ■ The questions should be written in natural and familiar language
>
> ■ You should avoid double-barrelled questions (two questions in one but offering only one response)
>
> ■ There should be appropriate use of open ended and closed ended questions
>
> ■ You should make an appropriate use of scales, class divisions and question response techniques.

44 Opinion polls

> *Tutorial note.* It is likely that our answer includes a rather longer discussion of the statement in the question than you may have written, but hopefully the examples will be useful for revision purposes. You may have focused rather more than we do on scales, association grids, error of central tendency, and so on in your answer to the second part of the question: this would be fine so long as the points you make are valid and relevant.
>
> See also **question 26** for more information on sampling for political opinion polls.

Are opinion polls more often wrong than right?

Opponents of opinion polls can indeed cite some very **spectacular failures**.

(a) In the 1920s and 1930s the US magazine *Literary Digest* became famous for its huge political polls. It sent as many as 18 million postcards to potential voters asking their preference among the presidential candidates and the magazine correctly predicted the election winners up until 1932. In 1936, however, it predicted that Franklin D. Roosevelt would lose to Alf Landon, whereas Roosevelt actually won a landslide victory. Partly as a result of this error, the magazine went out of business.

(b) In the 1948 US Presidential Election the polls predicted certain victory for Thomas Dewey. Without waiting for the official count of the votes, newspapers throughout the country proclaimed in their headlines 'Dewey Defeats Truman!'. In the event, however, Truman was elected.

(c) Opinion polls conducted before the 1970 General Election in the UK predicted a comfortable win for Labour but the Conservatives won with a majority of 30 seats.

(d) In the 1992 General Election in the UK, the Conservative Party was returned to power with a slender majority of around 2%. This result was the opposite of just about every published opinion poll in the run up to the election, and, suddenly, market research found itself having to defend its reputation.

These are famous cases, and for the foreseeable future instances like these are likely to trip very readily off the tongues of politicians – especially if the latest poll predicts that they will lose!

In defence of the opinion polling industry it should be pointed out in the first place that examples of opinion polls being **correct** are much more common, but they are **not newsworthy**: the examples above are in fact the **only** national elections that have been wrongly predicted by major national polls in either the UK or the US since 1936. In the second place, market research practice has been refined and developed over the years as a direct result of the problems that occurred in the cases mentioned. In the case of the 1992 UK election the Market Research Society set up a committee of enquiry to investigate the matter in depth, as will be explained later.

Here are some additional queries over the validity of the statement in the question.

(a) **How wrong is 'wrong'?**

Opinion polls will almost always be 'wrong' in absolute terms, in the sense that they will not predict an outcome with 100% accuracy. A poll might accurately predict the overall outcome of an election, but not the exact size of the winner's majority. Polls predicted that Winston Churchill would win the 1951 election in the UK and he did so, but by a much smaller majority than had been expected.

(b) **When is 'wrong' wrong?**

Another major problem with opinion polls that are intended to measure a specific **intended** behaviour, such as voting intentions in a particular election, is that they take place **before** the actual event. This means that there is a possibility that some external event that occurred after the survey was taken may cause attitudes and therefore behaviour to change. In politics the event may be anything from news of a major scandal to inclement weather on the day of the election. One of the findings of the MRS enquiry mentioned above was that subsequent research had established that a significant number of voters changed their minds at the very last minute, which no poll conducted in advance can predict.

(c) **Are polls self-defeating?**

What appears to have happened in the UK 1970 election is that the widespread predictions of a Conservative defeat led far too many Labour voters to stay at home and not bother to vote, confident that their party would win. This leads to the ironic conclusion that polls can best predict accurate results if people actually believe that they are 'more often wrong than right'!

(d) **Are polls more accurate than elections?**

Given that (in the UK, at least) an increasingly large proportion of the electorate fails to vote on election day, it could be argued that polls may be more accurate in reflecting public preferences than elections are.

Robust techniques to measure attitude and behaviours

First some definitions. An **attitude** is a learned predisposition to respond in a consistently favourable or unfavourable manner with respect to a given subject. **Opinions** are the expression of an underlying attitude often relating to a particular aspect of a subject. An individual's attitude will usually remain dormant until the object of the attitude becomes relevant, at which point the attitude is expressed as an opinion in speech or by some form of **behaviour**. In this question the behaviour that we are interested in is voting for political parties in a general election.

(a) Eliminate **bias** and **self-selection** from the sample

In the case of the massive *Literary Digest* samples the lists of people to whom postcards were sent were biased (not representative of all citizens) because they excluded many people of lower socio-economic status. Also, those who replied were a self-selected sample, and individuals who took the trouble to return the postcard were often more extreme in their opinions than the average person.

More scientific sampling methods were subsequently popularised by pollsters such as George Gallup, who used the **quota** method of sampling, in which individual members of the sample are chosen in accordance with a quota so as to roughly match the national population on factors such as geographic area of the country, urban versus rural residence, sex, age, race, and socioeconomic status.

Quota sampling is still problematic, however, because interviewers are allowed discretion in choosing individual respondents, and this discretion introduces a further possible source of bias.

A much better approach is the probability method of sampling, in which specific respondents are chosen by random selection methods. The result of this method is that no type of individual is systematically omitted from the sample, and the likely amount of error in the resulting data can be calculated.

In general, the larger the size of the sample, the more reliable the results. Most current polls use samples ranging in size from 1,000 to 2,000 individuals. A sample of 1,500 has an expected (that is, a 95%-certain) margin of error of plus or minus 3%.

(b) Take care not to **lead** respondents

Questions must be **carefully worded** and pre-tested in pilot studies to ensure their **clarity** and **impartiality**. Unclear, biased, or emotionally charged questions will produce misleading answers and weaken the accuracy of the results of a poll. Questions such as 'How do you feel about candidate X?' or 'You are planning to vote for candidate Y, are you not?' would be suspect. Questions must avoid biases in wording that suggest a socially desirable answer or lead respondents to agree with one side of an issue. **Interviewers** must be carefully trained to avoid influencing respondents' answers. The order in which questions are asked can also affect a poll's results.

(c) Determine **how well-informed** respondents are/will be about the issues

In the case of a general election respondents are regularly bombarded by the **media** with large amounts of information about political parties, and they have their own **past voting habits** to guide them.

But this does not always apply: in the UK, for example relatively few people are currently well-informed about issues like the **Euro** or the proposed new **European constitution**, and a poll taken today on such issues would most probably give widely different results from a poll taken the day before a referendum, by which time the pros and cons would have received widespread publicity.

Survey results will need to take account of the level of knowledge of the issues amongst the target population. It may sometimes be necessary to provide the respondent with background information, but this needs to be done with great care to avoid influencing opinion.

(d) Take proper account of **non-response**

The major finding of the MRS enquiry into the predictions for the 1992 election was that most pollsters had failed to analyse non-response and had followed the convention of excluding it from the results. An analysis of the demographic profile of those not responding showed a much higher correlation with the demographics of Conservative voters rather than those voting for other parties. Relevant in this context is the so-called 'spiral of silence' theory which suggests that people are reluctant to take part in polls if their first-choice party is unfashionable or unpopular. If they do take part, these people consistently make up the bulk of the 'don't knows'. In other words, more Conservatives than other voters were **not** counted in the 1992 polls. Together with the last minute switchers, this was sufficient to tip the balance in the direction of the actual election result.

(e) Assess **volatility or firmness** of attitude

Is the opinion a deeply held belief, or an off-the-top-of-the-head reply? Researchers have a number of techniques for trying to assess this. The most common is asking the same question twice, to see if opinions shift due to changes in wording or in response to issues raised or information provided between the two questions.

To understand how steady a particular opinion is, or how it changes over time, researchers sometimes ask exactly the same question to different samples of a target population at regular intervals ('longitudinal' polling).

(f) Use **attitude scales**

Pollsters now make considerable use of sociological and psychological theory in framing their research and computer technology is needed to analyse the results. Respondents will typically be presented with a list of very carefully devised attitude statements and be asked to grade each one on a scale ranging from 'Strongly agree' to 'Strongly disagree'. Statistical analysis is then carried out to see how far each response correlates with the others. This approach recognises that attitudes are highly complex and cannot be measured accurately by asking a single question.

45 Attitude research

An **attitude** is a learned predisposition to respond in a consistently favourable or unfavourable manner with respect to a given subject. An individual's attitude will usually remain dormant until the object of the attitude becomes relevant, at which point the attitude is expressed as an opinion in speech or by some form of **behaviour**.

If attitudes are proven **predictors of behaviour** and they can be **measured effectively**, then the researcher can provide the decision maker with a powerful predictive tool. However, **expressed** attitudes, ie opinions may only be a superficial reason for behaviour. For instance, the statement 'I do not want to go abroad because it costs too much' may actually mask a more deeply rooted attitude (eg "Foreign food makes me ill").

A deeper understanding of attitudes has therefore become important in the market research industry. This is in spite of the fact that attitudes are **extremely difficult to research**.

(a) They are based on numerous factors, such as beliefs, values, feelings, past experiences, personal and social characteristics (age, sex, socio-economic class and culture).

(b) They may vary with intensity, ranging from strongly-held views to those that are barely noticeable. They may change, sometimes very rapidly, as a result of external events, new experiences, fresh influences.

(c) Respondents may not be fully aware of their attitudes, or at least not be able or willing to articulate them in a way that would be directly useful to a researcher.

(d) Because attitudes are so complex, attempts to measure them may lack **validity** (it is not clear precisely what component(s) of the attitude the measure represents) and may also lack **reliability** (in other words not give consistent results: for example, if the same question is asked in two different ways the response may be different because the wording and context tap into different aspects of different attitudes).

Both quantitative and qualitative methods may be used to collect data on attitudes, depending on the research objectives.

(a) **Quantitative research**

Quantitative research will indicate the **range** of attitudes held by the population of interest, and the **prevalence of particular attitudes**, and will provide **some measures (albeit fairly crude ones) of the level of intensity** – the depth of feeling on particular issues

Researchers are likely to be asked to **map** the attitudes of the population of interest to other geo-demographic characteristics, for example to help a client accurately promote and market the product successfully to a chosen group of consumers.

These are the potential strengths of quantitative research into attitudes, but the **results are not easy to achieve**. As indicated above attempts to measure attitudes may lack validity and reliability. A single question cannot hope to cover all the possibilities and so researchers develop banks of questions or attitude statements that are intended to reflect or measure different elements of an attitude and then combine these statements in attitude scales.

Attitude statements are collected from initial, exploratory, qualitative research and formed into an 'item pool' or 'attitude battery' which respondents are asked to agree or disagree with.

An attitude scale may include a large number of statements and a standard response format such as the familiar **Likert scale**.

	Strongly agree	Agree	Neither agree nor disagree	Disagree	Strongly disagree
Statement 1					
Statement 2					
Etc					

This approach is intended to increase the validity of measurement, because many more components of the attitude are being measured, and also reliability, because the large range of statements supposedly has the effect of cancelling out the influence of wording and context.

Problems do arise with such scales.

(i) **Wording of statements**. This is subject to similar pitfalls to those that apply in conventional questionnaire design regarding ambiguity, jargon and technical language and so on.

(ii) **Error of central tendency**. This is the tendency for respondents to avoid the extremes.

(iii) **The 'halo effect'**. This is the evaluation of the subject of the question highly on many traits because of a belief that the subject is high on one particular trait (or downgrading the subject on all traits because of a low rating on one in particular).

(iv) **Patterns**. If the respondent thinks he or she can detect a pattern of ticks, such as all positive scores lining up on the left, there may be a temptation to follow the pattern rather than reading the statements and thinking about the answers.

Quantitative research is likely to **oversimplify** matters in the interests of presenting the data in a way that can be taken in at a glance. Scales, for example, might be taken to imply that people and their attitudes fall into neatly segmented categories and degrees of feeling, and this may not be the case at all.

(b) **Qualitative research**

Qualitative techniques will be used when the researcher wants to **understand the full complexity of an attitude in rich detail** – how the attitude interconnects with respondents' needs, wants, motivations, feelings, values and behaviour.

At the very least qualitative research will be help the researcher to understand how people conceptualise the attitude and thus to develop the content and wording of attitude statements that may be used in more extensive quantitative studies.

Qualitative research **may be the only way** of finding out about attitudes that people are unable or unwilling to talk about in response to direct questions. This may be a particular problem if the topic is a **sensitive** one or if the respondent is **concerned** that his or her **attitude may be frowned upon** by the researcher because it is socially unacceptable (at least in the respondent's perception of the world).

(i) **Group discussions** may be a useful way of getting a picture of a range of attitudes and also of the ways in which people may influence each other's attitudes. Arguments, so long as they are controlled, will help to indicate the intensity with which attitudes are held. There are, however, the usual drawbacks of peer pressure and reluctance to discuss sensitive personal topics amongst a group of strangers.

(ii) **In-depth (one-to-one) interviews** with a skilled interviewer may get deeper below the surface because the group constraints are removed.

(iii) The researcher may also use **projective techniques**, which can help to overcome reticence due to self-awareness, politeness and so on, although validity and reliability depend upon a skilled researcher's choice of an appropriate technique to suit the research objectives and his or her skill in using the technique and interpreting the results.

46 Measuring attitudes

Tutorial note. In part (a) you are expected to provide a range of difficulties and use examples to demonstrate your understanding of those difficulties. In part (b) your descriptions should demonstrate that you understand how the response formats operate and you should demonstrate the strengths and weaknesses of the formats you have described.

Our answer to the 'evaluation' aspect of part (b) is organised along the lines of the key points to cover, according to the examiner's report, because this seems a more useful approach for your revision purposes. This makes our answer a good deal longer than you could have produced in the time available. You are more likely to have addressed these points in the course of describing your two chosen formats: it would have been more natural to answer like this under exam conditions.

(a) **Difficulties facing the researcher when measuring attitudes**

Attitudes are based on a number of factors. They may be affected by an individual's personal and social characteristics such as age, sex, socio-economic class, education and culture and they may vary with intensity, ranging from strongly-held views to those that are barely noticeable. Most attitudes are part of a wider compound of values, beliefs and feelings.

There is a consensus that, for example, the more favourable the attitude of consumers, the more a product is used and the less favourable the attitude, the less the product is used, and this is why it is **desirable to measure attitudes**. But the sheer complexity of an attitude makes it extremely **difficult** to measure. The attitude may change in response to changes in any of the factors that gave rise to it in the first place and added to this, the intensity of an attitude can change over time.

Quantitative attitude research raises problems of reliability and validity.

(i) **Reliability** means that the measurement could be repeated a number of times with the same outcome. When researching an attitude, however, it may be found that if the same question is asked in a number of different ways a different answer will be given each time, because respondents are highly sensitive to the wording and context of the question: different versions evoke different values, beliefs and feelings.

(ii) **Validity** means that the measurement reflects accurately the data needed to solve the defined research problem. When researching an attitude, however, the rich web of components that make up that attitude cannot possibly be captured by means of a single question.

Researchers address these problems by developing lists of **'attitude statements'** (an 'item pool') and arranging them in **attitude scales**, but the development of statements and the choice of scale raise further problems of their own.

(i) **Carelessly-worded** statements and/or an inadequate range of possible responses may not get to the heart of the attitude being investigated

(ii) Badly chosen items may well evoke dishonest replies, especially if the issue is a **sensitive** one or there is some question over the **social acceptability** of an attitude.

(iii) The **ordering** of the statements may influence the respondent's thinking and bias the responses.

(iv) **Positive** views and **negative** views need to be carefully **balanced**.

(v) Reliability of measurement tends to **increase with the number of items included**, but as the number of items increases, so the time taken to complete the questionnaire will also increase, and this may **demotivate** the respondents. Generally fewer than 20 items may reduce reliability unacceptably, but more than 30 will begin to demotivate the respondent.

(vi) The results need to be carefully **analysed** using statistical techniques to identify how responses are correlated

Qualitative research into attitudes may seem to offer more opportunity to get to the heart of an attitude since matters can be discussed in depth and individual motivations and influences can be better understood. There are still problems however.

(i) Respondents may still be **unwilling to be open** and truthful about their attitudes to sensitive matters or attitudes that they hold but which they do not perceive to be socially acceptable.

(ii) Respondents may **not be able to articulate** their attitudes, or at least not in a way that is meaningful or useful for the researcher. **Projective techniques** may help, but great skill is needed in choosing and using an appropriate technique and interpreting the results.

Finally, it is **difficult to draw conclusions** from the research. There is no automatic link between holding a certain attitude and taking a particular action.

(i) A person may have a very positive attitude towards sports cars but that does not mean that he or she will buy one, because economic and family circumstances have to be taken into account too.

(ii) Two people may hold identical attitudes but they will almost certainly have arrived at those attitudes in response to a different combination of influences and they may behave in completely different ways.

(b) **Two response formats**

The two response formats most widely used today in market research are Likert's Summated Rating Scale and Osgood *et al*'s Semantic Differential Scale.

Likert Summated Rating Scale

With this method a large number of statements about the topic or topics of research are devised, often as a result of preliminary qualitative research. Statements are typically in the form of a **short sentence** such as 'Cars made by Toyota are more reliable than cars made by Ford'. Respondents are then asked to decide how they rank the statement, typically on a labelled five-point scale, as in the following illustration.

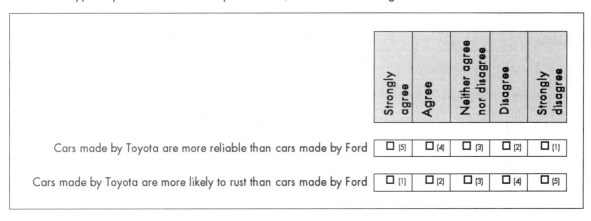

The **scores** shown here – the numbers in brackets – will **not normally be shown** on the questionnaire that is completed by respondents since they could be a distraction and influence the respondent's answer. Both positive and negative statements are used (as in this illustration), and they are scored accordingly.

Each respondent's overall attitude (in this example to Toyota as compared with Ford) can then be calculated by summing the columns. If there are 30 statements and a 1 to 5 score is used, the maximum score (most favourable attitude) is 150 (30 x 5) and the minimum (least favourable attitude) is 30 (30 x 1).

In addition the **average score** for each item, taking account of all respondents, can be calculated to establish the general strength of attitude towards individual statements.

Many other more complex statistics can be derived about the correlation between attitudes to different aspects of the question topic.

Semantic Differential Scale

A semantic differential scale is similar to the Likert technique but there are certain differences.

- The Semantic Differential scale consists of **pairs of bipolar (opposite)** words or short phrases for each item.

- The pairs (reasonable-unreasonable) are separated by a **seven-category response area**, but no verbal or numerical labels are given to the levels of response.

- There is a **mixture** of **favourable** and **unfavourable** descriptions on either side.

Here is an example of the physical layout.

Listed below are a number of pairs of words or phrases that you might use to describe cars. For each pair mark a T between the two words or phrases in the position that best describes your view of Toyota cars and an F between the two words or phrases in the position that best describes your view of Ford cars.

Reliable | | | T | | | | | | | F | | Unreliable

Rusty | | F | | | | T | | | | | Rust-free

The scales can be scored numerically at a later date in a similar way to Likert scales

However, a more popular method is to **re-organise the positives and negatives** and then give a **pictorial profile** as follows.

Reliable | | | | | | | | | : | Unreliable

Rust-free | | | | | | | | | : | Rusty

——————— Toyota

.... Ford

Usefulness to researchers

When deciding how to construct an appropriate itemised rating scale researchers will consider the following issues.

(i) **Number of categories**

Likert scales and semantic differential scales provide enough categories for the researcher to be able to judge respondents' degree of feeling towards the topic.

Some researchers argue that a seven point scale, with two additional extremes, gives greater accuracy. The theory is that some respondents are predisposed to avoiding extremes. Consequently a five point scale would unduly limit their options. It is important to take cultural differences into account: some respondents from one culture may be happy to respond to extremes (eg very strongly agree) while respondents from another culture may be more likely to use fewer scale responses.

On the other hand, both too few and too many categories can produce unreliable or invalid data. For example, three response categories are insufficient for someone to express her/his attitude to the quality of television in the 1990s (Good/Bad/Don't know), while ten response categories to express her/his opinion on bottled water is too many for such a simple topic.

Research suggests that somewhere **between five and nine categories** are manageable, although in telephone research, five categories are usually the maximum that respondents can comprehend.

(ii) **Balanced versus unbalanced scales**

The Likert scale illustrated above is an example of a **balanced** scale, which provides an **equal proportion of positive and negative responses** (Very good/Good/Neither good nor bad/Bad/Very bad). This type should be used when there is a wide range of opinions.

It is also possible to construct a **non-balanced** scale, which is **deliberately weighted**. For example, if exploratory research suggests that most attitudes towards Australian wine are positive, the researcher may wish to measure the intensity of that positiveness: Excellent/Very Good/Good/Fair/Poor. Here there are three positive words and only two negative ones.

This cannot easily be done with a semantic differential scale: it would be very difficult to interpret the results.

(iii) **Odd or even number of categories**

Both Likert scales and semantic differential scales use an odd number of categories, and **generally, odd intervals are preferred**. With, say, a six- or eight-point scale there is no midpoint for a genuinely 'neutral' person.

On the other hand a five- or seven-point scale gives respondents the easy way out. It is far easier to sit on the fence than to uncover one's true feelings on the subject. Also some respondents (and the researcher cannot know which ones) may tick the midpoint when they actually mean they don't know. There is a difference!

(iv) **Forced v non-forced choice**

One solution to this problem (with either Likert scales or semantic differential scales) is to give a category outside the scale for the genuinely unsure.

eg: Modern - Old fashioned   Don't know

Forcing a respondent to score something when they simply do not know or care can have serious repercussions for the interviewer. For instance, a respondent can quickly feel threatened if they feel forced into giving an answer on something they do not hold an opinion on and may simply walk away, terminating the interview.

(v)   **Degree of verbal description**

The use of pictorial profiling has made semantic differential scales very popular in market research. However, there are **two potential problems** with this type of scale that may limit their usefulness for researchers. Firstly there are no verbal descriptors of the response intervals, as there are with the Likert scale (Strongly Agree etc.) These are left open to interpretation for a semantic differential scale. The second problem once again relates to the precise meaning of the central spaces.

(vi)   **Physical form**

The illustrations above demonstrate some of the **practical difficulties** that can arise in laying out attitudinal questions together with a suitable number of response options on the page. In the Likert scale, for example, it is necessary to layout the column headings vertically. Semantic differential scales present fewer problems in this respect. In both cases there may be some temptation to reword the attitude statement or bipolar phrases merely for layout purposes, but if this is done it undermines all the careful research that has gone into developing the item pool in the first place.

47 Data coding and input

Tutorial note. This question can be answered solely on the basis of book learning. We have dealt with the issue of reliability at the appropriate point under the other headings rather than giving it a section to itself. Our answer is probably rather longer than you could have managed in the time available.

Editing

In **editing** the researcher is largely concerned with identifying and correcting **completion errors**, which are errors caused by the interviewer (or in the case of self-completion surveys, the respondent). There are typically four kinds of completion error, in order of difficulty to detect.

(a)   No answer selected when one is required.

(b)   More answers given than is permitted.

(c)   Answer conflicts with a previous answer (eg the respondent entered zero purchases, but the next question lists several purchases).

(d)   Wrong response selected or keyed by mistake.

No editing technique can hope to detect and correct all completion errors.

With **manual editing**, each questionnaire will be visually inspected to ensure that it has been completed properly. To assist the editor, the researcher should write descriptive editing instructions, ideally when the questionnaire is ready to go to field or when the first ones are going to data entry. In their simplest form, editing instructions can be a marked-up version of the questionnaire which either identifies what is correct or what is an error, and the action to be taken, if there is an error.

A common editing technique with **awareness and usage grids** is to use **back-coding** to fill in gaps in the recorded answers to the more general questions with the more specific answers from the other columns. It may often be possible to computerise this process.

Editing can also take place on the keyed-in data. In this case the editing instructions are programmed into whatever analysis system is being used as computer editing instructions, in order to produce a report of the errors. The report will normally show the error condition that has occurred and possibly the erroneous response as well as the unique questionnaire or case number.

Some errors can be corrected on the basis of this information alone. For others, it will be necessary to extract the individual questionnaire to see if the data have been mis-keyed.

The data are then corrected either by altering the values on screen or by running a further program that will perform the corrections.

It is always more **'controlled'** (where controlled means the ability to retrace editing steps if an editing error is made) to use a method that can be either repeated or undone, and one which keeps a record or **audit trail** of the changes that have been made. Not all software packages will permit this, so manual records should be kept instead.

With **automated editing (force cleaning)** the researcher's editing instructions are programmed in as instructions, read and executed by the tabulation programme to make automated changes to the data.

Automated editing and force cleaning is, in many analysis packages, a 'black box' technique – the user cannot actually see what is being done. Therefore, it is important to check the **reliability** of the results carefully to ensure that the force cleaning is being carried out correctly, and has not either failed to correct things or, at the other extreme, been too enthusiastic in its error correction and removed meaningful results. One way to do this is to request a simple frequency count or 'top-line report' on the raw, unedited data, and use this to compare with any tables based on cleaned data.

Coding

For closed questions – those where the respondent replies Yes or No or chooses from a limited list of options – simple numerical code values are normally assigned at the time the questionnaire is designed. Even if that was not done at the time of design in this case it is a simple matter to do it at this stage.

Question 1	Code
Yes	1
No	2
Not answered	3

Question 2	Code
Red	1
Yellow	2
Pink	3
Green	4
Not answered	5

Numerical codes are necessary for computer efficiency (both for storage of data and later analysis) but ideally the data entry software will make the job intuitively easy for data entry personnel by using a human-friendly interface that avoids the need to know the code that the computer is recording behind the scenes.

Question 1

Yes   ○

No   ◉

Not answered   ○

Question 2

Yellow ▾

| Select... |
| Red |
| Yellow |
| Pink |
| Green |
| Not answered |

Obviously if the questionnaire is **completed electronically** in the first place all of this coding work and input of data (and validation and verification: see below) will already have been done. This is by far the most **reliable** method. An alternative, if electronic completion is not feasible, is to design the form so that responses to closed questions can be scanned into computer via optical mark reading. If responses on some questionnaires have been spoilt in any way the OMR software will produce an exception report and these questionnaires will have to be examined manually.

Open-ended responses

Open-ended questions cannot be coded up until the answers have been examined: this process is called post-coding. Typically, the first stage in coding is to produce a **code frame**. This is a summary and composite list of the most frequently occurring written-in responses to open-ended questions: each composite response is assigned a unique code. It is used to classify the entire range of open-ended responses for quantitative analysis. For this, the researcher will use either all of the verbatim responses to an open ended question, or a sample of them (between 10% and 25% according to the size of the sample). A skilled coding specialist will then group similar responses together and produce a summary list which attempts to classify the responses and account for the majority of answers in as few classifications as possible. In the next stage, coding specialists will either work through the physical questionnaires, reading the answer, identifying the code frame answers that apply and writing their codes on the questionnaire, or (preferably) will perform the equivalent task on screen if the data originated from CATI, CAPI, web interviewing or scanned data.

There are some **specialist software tools** available to simplify this task, and even some **automated coding programs** that will mass code results by text string matching. Such automated coding programs achieve varying degrees of success.

Data entry

Manual data entry after the data has been collected is a major source of error in the survey process. If there is any possibility of entering data at the same time as it is collected this is much to be preferred.

There are two common methods used to **improve reliability** in the case of manual data entry from paper-based forms:

(a) **Validation**

Valid data are those which agree with one of the codes for the question the data refer to. Validation of data is usually carried out by computer operation. Data entry with validation will ensure that the person entering the data can only enter data that conform to the range of codes expected for the question or position being entered. Therefore, a "yes/no" question using codes 1 and 2 would not permit anything other than 1 or 2 (and not 1 **and** 2) to be entered. As already indicated the modern approach is for the interface to use natural language, so the operator does not even have to remember the codes.

Validation techniques may also be used to perform the back coding process referred to earlier, since this is a simple test of logic and consistency. Validated data entry can also take account of the routing structure of the questionnaire, and automatically skip over sections that will be blank due to an earlier response. Validation has the advantage that it will eliminate most keystroke error, but too much validation will slow down the data entry process considerably. Too little validation imposes editing duties on the data processor.

(b) **Verification**

With verification, some, or all of the data, are entered twice by different operators and the results compared. This is a method of determining the **reliability** of the data entry staff. Normally, the second operator will be alerted whenever there is a discrepancy with the data entered by the previous operator and must then confirm the correct value. Rather than verify the entire dataset, a good measure of the accuracy of the data capture can be achieved by double-entering a sample of 10% of the forms.

48 Pre-coding and post-coding

Tutorial question. This is quite an easy question if you happen to know about the topic, but apparently it was very unpopular when set. That is possibly because it is rather badly written: unfortunately it appears that in part (b) the examiner actually intended to ask what factors influence the decision whether or not to offer the respondent a **choice of ready-made answers** to a question in a questionnaire, it is not really asking **when** the codes should be added. At least, the former is the question that is answered in the examiner's report. If you realised this, then well done, but bear in mind that it is usually a bad idea to answer the question you wanted to see rather than the one actually set.

You need to describe the differences between the two types of responses and show knowledge of the practical application of coding, providing a few convincing examples to illustrate points. Stronger answers will demonstrate a clear, practical awareness of the issues involved in coding.

(a) **Pre-coded and post-coded responses**

Coding is the conversion of respondents' verbal answers to questions into numeric values. This is done because it makes data entry faster and less error-prone and because it makes it easier and quicker for computers to store and process the very large amounts of data that are typically collected in a research project.

Pre-coded responses are responses to questions that are allocated a code for use in data analysis **before** the questionnaire is distributed to fieldworkers or direct to respondents.

Can you swim?	Code
No	0
Yes	1

What is your annual income?	Code
Up to £20,000	1
£20,001 to £35,000	2
£35,001 to £50,000	3
Over £50,000	4

Which of these TV programmes have you watched in the last week?	Code
Eastenders	1
Coronation Street	2
Emmerdale	3
Hollyoaks	4
None of these	0

Note that computer programmers are likely to prefer No/Yes answers to be coded 0/1 as shown above, not 1/2, since the former method is the basis of much computer programming logic. Note also that even though the question may contain numerical values the codes do not need to match those values. Only one code should be selected for the question about income, but up to four codes might be selected for the one about TV programmes.

In some interviews the pre-coded responses may not actually be shown or read out to the respondent: the respondent will answer in his or her own words and the interviewer will record the code that is closest to what the respondent said.

Post-coded responses have codes applied **after** data collection when themes and trends can be more easily identified from the data that has been collected. This method is appropriate for open ended questions where the researcher cannot predict in advance what answers may be given.

Typically, the first stage in post-coding is to produce a **code frame,** which is a summary and composite list of the most frequently occurring written-in responses to open-ended questions. There are some specialist software tools available to simplify the task, and even some automated coding programs that will mass code results by text string matching.

(b) **Questionnaire responses**

Ideally as much pre-coding should be done as possible, in all circumstances, since this will improve the accuracy of data collection and saves time at the data entry and analysis stages.

(i)   All **closed questions** can be pre-coded. Examples are given in part (a).

(ii)   Pre-coded responses may also be used for certain types of **open-ended questions** if the researcher has some idea of the range of responses that might be received, perhaps as a result of previous research. However, there will need to be a code for 'Other' answers that were not anticipated.

If the question is asking about the decision as to whether or not to include responses for the respondent to choose from in a questionnaire (or whether an interviewer should prompt the respondent with possible answers), this will depend upon the following factors.

(i)   The **aim of the question**. For example 'Can you swim?' might be the first in a batch of questions about a sports centre's pool facilities. There are only two possible answers and routing to subsequent questions will depend on which one of the two is chosen. The question is only included for routing purposes, and would always be pre-coded. A question such as 'What is your annual income' would typically be included so as to determine the socio-economic grade of the respondent. The researcher will already know what income brackets are of interest in the research study so again there is every reason to include pre-coded responses, and this would be done in the style illustrated in part (a) since the precise amount is not of interest, just the range.

(ii)   The **scope of the research**. The question about TV programmes in part (a) is clearly from a questionnaire with **limited scope** about specific TV soaps: the researcher is not interested in other soaps or other types of TV programme and **pre-coded responses** are provided to avoid collecting irrelevant data. If the research has a **wider scope**, for example if it is about TV watching in general, it would be impractical to list every programme that might have been watched, and the researcher may only be interested in **unprompted recall**. Responses would be free-form and post-coded.

(iii) The extent of the researcher's **existing knowledge** about respondents. As already mentioned, previous research may already have indicated the most likely answers and if these are included as **pre-coded** responses in the questionnaire (whether or not they are actually shown to the respondent) it will be easier and quicker to record the majority of answers. If the research is not now restricted to those who give one of the anticipated responses an 'Other (please specify)' option must also be included with a space for free-form answers. 'Other (please specify)' is pre-coded but this is only an indication to the researcher that the questionnaire contains an **unanticipated response** that will have to be analysed further and **post-coded**.

(iv) If the choice of answers is defined in advance (**pre-coding**) this **reduces** the possibility of **interviewer bias**.

(v) If the research requires **verbatim** responses to be recorded then these can only ever be **post-coded**.

(vi) Open-ended (**post-coded**) questions require more time and effort on the part of the respondent, especially if it is a self-completion questionnaire. The researcher needs to take account of the fact that such questions are more likely to be **left unanswered** or that the questionnaire will **not be returned** at all because the respondent cannot be bothered to complete it.

(vii) Open-ended (post-coded) questions also require more time and effort on the part of **interviewers** and **data analysts**. If the **budget** is **restricted** and/or the **time-scale** is **tight** the researcher is more likely to use questions with **pre-coded** responses.

(viii) Open-ended questions do not lend themselves well to **computerised data collection** methods (though this may well change as voice recognition software improves). Pre-coded questions, on the other hand, are ideal for computerised methods.

49 Data editing

> *Tutorial note.* In part (a) you should state the aim of the editing process and mention some of the types of errors that are being checked for. You should note that there are differences in the process depending on whether manual or computer assisted recording methods are used and make some mention of points at which the checks are done. Credit would be given for additional checks which can be made on accuracy and/or consistency so long as they are clearly described and justified.
>
> In part (b) you should provide a clear and convincing definition of 'missing data' and give some examples of how it arises. You should describe a range of ways of handling missing data during data processing. Try to use examples to provide clear illustrations of your understanding of the process.

(a) **Data editing**

The aim of editing is to ensure the accuracy of the data collection process so as to deliver clean, error-free data to analysts.

In editing, the researcher is largely concerned with identifying and correcting **completion errors**. Completion errors are errors caused by the interviewer or, in the case of self-completion surveys, the respondent.

There are typically four kinds of completion error, in order of difficulty to detect:

(i) No answer provided when one is required (missing data).

(ii) Answers provided when none are required. This may happen if the questionnaire instructs the respondent to skip, say, Questions 7 to 9 if the answer to Question 6 is 'No', but the respondent answers Questions 7 to 9 anyway, in spite of answering 'No' to Question 6 (a **routing** error).

(iii) More answers given than were asked for. This may happen if the question asks 'Which ONE of the following …' but more than one option is ticked.

(iv) Answer conflicts with a previous answer (eg the respondent entered zero purchases, but the next question lists several purchases).

(v) Wrong response selected or keyed by mistake.

No editing technique can hope to detect and correct all completion errors.

Ideally data will be checked **at the time when it is recorded**. There is no way of ensuring that this is done with a manual self-completion questionnaire, but a diligent and well-briefed interviewer will make such checks for every question, as it is asked, and again at the end of the interview.

Far preferable is to collect the data by **computer** – via an on-line questionnaire for self-completion, using a handheld computer if the data is recorded by an interviewer face to face, or via a desktop computer if it is a telephone interview. In each case the data entry system can be programmed to prevent most errors **at the time of collection**.

(i) In some cases the computer will not allow the respondent to go on to the next question at all until the current one has been answered. This might be the case if subsequent answers need to be checked for **consistency** with the current one, or if the next question varies depending on the answer to the current one (**automatic routing**). Alternatively, or in addition, a check will be made that all questions have been answered when the questionnaire is **submitted** or **saved**. If not the missing questions will be asked again.

(ii) **Range checks** can be used. For example, if the options are 1, 2 and 3 then an answer of any other number (an 'out of range' answer) will not be accepted.

(iii) **Format checks** ensure that if a number is required the respondent cannot enter other characters such as letters or punctuation marks. Other examples include checking that a postcode is in a valid postcode format and checking that an email address contains the @ symbol and at least one full stop.

If data is not collected by computer these checks can still be built into the data **entry** program, but more flexibility is needed to deal with cases of **missing data** (see part (b)).

If computerised methods are used for data recording the program itself should be thoroughly checked before the system is actually used. Programming errors can result in it being impossible to complete a questionnaire even if all the answers are present and are legitimate, or can send the respondent or interviewer into a never-ending loop.

Checks that data is being recorded correctly are likely to be made again after the first few questionnaires have been returned – at the end of the first day, say. If there are problems there is still time to make amendments to the data collection process.

With **manual editing**, the researcher will visually inspect each questionnaire to ensure that it has been completed properly. To assist the editor, the researcher should write descriptive editing instructions, ideally when the questionnaire is ready to go to field or when the first ones are going to data entry. In their simplest form, editing instructions can be a marked-up version of the questionnaire which either identifies what is correct or what is an error, and the action to be taken, if there is an error.

Instead of working with the physical questionnaires, editing can also take place on the **keyed-in data**. The editing instructions will be programmed into whatever analysis system is being used, and a report of the errors will be produced showing the error condition that has occurred and the unique questionnaire number. Depending on the type of error corrections may then be made either by altering the values on screen, or running another program that will perform the corrections automatically.

(b) **Missing data**

The term is explained above: no answer is provided when one is required.

This may occur for a variety of reasons.

- The question may simply have been overlooked by the respondent or the interviewer.
- The question may not have applied to the respondent.
- The respondent may not have known the answer.
- The respondent may have refused to answer.
- The answer may have been recorded elsewhere.
- The computer program may be faulty

If data is missing and this is not dealt with then **subsequent analysis** – in particular statistical analysis – will be **invalid**. Missing data might be dealt with in the following ways.

(i) It is less likely to occur in the first place if the questionnaire is well designed and interviewers are thoroughly briefed and if there are **options on the original questionnaire** such as 'Not applicable', 'Don't know', 'No answer', 'Refused'. This at least provides assurance that the question was not simply overlooked.

(ii) It may be possible to **contact the respondent again** and obtain the missing data. Care is needed, however: if the respondent refused to answer and this fact was not recorded this is likely to be very irritating for the respondent.

(iii) As already mentioned, at the **data entry** stage a **code** should be available for the in-putter to record the fact that there is no answer, even if this was not available on the original questionnaire.

(iv) **Casewise** deletion means that any questionnaire that contains missing values is left out of subsequent analysis entirely. This reduces the sample size, of course, and all the data that was correctly completed is lost. In extreme cases it may mean that no data at all is left to analyse.

(v) **Pairwise** deletion only excludes the faulty questionnaire from analysis for the purpose of the question that is not answered.

(vi) The data analyst can calculate the **mean value** for the question (find out what the most typical answer was) and substitute that for the missing data.

(vii)   It may be possible to **infer** what answer would have been given on the basis of the respondent's **answers to other questions**, or on the basis of the answers given by other respondents who have similar profiles to the respondent who did not answer.

In the last two cases, of course, analysts are just **guessing** what the answer would have been, even though they are using the best available evidence. The guesses may be correct, or the results may be biased, and users of the research results should be made aware of this.

50 Tutorial question: Training handout

(a)   **Lifestyle research** is based around psychographic measurements. Two frameworks for such research are based around the AIOD framework (Plummer, 1974) and the VALS framework (Mitchell, 1983). These are outlined below with selected examples.

AIOD

Activities	**Interests**	**Opinions**	**Demographics**
Work	Family	Themselves	Age
Hobbies	Job	Social issues	Education
Social Events	Community	Politics	Income
Vacation		Business	Occupation

VALS

Need driven groups – survivors and sustainers

Outer directed groups – belongers, emulators and achievers

Inner directed groups – I am me, experiential and societally conscious

Combined outer and inner directed groups – integrated

The underlying motivation for this research is that increasing wealth has resulted in wide and varied consumption patterns that vary within the same class and age groups. Such classifications should reflect individual life styles. The above categorisation of consumers, if correctly researched and analysed should result in data and information that should assist firms to better satisfy customer needs in their chosen target markets.

(b)   **Survey research**

The objective of a **marketing information system** is to collect data from the firm's operating environment, including its customers. Were no financial constraints to exist, a marketer would probably get the most accurate data by asking questions of every relevant person. **Surveys**, if carefully and properly constructed according to best statistical practice, can obtain excellent results by referring to a sample of the whole population.

Survey research involves asking questions of the **target market**. In the design of a survey, it is important that the members of the survey sample are selected so that the sample is as representative of the whole target market population as possible, given the constraints of time, money and availability. A biased sample will give a misleading impression about the population.

Methods of **designing and constructing the sample** include techniques such as: random sampling, stratified random sampling or multi stage sample design (cluster or area sample). Determining the correct size of the population sample is important and using models derived from the central limit theorem / normal distribution, it is possible to determine the appropriate sample size for a required degree of confidence. Questions can be limited and highly structured, delivered by post, phone or personally. Such results are usually quantitative and provide factual responses. Alternatively questions can be of an in depth nature asked of a relatively small sample. The latter results in information of a behavioural or attitudinal nature.

(c) **Mall intercept interview research** refers to surveys carried out in busy populated areas, especially shopping centres. Questioners will stand in a prominent position and approach passers by, taking care to select potential interviewees as appropriately as possible to fit in with the selection criteria. Due to the 'cold calling' nature of the approach, the contact time is likely to be brief and the questions carefully designed, as complete as possible for the purpose and to the point.

When designing a research campaign for Campo Camping Ltd, an outdoor activities manufacturer and retailer operating from a chain of city centre stores, we may consider using the above techniques.

Campo wishes to undertake a marketing campaign to increase its market share in both current and potential trading areas. The objective would therefore be to obtain the information necessary to design a marketing promotional and/or advertising campaign. This could include the following.

(i) **Design a questionnaire** to discover the lifestyles of the local populations, to ascertain how many people undertake outdoor pursuits in their leisure time and to discover what their interests and opinions are. The questionnaire would also research the ages, income, education and occupations of the interviewees. For example, one of the questions might be – 'I enjoy camping' and the answer ranked could be on a scale of 1 – 5 with the outer parameters being totally agree and totally disagree. Other questions could be designed around the AIOD headings.

(ii) The researchers would first need to determine that a **mall survey** would be an appropriate method for the required survey outcome. They would need to design appropriate locations of the samples that reflect the area in which the shops are operational (area sampling). The number of interviewees would need to be sufficient to represent the population mix of the areas in question and for the results to give a (say) 95% degree of confidence.

(iii) The researchers would need to choose suitable **mall locations** (eg not areas with a low footfall) and times of day (suitably busy). Interviewers would need to be recruited and briefed on the appropriate approach (eg how many people to ask, what apparent ages to ask, what questions to ask and how to phrase them) and given other instructions on how to make the sample frame as representative as possible.

51 Report and presentation

(a) **Characteristics of a good research report**.

(i) The executive summary should be well written.
(ii) It should provide the answers to the research brief.
(iii) It should contain recommended courses of action.
(iv) The interpretations and conclusions should be fully stated.
(v) Relevant graphical representations should be included where appropriate.
(vi) It should be clearly structured and concisely written.

(b) **Research Report**

    (i)   **Title page**: this should list the title, the client for whom it is written, the name of the research organisation and the date of submission.

    (ii)   **The executive summary**: should give a concise summary of the report in approximately 250 – 650 words. This summary should give the busy executive sufficient information to understand the outline of the report and its conclusions.

    (iii)   **Contents page**: should present the sections and content headings with relevant page references. Where graphs, tables and appendices are used, the appropriate page numbers for these should be indicated.

    (iv)   **Preface**: this should give the outline of the agreed research brief, together with the statement of objectives, the scope and the research methods used.

    (v)   **Introduction**: should include the background to the research, people involved in the research, their roles and positions and the necessary acknowledgements.

    (vi)   **Research methodology**: showing the type of study, the purpose of the study, the definitions of population under consideration, sampling design and methodology, data collection methods adopted and the justifications of the method(s) used.

    (vii)   **Summary of conclusions and recommendations**: showing the summary of the findings, and, where appropriate, any creative interpretations of the findings and related recommendations.

    (viii)   **Appendices**: showing sample questionnaire(s), technical details and any other workings that need to be included to support the main body of the report.

> *Tutorial note.* There are acceptable variations on the above layout and sequence of the report

(c) **Format of the oral presentation**:

Introduction and audience welcome

During the introductory session the presentation team should be introduced and the format and structure of the presentation explained together with the rationale for the study and the objectives of the research.

Methodology

The methodology employed in the study should be described as well as outlining time scales and any limitations.

Findings

At this stage, the findings should be presented and where appropriate, these should be supported with graphs and tabular summaries. It is important that the structure of this section should be logical and easy to follow/understand.

Conclusions and recommendations

This section should follow on from the findings and should be presented in such a way that the audience can be persuaded by the logic and the key points which can be summarised at this stage.

Questions

The presenters can conclude the presentation with a question and answer session.

Presentation techniques

- Test all the equipment before starting and ensure that any computer software is compatible where PowerPoint type presentations are used.

- Have a back up light bulb where projectors are used.

- If you are using Powerpoint it is advisable to have a set of slides and overhead projector on hand in case of equipment/software failure.

- Rehearse the presentation and timings beforehand.

- Provide handouts but beware them being a distraction from the presenter.

- Ensure the conference administrators have provided pens and pencils where appropriate.

- Keep eye contact.

- Vary the content and pace: everyone will lose concentration after a maximum of 45 minutes, and the optimum concentration span is perhaps only 20 minutes.

- Keep it simple.

- Check understanding by asking questions of the audience where appropriate.

- Avoid Ums and Ers and mannerisms such as 'You Know' or 'OK?'

- If you don't know the answer to a question, don't waffle, but offer to find out the answer and convey it to the audience member later.

- Finish on an emotive point and remember that you are there to sell your work and research findings to your customer.

52 Presentation preparation

> *Tutorial note.* Even if you have never given a presentation yourself you are likely to have been to one so take the opportunity to liven up your answer with some examples from your own experience if possible. Our answer is longer than you could have managed in the time available: it probably contains too much on preparing the actual content, but we felt the points were useful for revision purposes.

A presentation of research results involves a **face-to-face meeting with the client**. The researcher will talk through the results, typically with a slide presentation, and will answer questions either during the presentation or at the end. This may be done on the day the full written report is delivered, as an introduction to it, or a short while afterwards when at least some of the audience have had a chance to read through the full report and will no doubt have some initial questions.

No matter how familiar the researcher may be with the research project, having worked on it perhaps for many months, **thorough preparation** will ensure that the presentation goes smoothly and communicates the results with appropriate impact.

Venue

It is most usual for the presentation to be delivered at the client's premises. The researcher will need to find out where the venue is and **how to get to it**. If possible travel arrangements should be made in advance, especially if the venue is a long way from the researcher's base and train or plane tickets and a hotel room need to be booked. At the very least the researcher should know the route, obtain a map and allow plenty of time.

It is important to find out at the outset what **facilities and equipment** are available at the venue, since this determines the format of the presentation. Hand-outs, flip charts or over-head projector (OHP) slides are possibilities, but it is most likely, these days, that the researcher will prefer to give a **PowerPoint** style presentation using a laptop computer with a projector and screen. If the client does not have a projector and screen the researcher will need to book out equipment from his or her own organisation or hire it from a supplier local to the venue. If hiring equipment this should be done well in advance and checked the day before.

Other facilities that may be needed include **audio and video** players, screens and speakers – increasingly such material is captured in digital form that can be played back by computer, but this may not be the case. If these facilities are needed they should be arranged in advance.

The researcher should also check the **size** of the proposed venue – slides will need to be legible for everybody and if it is a very large room this will have a direct impact on the amount of words that can be included on each one, the size of illustrations such as graphs and so on. It may even be necessary to consider arranging for voice amplification equipment, although this would be unusual.

Audience

The next step is to consider **who will attend** the presentation, in the light of knowledge of the client organisation. This will affect both the style and content of the presentation.

(a) What is their level of **knowledge of research procedures**, statistical analysis and so on? This will determine the technical level of the presentation content.

(b) What is their interest in the research project, in other words **what do they want to know?** If there will be representatives from several different parts of the client organisation the presentation may need to include a balance of matters of interest to each faction as well as matters of general interest.

(c) There may be some **politics** involved: it is a good idea to discuss in advance with the main contact at the client whether there are contentious matters that should be avoided. No matter how good the quality of the research the impact of the presentation could easily be ruined if it touches upon issues that are the subject of internal battles within the client organisation.

(d) What does the **client have to do** as a result of the presentation? The original research objectives must be kept firmly in mind. Although a presentation inevitably has marketing implications for the research agency – they are showing off their wares – the main purpose of the presentation is to explain to the client the benefits of the research to **their** business, not to show off how wonderful the research agency is.

Preparing the content

The first step when preparing the content itself is to check **how much time** has been allocated for the meeting as a whole. The length of the final report and the volume of the research findings should not dictate the length of the presentation. As a general rule people find it very difficult to concentrate on a single speaker for much longer than 45 minutes and so the presentation itself should last about 30 minutes. Besides the presentation itself account needs to be taken of discussion time and some allowance made for possible delays or interruptions.

The starting point for the content will probably be the final research report but this is likely to need to be **edited and restructured** for the purposes of verbal delivery. The researcher should select the most important information from all the data collected: as a general rule, if it does not help the client to reach a conclusion it should be omitted.

A good approach for keeping the audience's attention is to think of the presentation as a piece of **story telling** that leads clearly to the most important finding or implication. Signposts should be used so that the audience knows where the story is going and can make links between the different parts. **Narrative techniques** that may not be used in the written source material but are useful in presentations include two-sided arguments, hypothetical questions, simple repetition, reinforcement of points via anecdotes or analogies, and summaries of the story so far.

Graphs, charts and pictures should be used if they will emphasise and enhance the message, and draw attention to key elements of it, but they should not dominate the presentation. They do not necessarily speak for themselves unless the presenter points out what the audience should look for and talks around them. Badly-drawn graphics can undermine an otherwise excellent presentation: it is better to get them professionally done, and this will mean **advance planning**, especially if in-house experts are not available.

Packages like PowerPoint offer a range of easy-to-use bells and whistles such as **animations** and supposedly amusing clip-art, but these should be used sparingly and only if they actually further the audience's understanding of the topic, not for their own sake. (It is estimated that 30 million PowerPoint presentations are given every day – it is more likely, these days, that clients will be irritated and distracted by the technology than be impressed by the presenter's humour and technical wizardry!)

The audience may expect the presenter to have prepared **handouts** as a permanent reminder of the material presented and software such as PowerPoint makes the preparation of handouts easy. Nevertheless they are no substitute for a good verbal delivery with all the enhancement that tone of voice and body language can add. If they are handed out at the start of the presentation they can distract the audience's attention. They are perhaps best given to the audience when the presentation ends.

Rehearsal

An important part of preparation is to do a **timed practice run**, preferably with an interested audience such as other members of the research team. **Feedback** should be obtained on matters such as audibility, tone of voice, pace, body language, handling of visual aids and so on.

Even if this is not possible it is useful to speak the words aloud in front of a mirror to judge what works and what does not. If the links between sections are clumsy or the line of argument is weak this will often become apparent when the words are spoken because the presenter will feel him or herself hesitating or being tempted to ad lib.

The rehearsal is also a good opportunity to **anticipate the questions that are likely to be asked** and decide how to deal with them.

Finally the rehearsal, not the day of the presentation, is the time when the presenter should make sure that they are confident in using the technology and getting the equipment to work.

Contingency plans

Preparation should include planning for **things that could go wrong**. A backup of the presentation material should be made and stored on a separate disk. Acetates should be prepared in case computer equipment fails but an overhead projector is available. Paper copies should be prepared in case of power cuts. If possible an alternative venue should be considered in advance in case of problems with the chosen one on the day, such as noisy building work in the building next door.

On the day

The presenter should **arrive in plenty of time** so as to get equipment and materials organised, rearrange the seating if necessary, and get settled. Most people feel a little **nervous**, and it is a good idea to relax using techniques such as deep breathing, visualisation and positive thinking.

53 Municipal council

> *Tutorial note.* Presumably this question (set in March 2002) was inspired by the system of Comprehensive Performance Assessment (CPA) and local Performance Service Agreements that had recently been introduced in UK at that time. There are further tutorial notes in our answer that provide you with more information about this and other aspects of local government that may be unfamiliar.
>
> In our answer we have assumed that no arrangements to deal with the new government requirements have yet been put in place by the council, although in reality they would have had to have set up systems by 2004, and the option of 'starting from a clean sheet' would not be available – or at least if this exercise were undertaken it would be a profligate waste of money that could be better spent on meeting statutory reporting obligations and providing real services for council taxpayers!
>
> This question might appear to be a gift if you happen to work in local government in the UK, but in that case it will be hard to resist writing down everything you know. If you do work in local government research and you think we have missed something major in our answer please let us know: there is a feedback form at the end of this Kit.

(a) **Research into information that already exists**

(i) **Effectiveness in providing services that the community wants and needs**

'**Effectiveness**' means achieving the desired outcome.

The **key services** provided by a council will be set out (in broad terms) by legislation. For example, they will be statutorily required to provide education, social care, parks services, road and pavement maintenance, and housing services.

Whether the **specific services** provided by a council in trying to meet its statutory obligations are actually the ones **wanted and needed** by the community is a rather different matter: for example, if a library in a area comprising high net worth individuals installs a large number of computers for public use this may be neither wanted nor needed by local people, since they will have their own computers at home.

To some extent wants and needs will be measurable from existing data by looking at **usage** of the service (assuming that is recorded), but in many cases usage data will **not show why** people do not use a service or why they prefer one to another. For example, existing data may show that a youth club is not well attended but there may be all manner of reasons for this that cannot be determined without more detailed new research.

A full review should be conducted of any **complaints** received about current council services, and what, if anything, is being done about them.

It should also be possible to review the existing **background documentation** for any **new services** that are being developed, focusing in particular on **why** they are being developed (directly in response to community feedback or demands, in response to local environmental developments such as a new road, or for other reasons), on what level of public consultation there was, and what the response to the public consultation was – for instance, this may help to identify local pressure groups, and indicate the extent to which they are representative of general public feeling.

(ii) **Providing services that are value for money**

Value for Money (VFM) is usually said to consist of three E's: **Effectiveness** (desired outcomes, as above), **Economy** (avoidance of wasteful inputs), and **Efficiency** (the ratio of inputs to outputs).

In the UK, councils have for many years been subject to regular audit by the **Audit Commission**, who are concerned above all with value for money. Immediate research that should be undertaken, therefore, is to assess the extent to which data that is already collected, to satisfy audit and accounting requirements and for day-to-day management, will be suitable, in the light of the new reporting requirements. The new requirements themselves need to be analysed in detail and any **gaps** between the new and the existing reporting requirements must be identified.

Existing **methods of collecting and analysing data** should also be examined to see if accuracy could be improved in any way, for example by using more efficient collection methods or changing the method of sample selection or size of sample, if a census is not undertaken.

Previous **audit reports** should be examined to see what recommendations they contain and to what extent they have been implemented.

(iii) **Appropriate staff appraisal and relevant professional development support**

The terms 'appropriate', 'relevant' and 'support' need to be much more clearly defined. The first research task is to find out exactly what is meant by each: presumably the new government directives will contain further detail.

Assuming that the council already undertakes staff appraisals and supports professional development in some way a good deal of information should be available from the existing records of the **human resources/personnel department(s)**.

It may be that information required in the annual record (for example, total number of appraisals conducted) is not currently prepared on a council-wide basis, but it should be possible to **collect and collate** the information that is available immediately, from individual personnel records (including training records), from the records of departmental managers, and from records of training events organised and of expenditure on training.

Since this has not previously been a formal requirement, however, it is likely that there will be considerable inconsistencies between the type of information and the level of detail collected by different managers and different departments. The collation exercise should **identify inconsistencies and gaps** and it should then be possible to decide on what needs to be done to **standardise procedures** for the purposes of the new reporting requirements.

(b) **Regular research recommendations**

(i) **Effectiveness in providing services that the community wants and needs**

Usage of all existing services should be **measured continuously** and exception reports should be produced and acted upon sufficiently regularly to enable anomalies to be investigated on a timely basis, not months after whatever was causing the anomaly has ceased to be an issue. Measuring might already be done as a matter of course (for accounting purposes, where people pay separately for services such as transport, meals on wheels and so on), or some of the methods suggested in part (c) might be used.

General satisfaction surveys, covering all existing council services, should be carried out on a regular basis. Precisely how regularly this can be done will depend mainly upon budget factors, but also upon the size of the population served. The full survey might be preceded by a small number of **focus groups** to identify which issues are perceived to be most important and to find out if there are new **wants and needs** that the council was not previously aware of.

Alternatively, or in addition, more detailed surveys on **specific major areas** of council service, such as council housing, might be conducted.

> *Tutorial note.* In fact councils in the UK are **required** to carry out general satisfaction surveys and other prescribed surveys **every three years**. You can find examples of such surveys and their results on many council websites.

For ongoing purposes it would be useful to place a **feedback form** or forms on the council's **website** to collect complaints and suggestions. People are most likely to contact the council at the time when poor service is an issue, and may have forgotten about it by the time a formal survey is conducted.

Environmental monitoring should be **continuous**. External events (such as increased terrorist threats), and local issues (such as a large local employer closing down or local 'green' issues), will also affect wants and needs. The council should ensure that its research programme is flexible enough to include regular consideration of how events beyond its control might have affected consumer wants and needs. (*Ad hoc* research is of course *ad hoc*, but the **need** for it should be considered regularly.)

The purpose of all of the above is to identify areas that need to be researched in more depth on an *ad hoc* basis. For example, if usage of a service is declining an individual study will be needed to find out why.

(ii) **Providing services that are value for money**

Value for money is a concept that is easy to understand in everyday life. For example, we would typically describe an offer of 'two for the price of one' as good value for money because we get twice as much benefit for the same amount of input.

With a council service, however, it is much more **difficult to put a monetary value** on the benefit derived by citizens (for example, what is the value of the benefit per person of having their refuse collected, or of a street lamp?) and, although people will know how much council tax they pay overall per month, the **amount of expenditure per service is not generally known** (for example, how much of each person's council tax is spent on emptying a specific dustbin or running a specific street lamp?).

Moreover, many council services have **multiple outcomes**, for example a street lamp makes the footpath easier to for pedestrians to use, but it also helps to avoid road accidents and deter crime. Some in the community might argue that the benefits are outweighed by the negative consequences: a street lamp increases light pollution and exacerbates global warming; the noise of refuse collection is disturbing and the process slows down traffic.

If starting from a clean sheet the council would therefore need to develop a series of measures such as the following.

■ Cost of waste collection per household per year

■ Household waste collected per head of population in kg

■ Number of missed bins per 100,000 collections

■ Percentage of total waste recycled

■ Total tonnage of waste recycled

■ Percentage of population within 1 km of recycling facilities or kerbside collection

■ Number of complaints about noise of refuse collection

■ Number of complaints received about traffic disruption as a result of refuse collection

■ Percentage of population very/fairly satisfied with waste collection

■ Percentage of population very/fairly satisfied with recycling facilities

The majority of this information will be collected in the normal course of operating the service and the only extra research required is to analyse it sufficiently regularly to enable control action to be taken where needed. Information about satisfaction can be collected via the surveys mentioned in part (b)(i).

Additional VFM research that might be carried out includes **willingness to pay analysis** whereby members of the community would be asked 'if the council did not collect your refuse how much would you be willing to pay somebody else to do it?'. As before, precisely how regularly this can be done will depend upon budget factors and on the size of the population served. A second possibility is to find out the costs incurred by other councils and make comparisons: this should be possible on an annual basis in future, given that all councils are subject to the new requirements.

The research department should be continuously aware of **planned new initiatives**, so that before and after effects can be measured. It may be sufficient to ask for such initiatives to be **reported on a regular basis**, but the research department may wish to be more proactive and conduct regular surveys amongst the council's departments. For example, ease of use of footpaths may have been improved by a new policy of stricter enforcement of local bye-laws about parking on the pavement, but data may not have been collected that enables the council to judge the before and after effects of this policy, if there was previously no formal requirement to report on the issue at that level of detail.

> *Tutorial note.* In fact councils in the UK are required to report on over a hundred **Best Value Performance Indicators (BVPIs)** (a national measure of performance, set by central government). Some are indicated in our answer above. Others include: percentage of total footpaths that are easy to use; percentage of unfit private sector dwellings made fit or demolished; total expenditure on public libraries compared with total number of visits to libraries by the public; percentage of pupils achieving Level 4 or above in Key Stage 2 English; and all manner of others.
>
> The Government also expects councils to supplement the national indicators with local indicators, making use of the Audit Commission's *Library of Local Indicators.*
>
> Detailed guidance on how these things should be measured and on sampling procedures is provided by the Local and Regional Government Research Unit, now part of the Office of the Deputy Prime Minister.
>
> Thus there is absolutely no scope to 'start with a clean sheet' in the real world.

(iii) **Appropriate staff appraisal and relevant professional development support**

> *Tutorial note.* There is a vast amount of legislation that impinges upon this area of the queston, dealing with aspects such as discrimination, equality, fair pay, grievance procedures and so on. The Race Relations (Amendment) Act 2000 requires councils to monitor data on gender, ethniciity, age and disability of those benefitting from **training**. Under the Data Protection Act 1998 there is a code of practice dealing specifically with **monitoring at work**.
>
> The **ODPM** is currently working on standards and guidelines for collection of workforce data in association with organisations such as TOPSS which specialises in education and training standards for social care workers. The **Employer's Organisation for Local Government** conducts an annual Local Government Recruitment and Retention Survey which asks questions about skills gaps.
>
> We make these points to stress once again that the idea of 'starting with a clean sheet' is not practical.

The first step, as noted above, is to standardise reporting procedures. This process will be led by the human resources department but it should be done in consultation with researchers to ensure consistency and analysability of data.

The purpose of appraisal above all is to identify what needs to be done to maintain and hopefully improve an individual's performance. A by-product of appraisals is sometimes some kind of bonus system.

Regular research might therefore sample employees and discuss with them and with their managers the effectiveness of the appraisal process, including especially the validity and measurability of objectives that are set, actions taken by the employee, and support provided by the employer. Quantitative measurement is easier where the development objectives are concerned with hard and specific skills such as operating a machine, but much harder for competencies that involve behavioural skills such as interacting with the public.

A framework for measurement might be provided by adoption of a scheme such as the **Investors in People** standard. This sets out a series of principles (management commitment to staff development, planning, action and evaluation) together with sets of indicators for each principle and the type of evidence that could be collected. Again this would be led by the human resources department but ideally in consultation with researchers to ensure consistency and analysability of data.

The Employer's Organisation for Local Government takes the view that **staff attitude surveys** can provide an excellent overview of employee motivation and performance across the organisation, and also demonstrate to employees that the employer cares about what they think and, most importantly, acts on it. Their sample questions include a series of attitude statements on training and development such as:

- There are not enough opportunities for career development with the organisation

- There are not enough training and development opportunities available to me

- The training I have received will help me to develop my career

- The training and development needs highlighted in my performance management interview have been largely met

- My manager seeks regular evaluation of any off-the-job training I undertake

- The organisation is supportive of my individual training and development

- I understand the Staff Appraisal Scheme and how my performance will be measured

(c) **Data collection methods**

Usage data about many services will be collected from operational data (for example, information about library lending levels should be available from library records; computers also typically need to be booked), and financial data wherever a fee is payable for use of a service (for example, swimming pools, meals on wheels and so on).

Usage of free services such as libraries, museums and parks could be measured via pressure mats or automatic gates/doors at the entrance or exits. Usage data might also be collected by observation on an *ad hoc* basis at different times of day and different times of the year (for example school holidays v term time; exam periods and non-exam periods).

General **satisfaction surveys** will be carried out by **postal questionnaires** sent to, say 2,000 to 5,000 randomly selected addresses across the district. (The number will depend on the size of the population.) Surveys should be addressed to 'The Occupier' to take account of changes that are not yet reflected in the electoral register: it is the postcode that is being targeted not the individual.

Other more **specific surveys** may also be carried out on topics such as council house services: these would of course only be sent to a sample of council house tenants, or it may be practical to conduct interviews door-to-door or by telephone.

Regarding staff, it will be important to conduct **qualitative interviews** with individuals: these should cover the full range of the council's activities, which will be very diverse, and they would probably best be done in collaboration with staff in human resources.

Staff **attitude surveys** can be conducted by **self-completion questionnaire**, probably via the organisation's **intranet**. It is important that they are consistent for comparison purposes. The frequency of the survey may vary due to resourcing or size of authority, for example every two years, every eighteen months, every year, or every six months.

The problem with all kinds of regular research is **respondent fatigue** – people may be happy to take part on the first occasion, but less and less interested as time goes by. There is also a **political angle** where employees are involved: if some are sampled but not others, the others may resent the fact that their views are not being taken into account. The sampling therefore needs to be done with care and sensitivity.

54 Cereal manufacturer

Tutorial note. This is an excellent question that gives you the opportunity to demonstrate your knowledge of a number of aspects of market research. In part (a) you may have had rather more to say than we do about primary research that could be done and about sampling methods: this would be quite acceptable. In part (b) we have taken the view that people's propensity to snack is heavily influenced by their other eating habits. In part (c) we have assumed that the research described in part (a) has already been done and that the target segments have been identified as a result of the analysis of information in part (b).

(a) **Research design**

Research objectives

To provide the marketing team with robust information on snackers' eating habits and preferences. This is to be done alongside the marketing team's product development efforts over the next financial year.

We will assume that the research budget covers an entire year and is sufficient to fund a wide variety of activities.

Research design

Initial background **exploratory** research should be carried out to determine what existing sources of information there are on eating habits and preferences, in other words **secondary** research.

The topic is of **very wide public and commercial interest** and it is likely that there will be a wealth of good recent data from a variety of sources, including national **government statistics** and research conducted by **regional and national health and nutrition bodies**. **Panel** data such as TNS SuperPanel and AC Neilsen's Homescan will give valuable insights, and there are also highly likely to be a number of recent **Mintel** reports that are relevant to the topic, exploring trends and lifestyle changes in different age groups.

Given that the organisation is a major cereal manufacturer it would be surprising if they did not already conduct this sort of secondary research on a continuous basis in any case, regardless of the current project.

This initial research should help to clarify and understand the key issues, the language used, and the wider context. To get the most **up-to-date** picture and to **flesh out** details where necessary it would be advisable to conduct a small amount of **primary**

exploratory or descriptive research too, perhaps via **in-home interviews** with a representative sample of households (single persons, couples and families at various life stages, the elderly and so on.).

Depending on the extent to which existing published data answers the marketing department's questions it may also be necessary to carry **its own quantitative surveys** amongst various groups such as schoolchildren, office workers on their lunch break and so on. If external events such as government health campaigns are influencing opinion and habits it may be necessary to carry out **repeated waves**, throughout the product development process. Alternatively the organisation could commission questions in regular **omnibus** surveys such as NOP's ParentBus and Young Generation Omnibus.

(b) **Information for successful profiling of snacker segments**

The organisation will also need to collect information such as listed below, all of which will be analysed in terms of **demographics** (for instance, percentage of male non-manual workers aged over 35 whose buying habits are influenced by a food product's fat content) and in terms of **behaviour and lifestyle** (for example, number of people who leave home before 7.30am on weekdays who eat breakfast, and as compared with their weekend breakfasting behaviour).

(i)   Food **shopping patterns** (type of store, time and regularity).

(ii) Factors that influence **buying behaviour** such as cost, convenience, diet and nutrition, habit, children's preferences, labelling, advertising, branding and so on.

(iii) **Main mealtime patterns**, for example whether families eat meals together, eat the same food at different times or cook different foods.

(iv) **Breakfast eating** patterns: weekday and weekend behaviour is likely to be different and age will be a factor (the retired will have more time for breakfast). Location will also be important (at home, while travelling, at work, in a café or canteen). A proportion will snack rather than eating breakfast.

(v)   **Lunchtime** eating habits: consumption of school meals or food in work canteens, packed lunches, takeaway items such as shop-made sandwiches or pastries, location (at the desk, at home, in the street or a park or a playground, etc).

(vi) **Eating out** and **takeaway** meals: how often people eat in a restaurant or pub and how often they have meals such as fish and chips, burgers etc, with the information broken down demographically as usual.

(vii) **Food type**: categories might be divided into (portions of) fruit and vegetables; bread, cereals, potatoes rice and pasta; meat, poultry and fish; milk and dairy products; and of course **snacks** of various kinds (fries, crisps, biscuits, cakes, confectionery, fizzy drinks, supposedly healthy snacks like cereal bars, etc.)

(viii) **Awareness of healthy eating**: information needed here would be what people perceive to be healthy or unhealthy, not what actually is according to nutrition experts.

(ix) **Changes** to eating patterns in, say, the last year: for example, whether people were attempting to eat less salt and sugar, or more fruit. Information would also be needed on the reasons for trying to change (weight-loss, appearance, health, medical advice etc), and factors that prevented people from changing such as lack of time for proper cooking, cost, children's refusal to change.

(c) **Research plan to provide feedback on a proposed new snack**

Once the new products are under development it will be necessary to test the various market segments. Both **qualitative** and **quantitative** information will be needed. Clearly the product will have to be **taste-tested** amongst a **representative sample** of people in **each of the segments** identified as a result of the analysis in part (b). It will also be important to obtain feedback on **packaging** and on proposed **advertising**.

(i) **Research objectives**

To obtain feedback on the proposed new snack.

(ii) **Methods for obtaining the information and data collection**

The following methods might be used.

(iii) **Hall tests**

Hall tests involve interviewing people in church halls, hotel reception rooms and so on. Often nowadays there may be facilities set aside for this purpose in shopping centres, and that is probably most appropriate in this case.

Hall tests can include observation and qualitative techniques alongside a structured questionnaire. In this case the test will include usage (ie consumption) of the product and an interview during which a respondent is asked to give his or her opinions about the product and evaluate it, as well as make a future usage and purchase declaration. An individual test usually lasts about 20 minutes, although the simplest versions may only involve tasting the snack product and evaluating it on a scale.

Respondents can be recruited in advance to come along at a certain time, but in the typical hall test, interviewers approach potential respondents on the street in the vicinity of the hall, and invite them inside to be interviewed.

A useful approach with **young families** is to hold an initial session that includes watching TV programmes (such as cartoons) interspersed with advertising for the new product. The parent and child will then be sent around a supermarket into which the new snack product has been placed. CCTV cameras can capture buying behaviour including the influence of pester power.

(iv) **Product placement tests**

This approach, whereby samples of the product are 'placed' with respondents for use when and as they wish, might be more successful than hall testing, given that snacks are typically eaten **when people feel hungry** between meals: the researcher cannot easily control whether or not respondents chosen at random on the street are feeling peckish!

Moreover parents of young **children** may be reluctant to allow them to take part in a test that will disrupt their normal eating pattern.

Home testing could also be considered more appropriate because respondents may be reluctant to express an opinion unless the **whole family** have a chance to try the product.

Respondents may have an initial interview to determine product awareness, obtain a preliminary assessment and perhaps carry out a price test, then be given the product to try for, say, a week. A self-completion questionnaire may be used to obtain feedback or perhaps a second interview at the end of the test.

(v) **Data analysis and reporting**

Analysis would determine how much the product was liked by different segments, likely patterns of consumption and the importance of different factors such as labelling, perceived healthiness.

The report might contain recommendations for changes to the product itself or its packaging, pricing proposals, and recommended retail outlets.

55 Geo-demographic and lifestyle data

Tutorial note. Part (a) allows you a lot of leeway: your two questions may have been quite different to the ones in our answer, but equally valid. Parts (b) and (c) should be quite straightforward. For part 12 (c) think about retailers that you are familiar with such as Boots and Superdrug.

(a) **Two questions**

(i) **Shopping preferences**

We'd like to find out what is most important to you in choosing where you shop for pharmaceutical and health products. Below are a number of descriptors about retail outlets. Please select the answer that best expresses how important you think the factor is to you in selecting where you shop for pharmaceutical and health products.

	Not At All Important	Somewhat Unimportant	Neutral	Somewhat Important	Extremely Important
Fast checkout					
Low prices					
Close to where you live					
Close to where you work					
Courteous, friendly employees					
Offers generic products					
Makes it easy to get cash back					
Offers several brands to choose from in a category					
Provides medical advice					
Convenience of parking					
Processes prescriptions in store					
Open early in the morning					
Open late in the evening					
Wide selection of own label goods					
Has well stocked shelves					
Provides nutritional information about products					
Wide selection of national brands					

(ii) **Brand preferences**

We'd like to make sure that our stores stock the brands that you prefer. Which brand are you most likely to buy for each of the following products?

Cough and cold medicines

	Unprompted	Prompted
Don't buy	☐	
First one I see (ie no preference)	☐	
Brand A	☐	☐
Brand B	☐	☐
Brand C	☐	☐
Brand D	☐	☐
Brand E	☐	☐
Can't remember		☐
Other		

Facial moisturisers

	Unprompted	Prompted
Don't buy	☐	
First one I see (ie no preference)	☐	
Brand B	☐	☐
Brand D	☐	☐
Brand F	☐	☐
Brand G	☐	☐
Brand H	☐	☐
Can't remember		☐
Other		

This question is designed to be administered by an interviewer who will prompt respondents by showing them a list a brands if they cannot recall the brand they buy without prompting.

Unprompted answers will be sought initially. Similar questions would be asked for the full range of products that are sold by the retailer, such as pain relief products, vitamin supplements, cereal bars and so on. The brands listed in each case would be different, depending on the leading brands in particular categories. If the retailer has its own brand this should be included. The 'Can't remember' option is for those respondents who do buy the product, but cannot recall the brand name of the product that they do buy even after prompting. If the answer is 'Other' the name of the brand should be recorded.

(b) **Data that would be best collected confidentially**

Under the **MRS Code of Conduct** data that is confidential should not be collected at all unless it is **appropriate and relevant** to the purpose for which it will be collected. Respondents must be assured that no information which could be used to identify them will be made available without their agreement to anyone outside the agency responsible for conducting the research. They must also be assured that the information they supply will not be used for any purposes other than research and that they will **not be adversely affected or embarrassed** as a direct result of their participation in a research project.

The Code also makes it clear that all indications of the **identity** of respondents should be physically **separated** from the records of the information they have provided as soon as possible after the completion of any necessary fieldwork quality checks. The researcher must ensure that any information which might identify respondents is stored securely, and separately from the other information they have provided; and that access to such material is restricted to authorised research personnel within the researcher's own organisation for specific research purposes.

In deciding what information needs confidential handling in this case it is relevant to consider the categories of **sensitive personal data** defined in the UK by the Data Protection Act 1998, most of which are likely to be relevant to this client's purpose.

(i) The racial or ethnic origin of data subjects (cultural issues may affect whether customers are willing to purchase certain types of products, or products containing certain ingredients).

(ii) Their political opinions – customers' buying habits may be influenced by opinions on matters such as testing products on animals, exploitation of foreign workers, green issues and so on.

(iii) Their religious beliefs or other beliefs of a similar nature (again, this may affect whether customers are willing to purchase certain types of products, or products containing certain ingredients).

(iv) Their physical or mental health or condition: customers' purchasing habits in the client's stores may reveal confidential information about this.

(v) Their sexual life: again, purchasing habits may reveal confidential information about this.

(vi) The commission or alleged commission by them of any offence, and any details of court proceedings or sentences against them (possibly relevant where drugs are used for illicit purposes, or in the case of animal rights activists).

In addition to the above, **income** is a sensitive issue with many people. In this case, however, it is unlikely that the client needs any more than a general indication of income level and it should be possible to choose a response format for the 'income' question that the respondent will be prepared to answer on a non-confidential basis.

The question refers to the **collection** of data in a confidential manner, which presumably means that it should not be possible for the respondent to be overheard. This is most likely to be an issue where the questions are potentially embarrassing for the respondent, notably health-related questions, questions about sexual practices, and questions about opinions that might be perceived as socially undesirable.

In these cases the data collection method that is most likely to be acceptable to respondents and successful in eliciting the required information is the **one-to-one in-depth interview**. This is because in an in-depth interview rapport can be established with the moderator and the respondent is more likely to talk openly and freely. The interview may be conducted via telephone to increase anonymity (and also cut down on costs).

(c) **Question topics to help understand required changes in the pattern of retail outlets**

Topics could include the following.

(i) **Preferred location** of retail outlets. Customers may wish to have the option of large out-of-town stores for their main shopping and also smaller convenience stores near their place of work and/or home for ad hoc purchases. Sub-questions may ask about matters such as the importance of car parking, the importance of other types of shops in the same vicinity (eg in shopping malls), the desirability or otherwise of purchasing pharmaceuticals and health goods in non-specialist shops such as supermarkets.

(ii) Questions about **accessibility** of stores. This is likely to be an important issue for certain key customer groups such as the disabled, the elderly and people with young children.

(iii) **Regularity of purchases** of different types of product (eg *ad hoc* to treat specific ailments, part of regular weekly shopping etc.) This data will help with decisions about levels of stock to hold, store layout and so on.

(iv) **Time of purchase** (eg *en route* to or from work, at lunchtime, at the weekend, and so on). This data will help with decisions about store opening hours, shelf-filling, number of checkouts open, and so on.

(v) Questions on **shopping behaviour** such as whether consumers wish to browse or go straight to the product they need, the extent of impulse buying, whether they wish to have advice on purchasing decisions from trained staff such as pharmacists. This will help with decisions about store layout and staffing.

(vi) Questions on the influence of various **marketing communications** such as packaging, TV advertising, promotional offers and so on.

(vii) Attitude to purchasing different types of products by **mail order** or over the **Internet**. This is likely to vary considerably from product-to-product. For example, sun-tan lotion and other holiday-related pharmaceuticals might well be purchased in this way, since there is plenty of time for consumers to prepare in advance. If a consumer has a headache, however, they are unlikely to be willing to wait for aspirins to be delivered in the post!

(viii) Level of **interest in health goods**. Questions might tackle issues such as: awareness of government health initiatives; perceptions of how healthy different types of food are; response to 'scares' about certain types of food (eg food with high salt or sugar content) or certain types of product (such as vitamin supplements); factors that cause changes in eating habits, such as increasing age or weight or specific occurrences of health problems.

(ix) Suggestions for **other products** that could be offered. For example, exercise equipment might complement other health-related products, but such items are typically bulky and need to be displayed and warehoused in a different way to off the shelf packets.

56 Awards scheme effectiveness

(a) **Secondary research about other similar awards schemes**

In each case of another scheme the **information** that the agency should collect will include who runs the scheme, who is eligible to enter it (type of organisation, geographical location, turnover limits etc.), criteria for winning an award, what the award consists of (usually money and or a title), how well publicised it is, and (if possible) how highly regarded it is. General information about schemes will be available from the organisers (for example, by contacting them directly or reviewing their **websites** or other published materials). Information about how prestigious an award is felt to be might be obtained from **press coverage** and from talking directly to previous entrants and winners.

The purpose of gathering this data is to make **comparisons** with the awards that GlobalSustain organises, so it will be wise to begin by drawing up a **checklist** of the features of their scheme to help focus the research.

Either the **brief**, or subsequent **discussions** with GlobalSustain staff, may have already identified one or two similar schemes and if so these are the obvious starting point for research.

Assuming that GlobalSustain subscribes to, or has access to, a variety of **magazines and other publications** connected with sustainable development a review of past editions would be a good and very focused starting point for a search about similar awards schemes, and given that most award schemes are run annually it should only be necessary to review a maximum of two year's worth of copies. Many such publications publish searchable archives online, which will make searching even easier.

If the **charities and voluntary groups** that GlobalSustain is involved with have their own websites these should be searched for mention of other awards schemes. If not information may still be available in the form of other publications, annual reports or marketing material, or obtainable via a short conversation.

Likewise the websites or other publications of **current and potential sponsors**, especially large companies involved in some way in issues connected with sustainable development, should be consulted with the aim of finding out whether they sponsor awards schemes or even whether they have won awards themselves.

There are a variety of large **global or national organisations** who are involved in development programmes, such as the International Development Research Centre (IDRC), the Global Development Network, the United Nations, the International Monetary Fund, the Organisation for Economic Co-operation and the British Council. These may run their own schemes or their websites and other publications may contain mention of the topic.

Government sites and the sites of organisations such as the **EU** should also be good sources of information (though this will vary from country to country), and such bodies are likely to have awards schemes of their own.

More **general Internet searches** should also be conducted at some stage during the research, initially using a search engine such as Google or Ixquick, and subsequently following up promising links within portals and individual sites. Search terms could include phrases such as 'sustainable development', 'corporate citizenship', 'corporate social responsibility', 'business award schemes' and so on. This may be done very quickly at the outset of the research to obtain an overview but – reliable though tools like Google and Ixquick may be – they are also likely to turn up a **large number of less relevant results**, so the **more focused methods** described above should be commenced as soon as possible.

(b) **Programme of primary research**

Objective

To understand how effective the Business Awards Scheme is in raising the profile of the charities and voluntary groups.

(The expression 'raising the profile' means obtaining the attention of potential sponsors (increasing awareness) and so helping to raise funds.)

Research design

(i) Initially, the agency will need to **explore** the context and the key issues: some of the issues are likely to be highly emotive and/or political and this could have an important impact on the language that should and should not be used in subsequent research for questionnaire design, interviewer scripts and so on.

Interviewees should include representatives of existing and potential sponsors (people with decision making responsibilities), past awards scheme entrants and winners, managers of charities involved in projects that need funding or have received funding, and journalists with a particular interest in sustainable development. It may be possible to include opinion leaders such as politicians, senior civil servants and/or celebrities with a interest in the topic.

Questions that might be explored include what benefits sponsors expect to get out of their sponsorship, the type of support that the charities and voluntary groups need (perhaps not only financial support), the kind of stories that journalists are most interested in covering, and the kind of issues that opinion leaders wish to be associated with.

(ii) This initial qualitative study will inform the design of the **conclusive** research, a cross-sectional quantitative survey that aims to gather evidence about the effectiveness of the awards scheme.

The populations of interest for this second stage can be divided into four main segments.

(1) **Existing sponsors** of charity groups and voluntary groups represented by GlobalSustain.

■ To what extent do they consider their sponsorship was influenced by GlobalSustain and its awards scheme?

■ Do they only sponsor the winners?

■ What other sponsorship activities are they involved in?

(2) **Potential sponsors**. The agency will wish to measure their current awareness of and interest in the following.

■ Sustainable development issues in general
■ Charities and voluntary groups involved in sustainable development
■ GlobalSustain and its activities in general
■ The GlobalSustain awards scheme in particular

(3) Organisations **seeking sponsorship**.

■ How successful are they at present at obtaining funding?
■ To what extent are they aware of the GlobalSustain scheme?

(4) Organisations **receiving sponsorship**.

■ To what extent are they aware of the GlobalSustain scheme?

■ What role, if any, was played by the GlobalSustain award scheme or any other scheme in obtaining funding?

■ If none, how did the sponsorship come about?

■ What difference has the sponsorship made (ie how successful were they at raising funding before)?

Sampling

GlobalSustain is likely to have **existing** press contacts and government contacts and its **own databases** of contacts in sponsoring organisations and organisations needing sponsorship and receiving sponsorship. These lists may need to be supplemented by further research, for example to identify new potential sponsors and new charities and groups.

For the initial exploratory qualitative interviews it will probably only be possible to include a small sample. Some kind of judgement sampling is likely, although this will attempt to make the respondents as representative as possible.

For the quantitative research a **random sample** from lists of sponsors and (would-be) sponsored organisations can be taken. This should be **stratified** in each case since the population of interest is not homogeneous: various types and sizes of organisations will be approached so a simple random sample would not be truly representative of the whole. (To avoid the potential error the populations will be first be divided into their different strata and then random samples are taken from within each stratum.) Examples of sub-groups in the case of sponsors might be different sizes of organisation, different industry sectors and different locations. In the case of organisations wishing to be sponsored sub-groups may include GlobalSustain award nominees and winners, winners of other awards, non-entrants/non-winners. Again it may also be necessary to stratify by type of activity, location and so on.

The size of the sample in the latter case will depend on the extent of stratification necessary, the time available to collect data and analyse results, and the budget.

Data collection methods

The **exploratory** research will need to be conducted by means of **qualitative in-depth interviews**. Given that the participants required are busy executives, and assuming that they are very widely dispersed (as the name 'GlobalSustain' suggests), the most practical way of doing this will probably be by means of **telephone interviews**. Telephone numbers may already be recorded in GlobalSustain's database or will be readily available from websites or other published data. Interviews will probably be recorded to ensure accuracy in recording responses and to ensure that note is taken of non-verbal responses such as tone of voice.

An alternative might be **focus groups** conducted via **teleconferencing**, **web conferencing** (eg Webex) or **video conferencing** (depending on resources available). The advantage of this approach is that sponsors, politicians and the like may give richer responses if they are stimulated by what those seeking sponsorship have to say, and *vice versa*, although skilful moderation will be required to keep the peace and preserve impartiality.

The **quantitative** research is probably also best conducted via **telephone interviews**, especially if results are required before the next awards ceremony, which is due next month. The survey will be conducted centrally (from wherever GlobalSustain is based) to facilitate control and monitoring.

Self-completion questionnaires are an alternative: these may be distributed by post or via the Internet (email or a web link). However, either of these, particularly the postal approach, is liable to have a lower response rate and to take a good deal longer to complete.

(c) **Using the awards ceremony to conduct research**

On the face of it the awards ceremony would appear to be an ideal opportunity for research of various kinds because many of the interested parties will be gathered together in a single location: uniquely there will be a captive audience of people from widely different locations who represent widely different segments of the target population.

On the other hand GlobalSustain's current research problem is to measure the effectiveness of the awards scheme in absolute terms, but it is inevitable that those who attend the ceremony will be people who are **already aware** of it and who **view it** (the awards ceremony, not necessarily the cause) **positively** enough to turn up. It is highly unlikely that research will be representative of GlobalSustain's entire target population: it will be **heavily biased** towards those who favour the cause and the scheme. This bias is a very **major limitation** of any research that may be undertaken.

(i) At the very least, the **names** of all people who actually attend should be collected: it may be that many invitations were speculative and there may be new names to add to the database of contacts. This could be done very quickly and unobtrusively if invitations include barcodes that can be scanned at the entrance. A possible problem with this approach is that it could deny access to 'gatecrashers' who are desirable in other ways, for example journalists and photographers if a major celebrity attends. GlobalSustain need the publicity and research should not get in the way of business needs.

(ii) **Questionnaires for self-completion** could be left on chairs or tables in the auditorium. Because of the setting and the 'distraction' of the ceremony itself and of others company these will need to be short and simple, so there is a limit to the kind and volume of data that can be collected. Some attendees may simply be guests of the persons GlobalSustain wants to target, and not part of the population of interest at all.

(iii) Some participants may be willing to take part in **qualitative mini-depth interviews** (20 to 30 minutes). As already mentioned this may be a unique opportunity to obtain the views of key opinion formers such as politicians and senior civil servants. These could perhaps be pre-arranged. The **limitations** are mainly practical: because of the **time** involved a large number of interviewers will be needed to achieve a representative sample, and it may not be possible to cover all the issues in adequate depth.

(iv) Interviewers could be placed at strategic points such as in the reception area and the bar and conduct **short quantitative interviews** with anyone who is willing to take part. The **problems** are partly those of self-completion questionnaires (not everyone will be part of the target population, and there is a limit to the kind and volume of data that can be collected) and partly those of mini-depths (persuading people to take part when they are otherwise occupied and achieving adequate coverage).

57 Pickles and chutneys

Tutorial note. In part (a) you are expected to identify a range of pros and cons for each method and give a clear and convincing recommendation of which method you would recommend and why. You may choose to recommend neither, but again, a clear rationale needs to be given. Better answers may identify that, although they have recommended one over the other, there are limitations to both. Good answers may suggest the role which such a survey could play in a wider programme of research.

In part (b) you should provide two appropriate questions for a self-completion questionnaire, along with appropriate response formats. Where appropriate, clear instructions should be given on how to complete each question. The questions should be easy to understand with no double negatives, complicated wording, technical jargon, or abstract concepts. They should be unambiguous and shouldn't be two questions in one. They should be relevant to the stated objectives. Response formats should be clear and include 'don't know', no opinion, not appropriate options where appropriate. Layout should be easy to follow.

In part (c) you are expected to identify a range of sources of secondary data and link those to the research objectives stated in the question. You should mention what kind of data you are looking for, where it might be found and why it might be useful. Better answers will provide a wide range of ideas.

As often, our answer is a good deal longer than you could have managed in the time available, on the grounds that we need to cover a wider range of ideas to help you mark your own answer.

(a) **Data collection methods**

(i) **In restaurant**

Collecting information when diners visit the restaurants has several **advantages**.

(1) It is very easy to access members of the target population.

(2) Response rate should be high and responses will be received very quickly (within minutes, or hours at most) after questionnaires are issued.

(3) Respondents can sample the products at the time when they are completing the questionnaire, rather than having to recall their likes and dislikes at a later time.

There are also a number of **disadvantages**.

(1) Respondents may be influenced by factors not directly related to the pickles and chutneys, such as the quality of their meal as a whole and the ambience of the restaurants.

(2) The sample includes only people who eat out in the restaurant. They will be representative of people who live or work in the local area and like to eat out, but they may not be at all representative of a market for chutneys and pickles for home use.

(3) Regular customers may be surveyed several times and, being regular customers, they are more likely to have favourable views.

(4) Questionnaires are liable to completed in a group setting, since most people do not dine out alone. Groupthink may distort responses. This may not be important, depending on the question topics, but if general demographic questions are asked there is no way of knowing who actually filled in the questionnaire.

(5) Some customers may resent the intrusion: they have visited the restaurant to eat and enjoy others company, not to fill in questionnaires.

(6) Restaurant staff may influence responses, for example if they are asked to recommend accompaniments for meals: it is unlikely that they will be impartial. It is also unlikely that they would risk antagonising 'difficult' customers further by asking them to complete a questionnaire, so once again there is a strong risk that responses will not be representative of the total population of interest.

(7) The exercise is apparently so easy to do that it may be done by amateurs who do not understand the difficulties of questionnaire design, and the ethical issues involved.

(ii) **Using the customer database**

This approach has some **advantages**.

(1) The questionnaire can be longer and more elaborate. For example, it may include more open-ended questions that require thought, whereas this would be too much of an imposition on customers who have come out to dine.

(2) Respondents are not distracted by unrelated factors (the meal, their company) and are not influenced by restaurant staff.

(3) Responses can be overlaid accurately with geo-demographic data, since the postcode of respondents will be known (a question could be asked in an in-restaurant survey, of course, but there is no way of checking that it is answered accurately).

Problems include the following.

(1) The database will only include past customers of the restaurant, and in fact it is only likely to include regular customers who like the restaurant so much that they have opted to receive mailings, so it will be heavily biased. It is not usual for restaurants to collect any more information about customers than the name of the person booking the table and a contact telephone number. Many regular customers may not be listed and no casual customers.

(2) The database is unlikely to be completely up-to-date. For example, those included may have worked in the area when their details were recorded but they may have moved on by now.

(3) Contact addresses may be work addresses which cannot be used for geo-demographic analysis.

(4) The response rate is likely to be considerably lower than it would be with an in-restaurant survey, even if reminders are sent, and very much slower. A cut-off point will be needed (so that Mr Sharma can get on with product development), but this may mean that valuable responses received late are not taken into account at all.

(5) It is more expensive because of postage and printing costs.

(6) It relies on customer recall, perhaps some time after the experience. Customers may not even have known what they were tasting and responses such as 'I didn't like that green one' may not be helpful!

(iii) **Recommendation**

An **in-restaurant survey** is the **recommended first step** in preference to a postal survey because it is likely to include a more diverse range of people and because of the major advantage that respondents can try out the products at the time they complete the questionnaire. Speed and low cost are also very significant reasons for preferring this approach.

The **disadvantages** of this method must be **recognised** however, and the results must not be regarded as conclusive. The next step could be to develop a truly **representative sampling frame**, for example by buying a list from a broker and conducting either a postal questionnaire or a telephone survey. **Alternatively**, or in addition, a **hall test** is recommended since this would allow respondents to try the products. The initial in-restaurant research will nevertheless have been useful in determining the direction of questions in subsequent research.

(b) **Two questions**

(i) **Which flavours are most popular?**

We produce pickles and chutneys in five different flavours as listed below. For each flavour please mark an X in the box in a position that best reflects how much you like that flavour, or if you have not tried it please mark an X in the 'Not tried it' column. Please tick one box only for each flavour.

Rationale for this question format

Asking the question in this way has advantages over simply asking 'What is your favourite flavour?' (which does not give any information about any other flavour), or asking for a 1 to 5 ranking (which is more difficult for respondents to do, which can be error-prone in a self-completion questionnaire, and which may discourage respondents from saying that they like or dislike certain flavours equally). The 'not tried it' column needs to be there to cover this situation, and gives a certain amount of information about popularity, although it does not explain why respondents have not tried a flavour: it may simply not have been available when they visited the restaurant.

(ii) **Where customers would expect to buy the products**

Where would you expect to be able to buy our pickles and chutneys?

Please tick as many boxes as apply.

In our restaurants	☐
From our website	☐
Delicatessens	☐
Speciality Asian stores	☐
Open air markets	☐
Asda	☐
Co-op	☐
Marks and Spencer	☐
Morrison	☐
Sainsbury	☐
Somerfield	☐
Tesco	☐
Waitrose	☐
Other (please specify)	☐ ....

Rationale for this question format

We have listed specific supermarkets since the product is liable to be considered as somewhat specialised and confined to the more up-market outlets. We have included the option of Mr Sharma distributing the products himself (via a website), but if this is not practical due to lack of resources this option should be omitted to avoid raising customer expectations.

(c) **Programme of secondary research to help understand the structure of the potential market**

Some **secondary research** may have been **carried out already** in connection with the previous venture referred to in the question. This should be **reviewed** and **checked** for relevance to the current project. It is likely to be somewhat out of date, but it may suggest useful sources for new research.

Trade magazines such as *The Grocer* are likely to have covered the market and they may have online archives allowing fast searching. In particular they are likely to report on the key features of recent research that has been carried out.

A search of **Mintel's website** is likely to be very fruitful. A Mintel report will typically contain information and statistics about market size, market segments, supply and distribution information (including information about the major players in the market), and consumer information. Detailed information is likely to cost in excess of £500, but the contents page (at the very least) will be available online and may help to provide directions for further search topics. The full report will be available for immediate download on payment of the fee.

Reports may also be available for download or purchase **from other publishers** of **syndicated research** on packaged goods such as Key Note Publications, and **from specialist agencies**. Care is, of course, needed to ensure that reports are relevant to Mr Sharma's market (presumably the UK, at least initially), and that they are reasonably up to date. It is also important to be aware of possible bias – for example, published results from research conducted on behalf of Sharwoods, who would be a major competitor, are likely to portray Sharwoods in a favourable light. Depending on the source of the report and the intended market for the information it may be necessary to look in some detail at the research design and methodology to check on the accuracy and representativeness of the data.

Major branded competitors can be identified simply by visiting potential retail outlets and seeing what is currently available. **Competitors' websites** should be consulted for more detailed information about existing products (range, price) and news of new products. It may also be possible to draw some conclusions about the profile of consumers who are being targeted by different competitors from the contents of their websites, for example if foreign language versions are available, or if specialist recipes are provided. Information may also be available about distribution methods (perhaps aimed at retail outlets). Shareholder information may be available: annual reports may contain assessments of trends in the market, market shares and so on.

Own brands may be more difficult to research in detail but the websites of supermarkets should be checked to get a more complete picture of the competition.

Sites of **online distributors** of Asian food products may help to identify additional competitors and imported products.

Government information relating to the market itself is likely to be limited, but it may be useful to consult government sites like the Food Standards Agency to find out about regulations for manufacturing, storing and distributing food items, labelling requirements.

Finally, articles in **food-related magazines and supplements**, for example in weekend newspapers, will give an indication of current consumer trends. Advertising in such sources may also be informative since it will indicate what other manufacturers perceive to be worth promoting.

58 EduWeb's new market

> *Tutorial note.* This is a rather poor question, in our opinion.
>
> In part (a) you may include some or all of the suggestions in our answer. Better candidates will provide a convincing justification for each change suggested and link this to the business objectives.
>
> For part (b) the examiner commented that there are many different ways of writing up a report based on this information and was looking for reports that would aid comprehension. You may have struggled with this part, given that the data is quite unsuitable for the purpose stated in the question!
>
> Your answer to part (c) should include a range of points and accompanying rationale.
>
> Incidentally the table is not an exact reproduction of the one in the BMRA report and the question paper even contained an error. We have assumed this was deliberate so we have mentioned it in our answer, but you would have to do some quick calculations to be sure so don't worry if you missed it. The original report can be viewed on the BMRA website (www.bmra.org.uk).

(a) **How to reorganise/rework the table**

The **objective** of EduWeb is to find out about market research in the UK and know about the best way for them to gather data.

The **table does not give any information** about what is the best way in different circumstances, simply about the relative income earned by around half of the UK market research industry from usage of various methods in 2001.

The **table could be made easier to interpret** in the following ways.

(i) The first two columns could be headed with percentage signs and the individual percentage signs could then be removed, since they make the data look cluttered. The pound signs in the third column are not necessary at all. There is no reason for the first column to be in italics.

(ii) More space should be allowed for the row labels. In the current layout it is not clear whether 'Qualitative' means qualitative research in general or qualitative telephone research as opposed to quantitative telephone research.

(iii) The data could be listed in order of market share: this would make it easier to see what were the most and least profitable methods for the market research industry.

(iv) In a table listed in order of market share the year on year change figure could be replaced by words, such as 'Growing significantly', 'Growing', Declining', 'Declining significantly'. This would avoid having too many numbers in a single table, and in any case minus signs are quite hard to see.

(v) The data could be listed in order of year on year change to show which methods were growing the most and which declining the most. This would make it clear, for example, that although Web/Internet had only a small market share in 2001 it is likely to have grown significantly since that time.

(vi) The data could be grouped into similar categories of research, for example: quantitative and qualitative; Internet and Postal (both self-completion methods); Consumer Panel + Retail Audit (both panel-based methods).

(vii) The turnover figures are probably not relevant for EduWeb's purposes and could be omitted entirely – the information is already provided in relative terms in the Market Share column. (The column headed '2000 Turnover' should be headed '2001 Turnover', since the percentages match up precisely.)

(viii) The figures could be rounded up to whole numbers. This would not affect the order of items in any way, except in the case of the two items that are less than 1%, where the decimal percentage might be given in brackets next to the label to make it clear that Web/Internet comes slightly above Retail Audit.

(ix) The categories that have a market share lower than 4.9% – Retail Audit, Web/Internet and Observation/Mystery shopping – *could* be grouped together under 'Other'. However, each of these categories shows significant growth or decline, so this is not recommended because it would remove information that is valuable for the purposes of an online training company such as EduWeb.

(x) Further changes would be possible if more information were available: this is addressed in more detail in the answer to question 3.

(b) **Summary of BMRA data and conclusions about data collection methods in the UK**

REPORT

To: Senior Management of EduWeb
From: MRS Candidate
Date: 30 September 20X3
Subject: Data collection methods in the UK

Based on data obtained from the British Market Research Association (BMRA) the most popular methods of data collection in the UK in 2001 were as follows.

	Market Share %	Growth %	Decline %
Face-to-face Quantitative	41		(4)
Telephone Quantitative	20	5	
Qualitative	13		(8)
Consumer Panel	10	9	
Postal/Self Completion	8		(1)
Other	5	8	
Observation/Mystery shopping	3	21	
Web/Internet (0.5%)	1	18	
Retail Audit (0.4%)	1		(42)

The market share is shown in the form of a **pie chart** and growth or decline is shown in the form of a **bar chart** at Appendix 1 [not included in this answer].

The growth or decline represents the change from the previous year, only: it should not necessarily be interpreted as a long-term trend. Arranged in order of growth or decline of the different methods the information is as follows.

	Year on year change %
Observation/Mystery shopping	21
Web/Internet	18
Consumer Panel	9
Other	8
Telephone Quantitative	5
Postal/Self Completion	(1)
Face-to-face Quantitative	(4)
Qualitative	(8)
Retail Audit	(42)

The figures are **not necessarily representative of the popularity** of different methods at all: they are distorted by the fact that some methods are far more expensive than others (and therefore earn more income for the market research industry).

However, if we assume that the figures are somewhat indicative of the extent to which each method is used, we could draw the following **conclusions**.

(i)   Interviewer-based methods, whether face to face or by telephone are by far the most widely-used methods, accounting for nearly 75% of market share. These methods are likely to be relatively easier in the UK than they are in the United States, given factors such as the small size of the country and the absence of differences in time zones.

(ii)   Growth in quantitative telephone interviewing is almost exactly matched by decline in face-to-face quantitative interviewing. This may indicate that telephone interviewing is becoming more acceptable to respondents in the UK.

(iii)   Although Web/Internet research (which is particularly relevant to EduWeb's business) had only a 0.4% market share in 2001 it was growing significantly. Computer ownership and broadband connections in the UK lagged significantly behind the US at that time, so it is likely that the share has continued to grow, possibly at an even faster rate.

(iv)   Retail Audit is presumably not relevant to EduWeb's business, but for completeness it may be observed that this method shows a significant decline.

(c)   **Other information that would be useful**

As indicated in the previous answers, although information about the income of the market research industry may be of great interest to market researchers it is not very useful at all for the purpose of showing EduWeb what the best way is for them to gather data in a new market.

Presumably the 'best way' of researching is the way that produces the most useful, accurate and representative information to solve the business problem, and although country-specific factors and the skill and experience of practitioners in the country are relevant, the **key determinant of which method to use will be the nature of the business problem**.

The information given is only an extract. The **survey** itself could usefully contain the **following additional information**.

(i)   Information about the volume of usage of the different methods, in other words figures not distorted by money amounts.

(ii)   Information covering more recent years.

(iii)   Longer term trends, in other words information covering, say, the last five years.

(iv)   Less aggregated information: for example, it would be useful to know the split between mystery shopping and other types of observation. It would be useful to know the relative proportions of different type of face to face interviews (in-street, hall tests, door-to-door, etc). It would be useful to know what methods are included in the 'Other' category.

(v)   A copy of the survey questionnaire. This would help to answer questions such as who in the organisations surveyed was asked to return the information, whether evidence was required to support the information provided, and whether it was clear to respondents how to categorise their research methods (for example, some respondents might include self-completion questionnaires in web surveys). All of this would be helpful in judging the accuracy of the information.

A **report** to EduWeb management based on the data should include the following **additional information**.

(i)   Information about the BMRA and their membership. A US company may well know little about them and how representative they are of the UK industry as a whole. We are told that the information is representative of firms whose income amounts to around 50% of the UK industry's turnover, but this could comprise a few very large firms or a very large number of small firms.

(ii)   We are also told that responses represent only 66% of BMRA members' turnover. It would be useful to know if the 33% of non-responders includes members whose replies would have altered the findings significantly.

(iii)   Information about other professional bodies in the UK. These might be more representative of the industry as a whole, and may produce their own figures and other information that would be more helpful for EduWeb. In particular the MRS's *Research Buyer's Guide* would appear to be a useful source of information. (This is not to criticise the BMRA or their report: it is clearly not intended for EduWeb's purpose.)

(iv)   General information about the market research industry in the UK: who are the leading players, for example, and what specialist skills are available? What is known in general about consumer attitudes to market research? What is the state of technology used in market research (telephone ownership, Internet-connectedness, prevalence of CCTV)? What legal restrictions are there?

Test Papers

Advanced Certificate in Market and Social Research Practice Examination

February 2004

TEST PAPER 1

Instructions for Candidates

Time allowed 2 hrs 30 minutes

Answer _ALL_ questions in Section 1

Answer _TWO_ questions from Section 2

Section 1 accounts for one third of the final result.

Section 2 accounts for two thirds of the final result.

Section 1: Compulsory question

(Recommended time: 50 minutes)

This section tests problem identification and problem solving using a number of skills. The answers in this section account for one-third of the total marks.

Read the following case study and answer ALL the questions below.

LiveSport! is a not-for-profit organisation which aims to encourage young people to participate actively and safely in a wide range of sports. One of its main objectives is to raise awareness of ethical issues surrounding sports participation, in particular the problems surrounding the illegal use of performance-enhancing drugs. LiveSport! has representatives in all countries across the European Union and aims to use the interest generated by the Olympic Games held in Greece in 2004 to further promote its activities.

Prior to briefing its advertising agency on any changes to its current activity, LiveSport! wishes to assess how successful its current communications strategy has been at government level and with key groups of opinion formers, such as the governing bodies of individual sports, leading sports companies and journalists.

You have been commissioned to undertake a quantitative survey in 4 European countries (UK, France, Germany and Spain) to assess awareness of and attitudes to the work of LiveSport! Funding for this project will be spread across all countries involved in LiveSport! The survey will be conducted from a UK telephone centre using CATI (Computer-aided telephone interviewing). You have 3 months to report back.

1. What are the benefits and drawbacks of co-ordinating such a telephone survey out of the UK rather than having fieldwork conducted separately in each of the countries concerned?

    (Weighting: one-third of marks for Section 1)

2. What are the main issues you would need to consider when recruiting the sample?

    (Weighting: one-third of marks for Section 1)

3. LiveSport! is keen to get maximum benefit from the project and wants to make sure that reporting takes on the most appropriate form to achieve this. Outline the approaches you would take to reporting the results, giving reasons for the choices you have made.

    (Weighting: one-third of marks for Section 1)

Section 2: Optional questions
(Recommended time: 100 minutes)

The answers in this section account for two-thirds of the total marks.

Answer any TWO questions from the six listed below. Give a full answer to each of the questions you choose.

---

1   When designing research projects, compromises in some areas are often required in order to keep the project within budget. Would any of the following approaches reduce the cost of a quantitative survey? Discuss the potential limitations on the usefulness of a quantitative survey through the following compromises.

(i)	Smaller sample size	(Weighting: 25%)
(ii)	Broader sample definition (who precisely to interview)	(Weighting: 25%)
(iii)	Shorter questionnaire length	(Weighting: 25%)
(iv)	Shorter timescale	(Weighting: 25%)

2   A colleague is unfamiliar with qualitative research and wants to know more about it. Prepare a briefing document for them that describes the following:

(i)	The main differences between qualitative and quantitative research	(Weighting: 50%)
(ii)	The strengths and limitations of qualitative research.	(Weighting: 50%)

3   For the last five years, your client has conducted an employee attitude survey using a postal questionnaire. This year she would like to collect data from employees using the organisation's email system:

(i)   Outline the advantages and disadvantages of using the email approach compared to the previous postal method.   (Weighting: 50%)

(ii) Describe how this email survey might be conducted and the issues involved in designing and setting up a survey for this medium.   (Weighting: 50%)

4   Describe what is meant by each of the following and give examples of how you might use each of them in analysing data from a survey:

(i)	cross tabulations	(Weighting: 25%)
(ii)	frequencies and percentages	(Weighting: 25%)
(iii)	measures of central tendency	(Weighting: 25%)
(iv)	measures of dispersion	(Weighting: 25%)

5   (a)   Below are some of the principles which underpin The Market Research Society Code of Conduct. Describe briefly what is meant by each one, and outline the relevance of each to the research process.

   (i)   informed consent
   (ii) anonymity and confidentiality
   (iii) not deceiving respondents   (Weighting for Part (a): 50%)

   (b)   You are planning a qualitative study among children aged 12 to 14 about use of mobile phones. Outline the key ethical considerations in conducting research among this age group.   (Weighting for Part (b): 50%)

6   You have just taken on the role of a market researcher in a client company. One of your first tasks is to review and then summarise the findings from a supplier's final report on a research project. The project had qualitative and quantitative components and was commissioned before you joined the company. Describe and give a rationale for the steps you would take to evaluate the quality of this research.

Suggested answers

DO NOT TURN THIS PAGE UNTIL YOU
HAVE COMPLETED THE TEST PAPER

Section 1

ANSWER

Tutorial note. To pass question 1 you would be expected to include a minimum of two benefits and two limitations, but you would get extra credit if you can suggest more. Your answer to question 2 should recognise the practical problems associated with constructing a sample frame for this particular situation. In question 3 you should mention a range of delivery mechanisms which would help the client to understand the results clearly and you should provide a rationale for each point you make.

The examiner reported that many answers to this question were limited in scope and lacked real depth. There was limited evidence of a thorough understanding of the key issues relating to recruitment and the representativeness of the sample. In addition, many students could not identify the main benefits and drawbacks of co-ordinating the survey from one location and lacked creativity in terms of suggesting a range of reporting mechanisms.

1 **Co-ordinating a telephone survey out of the UK rather than having fieldwork conducted in separately countries**

The **benefits** of this approach include the following.

(a) **Cost-effectiveness**. Central telephone interviewing is likely to be much cheaper than conducting fieldwork separately in each of the countries because resources (equipment, management) do no have to be duplicated in each country. Given that LiveSport! is a not-for-profit organisation this is likely to be a very important consideration.

(b) **Control**. A centrally co-ordinated approach allows much more control over the project as a whole. Interviewer briefing will be quicker and cheaper, and will be totally consistent because there is no need for multiple briefings in each different country. Monitoring interviews for quality and consistency of approach (adherence to interviewing protocols, consistent coding and so on) will be easier and any changes needed in the process can be implemented much more quickly. CATI (computer aided telephone interviewing) allows the use of filters, greater control and less interviewer bias. It will also be easier to control the number of surveys conducted – in other words the facility can stop interviewing a particular cell as soon as its quota is full – and to monitor progress towards the individual and overall targets.

(c) **Time**. Telephone fieldwork from a central facility is likely to be completed more quickly than if it were conducted by separate agencies in each country. All responses will be recorded in a consistent way and stored in a central computer, and this means that turnround times from data collection to analysis of the data will be much faster.

There are a number of possible **drawbacks**, however.

(a) The researcher will need to recruit **interviewers** who can are fluent in one or more of English, French, German and Spanish. **Bi-lingual or multilingual** staff will be more difficult to find and more expensive.

(b) Centrally based interviewers may be multi-lingual but they will have **less local insight** and sensitivity to local issues, and they will only be aware of LiveSport!'s activities in individual countries to the extent that this can be included in the briefing.

(c)   The questionnaires will need to be **translated** and carefully checked to ensure that the meanings of the questions are fundamentally the same and measurements are consistent. Of course, this applies whatever method is used, but it will be more difficult to control from a central location, since those monitoring calls will also need to be multi-lingual.

(d)   The research may be perceived to be **UK-centric** and local branches of LiveSport! may therefore find it more difficult to accept the results of the research and take any actions that the research proposes.

(e)   Some of the costs and time saved by co-ordinating the process centrally may be offset by the extra costs of **requiring the client to travel** if they wish to attend the interviewer briefing and for progress reports and the final report.

(f)   Possible minor drawbacks are that the **cost of calls** may be slightly higher from a central location, and there are small differences in **time-zones**. The differences will be fairly **negligible** in this case, however, given the countries involved.

2   **Issues to consider when recruiting the sample**

The population of interest is defined in the question as people at government level, key groups of opinion formers such as the governing bodies of individual sports, leading sports companies and journalists. It would be useful to **define the target groups** more precisely, for example what groups are considered to be 'opinion formers', which individual sports are included, what is a 'leading' sports company, and what range of newspapers and other media is to be included?

Given that it already has a communications strategy LiveSport! is sure to have its own **databases of contacts** in each country and the first step is to obtain and examine these for completeness and up-to-dateness and also for consistency, since the data may be stored in different ways, with more or less detail, in different countries.

If the existing databases are not considered to be complete **further information** can be gathered from a **variety of sources**. Government websites are likely to have up-to-date lists of contacts, as are the sites of sports bodies and leading sports companies. Telephone directories and sports directories may also be used, so long as they are up-to-date. Many newspapers now contain the email addresses of its journalists, and even if this information is not universally available it should be relatively easy to obtain from the newspapers themselves. Magazine writers and local and national radio and TV journalists and presenters should also be included in the list.

Once the sampling frame is as complete as possible decisions will need to be made about **sampling method** (probability or non-probability) and the size of sample to recruit. These decisions will depend upon the precise information needs of the client.

The **representativeness** of the sample must be considered. For example, cricket is a major sport in the UK but not in the other countries: to what extent should the cricket world be represented? Weighting may also be necessary to take account of the different sizes of the countries in question and other national differences such as the relative importance of different media.

The researcher needs telephone numbers, of course, so **initial contacts** will need to be made in many cases, probably by email, inviting the potential respondents to participate and asking for their up-to-date details.

There may be difficulties in contacting some of the chosen sample including simple logistical problems such as differences in working hours and national holidays, and also problems in getting past gatekeepers (personal assistants) in the case of some of the sample, such as MEPs or famous TV presenters. This is of particular concern if a random sample is required, less so if an approach such as quota sampling is used.

3   **Approaches to reporting the results**

The approach to reporting will depend on the nature of the research and the research objectives (in this case to assess how successful LiveSport!'s current communications strategy has been amongst various groups), and on the client's requirements.

The most common ways of reporting research findings are via an oral presentation and a written report. Typically both methods will be used.

Presentations

The researcher will need to discuss with the client whether to give a **single presentation** in one of the countries involved (probably the UK, delivered in English) or whether to give **individual presentations in each country**, or whether to do **both**.

The choice may depend on the findings: if there are considerable differences between countries individual presentations may be more beneficial for LiveSport!, but each presentation would need to be in the language of the country in question. Clearly this would be more costly, but it would give the researchers a better chance of demonstrating the relevance of the findings to local managers and to answer questions on country-specific issues.

For a single presentation to client representatives in all countries it may be possible to present via a video-conference or a web-conferencing system such as Webex. This would save on travelling costs and time and allow more people to attend and participate.

The purpose of the presentation(s) would be to communicate the key messages of the research to key individuals within LiveSport! and to give the client the opportunity to raise questions.

The presentation could be in **multimedia format** including not only the charts, diagrams and tables that illustrated the key results most clearly, but also possibly audio clips of the telephone interviews (if permission had been obtained). Obviously the clips would differ depending on the language of the country having the presentation.

Written reports

Again the issue of language arises: should a single report be produced or should it be translated into other languages?

(a)   The abstract or **management summary**, the **conclusions** and the **recommendations** for further action are the most important parts of the report – they will highlight the greatest and lowest awareness areas and help in directing future resources. These, at least, should be in **all languages**, even though this will add to the costs. In addition the appendices might well include each of the different language versions of the **questionnaires**, and if results are reported country by country then individual tables can have questions and cross-breaks in the relevant language.

(b)   It may be desirable to include **verbatim answers** to add depth to the report (in the same way that audio clips would enhance a presentation): these should be in the original language, but if some of them were of general interest to all countries they may need to be **translated**.

(c) More detailed parts of the report might be in English (the international business language) only. This would include the details of the research methodology and the in-depth analysis, discussion and interpretation. **Summary data**, covering all countries, would almost certainly have to be produced in one language only otherwise it would be extremely complex to lay out tables and so on in a comprehensible manner that could be taken in at a glance.

The issue of **cross-tabulation** of the questionnaire results will need to be addressed in consultation with the client. It may be most beneficial to present comparisons across countries, or it may be better to focus on topic areas within each country.

Publicity

The research findings will be owned by LiveSport! but if they include matters of general public interest it could be beneficial for LiveSport! to make the information more widely available: this could be a useful source of free publicity. The researchers may be asked to prepare a slimmed-down version of the report for public consumption and a press release to draw attention to it.

Section 2

(Remember — in the examination answer TWO questions only from Section 2)

1

> *Tutorial note.* To pass on this question you should have identified a minimum of two limitations in each section and discussed each one in some detail. A strong answer would provide a comprehensive list of the issues involved and give examples highlighting the magnitude of the change. You would get credit for the range of ideas you include and the level of justification given for the inclusion of each. To help with your revision our answer includes a wider range than you could have written about in the time available, so don't be intimidated by the length of our answer.
>
> This was a popular question and the majority candidates who attempted it achieved a pass mark or above.

(i) Smaller sample size

A smaller sample size would reduce the cost of a quantitative survey because data would not need to be collected from as many respondents and there would be less data to analyse at the end of the process.

However it could limit the usefulness of the survey in the following ways.

(1) In probability sampling the margin of error is directly dependent upon sample size: the smaller the sample the larger the margin of error. In other words it **reduces** the **level of statistical confidence in the accuracy of the results**. The impact would depend on the size of the sample proposed originally and the size of the proposed reduction.

(2) The smaller sample may be **less representative** of the population of interest: some views may not be represented at all; other views may be over-emphasised because the full range of the population has not been surveyed.

(3) **Certain kinds of analysis may not be possible** if the sample size is reduced. For example, the client may require analysis by particular sub-groups such as regions or age-groups, but the smaller sample may not be sufficiently well balanced to permit this.

(4) The possibility of **interviewer bias** is increased. Fewer interviewers will be needed but each one will be potentially more influential on the overall result.

(5) In **longitudinal studies** where the intention is to measure the impact of environmental changes over time a smaller sample could **distort results**, simply because it will be possible to conduct the research over a shorter (unrepresentative) timescale.

(ii) Broader sample definition (who precisely to interview)

A broader sample definition would reduce the costs of finding suitable respondents to interview. No other costs would be reduced and some may be increased.

This approach could limit the usefulness of the survey as follows.

(1) **Some aspects** of the research **may not be applicable** to some respondents. This means that the sample size is reduced for questions that are not applicable to everyone and as in the previous case this reduces the level of statistical confidence in the accuracy of the results. Alternatively, the researcher may need to collect answers

that are based on impression rather than direct personal experience, and this is likely to be less accurate.

(2) More **routing** will be needed on questionnaires since some questions will not be applicable. There is therefore more chance of response error and data analysis will also be more complex.

(3) The level of detail may have to be reduced and ultimately the data gathered could be **too general** to be useful.

(4) If the sample definition is broadened by accepting respondents who have experience of the matter under research over a longer timescale (for example, within the last year rather than the last month) there is more chance that the details of the experience will **not be remembered** accurately or will have been forgotten completely.

(iii) **Shorter questionnaire length**

Of the four options this is the one most likely to give significant cost savings. It will be quicker and therefore cheaper to design, produce and distribute the questionnaire (or quicker and cheaper to conduct interviews), there will be less data to edit and enter, and less to analyse.

On the other hand this approach could limit the usefulness of the survey as follows.

(1) It will be necessary to **omit questions** that the researcher would like to ask (and no design time will be saved if these questions were devised but then omitted at a later stage).

(2) Information may be collected in **too little depth** and detail to add to understanding of the issues and be of use to the client. A shorter questionnaire will need to focus on proving or disproving current hypotheses only and this leaves little or no opportunity to include exploratory questions and investigate alternative hypotheses.

(3) If the questionnaire is too superficial (because the more in-depth questions have been omitted) the **respondent may not take the questionnaire seriously**. This could be especially true of business surveys since the respondents may well have some experience of market research themselves and will be able to see that the data they are asked to provide will not help the researcher to get to the heart of the matter. More diligent respondents may be inclined to provide deeper information even if it is not asked for, but that will make data entry and analysis more difficult.

(4) Alternatively, if general questions are omitted in favour of the deeper questions this will make it more **arduous** for the respondent to provide answers: they may not complete the questionnaire or they may withdraw from interviews if the experience is too intense and pressurised.

(5) It may be **difficult to interpret** some of the data that is gathered because key pieces of information are missing. If assumptions are made, for example about socio-economic circumstances, these may be invalid.

(6) In longitudinal studies it may be important to collect information on views and how they change over time, but if a particular topic is not topical at a certain time there may be a temptation to remove the question in favour of other more topical issues. The problem is that this will impair the researcher's ability to **compare** results over several waves of research.

(iv) **Shorter timescale**

Reducing the timescale will only reduce costs if there is an equivalent reduction in the amount of work to be done.

(1) If the workload is reduced by any of the means already discussed in this answer then we have seen the problems that could arise.

(2) If the workload is not reduced, just the time available to complete the work, then the researcher may quite legitimately charge overtime fees and may have to employ extra resources, so **costs will increase** rather than decrease.

Arguably a research agency should be flexible enough and employ (or have access to) sufficient resources to enable it to respond to tight deadlines. Otherwise the agency should renegotiate the research objectives, or the deadline, or turn down the work if it cannot complete the work so as to meet the client's needs in the time available. If the client makes demands that cannot realistically be met then attempting to meet them and failing will only damage general perceptions of the research industry.

We will assume, however, that the work will go ahead even though the client has been advised as to how the short timescale could limit the usefulness of the survey: in other words, as follows.

(1) The researcher may cut corners under time pressure from the client and therefore the **initial parts of the research process** may be rushed. It is likely that the general feeling will be that the sooner the fieldwork begins the better and this could mean that the researcher does not take enough time to understand the business issues fully and review any previous research. The overall research design may therefore be less appropriate than it might otherwise have been. Compromises may be made at important stages such as design of questionnaire content and wording and/or piloting of questionnaires to ensure ease of use in the field and to assess and address subsequent processing issues.

(2) At the **fieldwork stage** further compromises are likely. For self-administered questionnaires it will be necessary to set a short deadline for receipt of responses: extra incentives may help as may more follow-ups (these both entail extra cost), but it is likely that the response rate will still be lower than might otherwise have been the case and a representative sample may not be obtained.

For telephone or face-to-face fieldwork more interviewers will be needed. It may be difficult to recruit, train and brief sufficient good quality interviewers in the time available. It will be more difficult to monitor their performance, even though this is especially important if less experienced interviewers are used. Each interviewer will have less opportunity to become fluent in administering the questionnaire because they will conduct fewer interviews.

If the time available for fieldwork is limited the particular time chosen to conduct it may be inappropriate because of any number of uncontrollable external factors ranging from inclement weather to terrorist activity. Quotas may be impossible to achieve or the sample may be highly unrepresentative.

(3) If time is limited at the **editing** and **data entry** stages there is a high risk of **human error**. Automated data collection methods and pre-coding will help, but they may not be possible in some types of research.

(4) At the **analysis stage** time pressure could lead to a number of problems. At worst the results could be completely misinterpreted, especially if corners were also cut at

the initial stages when attempting to understand the problem facing the client. The analysis will almost inevitably be more superficial than it could have been. It will tend to focus on the most obvious issues and simply confirm expectations. There will be less time to put the results into context and cross-reference to other research; there will be less time to discuss the findings with the client and with other experts and consider alternative interpretations.

(5) **Reporting** may also be impaired. There will be less time to consider how to communicate the findings most effectively to the client (and to different factions at the client organisation) taking account of the client's knowledge or lack thereof of research methodologies, statistics and so on. There will be a temptation to focus on a few key findings that have impact rather than exploring the data from different angles, using a variety of analysis tools, and considering the relevance of the results for other possible client issues. In other words, if time is limited the final product could be poorer value for money than might otherwise have been the case.

2

> *Tutorial note.* This was a very popular question and a large majority of candidates achieved a pass mark. The strongest answers were those that addressed a comprehensive range of differences between the two types of research and provided a comprehensive account of, the strengths and, the limitations of qualitative research, with examples.
>
> In part (i) you are expected to compare the different approaches and identify a range of differences, preferably organising them into categories (as in our answer). In part (ii) you should identify a minimum of two strengths and two limitations, but the more the better: you will get credit for the range of points included and the clarity of explanation of each point. You may mention points made in relation to the comparisons required in part (i): in fact it is difficult to avoid this.

(i) **Differences between qualitative and quantitative research**

QUALITATIVE	QUANTITATIVE
Aims	
Qualitative research aims to provide information about **why** people think, buy or act the way they do.	Quantitative research aims to provide information about **how many** people think, buy or act in a certain way.
It aims to explore, describe and understand behaviour in **verbal**, **narrative** terms.	It aims to explore, describe and explain the causes of behaviour by means of **measurement** and **testing**.
Findings are **not intended to be conclusive**: for example, as a result of a qualitative study, we may discover that there are a number of features that consumers consider when buying a brand, but we cannot say how many people in the population consider which features important or how important they are in relative terms.	Quantitative research **is conclusive** research, intended to measure the incidence of various opinions in the chosen sample so as to verify insights and to aid decision makers in selecting a specific course of action. Findings are descriptive, unless an experimental design has been used in which case causal relationships between variables might be identified.

QUALITATIVE	QUANTITATIVE
Data types	
Data is in the form of **words and drawings**. Statistical inference is not possible.	Data is in the form of **numbers, percentages and summary and descriptive statistics**. Ideally, **statistical inference is possible**.
Data is **detailed** and **in depth**, and rich in **contextual** information. There is more scope to explore in depth inner feelings to provide rich data.	The data has **less detail or depth** and is relatively **poor in terms of contextual information**. There is little or no scope for lengthy responses.
Data is **high in validity** (in other words, it measures what it claims to measure), but **low in reliability** (it may not give consistent results if it is repeated with a different interviewer).	Data is **high in reliability** (consistent results are obtained when the research is repeated), but tends to be **low in validity** (see opposite) because questions are closed and do not go into enough detail to detect subtle differences.
Data collection methods	
Interviews and observation. Interviews are generally face-to-face, although the web is increasingly being used for group discussions.	**Interviews, observation and self-completion questionnaires**. Interviews may be conducted over the phone, on the Internet, via the post, on street, or in hall tests.
Usually qualitative research is a **one off** experience.	Respondents may often be **re-contacted**, especially for longitudinal studies.
Collection methods are **non-standardised** and only **semi-structured**. Questionnaires are often in the form of a discussion guide.	**Collection methods** are **standardised** and very **structured**. Questionnaires can be repeated.
Questions are **open-ended** and **non-directive**. They ask how and why people feel the way they do, have attitudes to a topic and behave in certain ways. A wider variety of techniques will be used such as the use of audio, video, and products and projective techniques.	**Questions** are mostly **closed**. They ask how many, how often, how much, how long, what people like best and least.
Qualitative research uses a **moderator** who would normally transcribe and analyse the data themselves.	In quantitative research the **fieldworkers** will only collect data not analyse it.

QUALITATIVE	QUANTITATIVE
Sampling and sample size	
Qualitative research is more likely to be content with **non-probability random sampling techniques** such as quota sampling, convenience sampling, judgement sampling.	Quantitative research is more likely to use **probability random sampling techniques** such as stratified random sampling, disproportionate random sampling, cluster sampling.
Sample size will be **relatively small**.	**Sample size** will be **relatively large**.
Data analysis	
Coding is normally applied **after the event**.	**Coding** can often be done **beforehand**.
Data analysis is normally carried out **afterwards**.	**Data** may be **collected** and **analysed at the same time if computerised methods** are used.
Analysts aim to **understand, explore attitudes, behaviour, and complex issues** such as why people make certain decisions. They are trying to gain insight into how humans react to ideas and hypotheses.	Analysts aim to **measure, quantify, and validate and produce statistics** and **conclusive answers**.
Cost and speed	
Cost per respondent is **relatively high** but **project cost** is **relatively low**.	**Cost per respondent** is **relatively low** but **project cost** is **relatively high**.
Qualitative research tends to be **quicker** to turn round.	Typically it takes **longer** to set up and conduct a quantitative research project.

(ii) **The strengths and limitations of qualitative research**

Strengths

It is a very **flexible** approach in the sense that it can be combined with quantitative research in a variety of ways. It can provide useful insights into what hypotheses and ideas should be researched quantitatively where there is no previous research available (potentially saving a large amount of money at the quantitative stage), but it can also help to provide answers after the event, if some of the results of quantitative research are unexpected and need further exploration.

Qualitative research offers the researcher the ability to **explore issues in depth** when a detailed understanding of complex attitudes, behaviours and buying processes is needed. Issues can be discussed in a much wider context, taking full account of other circumstances in the respondents' lives that may have led to different behaviours.

The research topic can be **explored from respondent's perspective**, in the respondent's own words, whereas quantitative research is typically more directive and relies on the researcher's pre-conceptions of what issues are important. Qualitative research allows the researcher to get below the surface and understand attitudes and draw out opinions that respondents may not fully understand or may not be willing or able to articulate themselves. **Projective techniques** (speech bubbles, picture categorisation, word association etc) may be used to help respondents to express what they really feel.

One-to-one in depth interviews may be used to explore **sensitive issues** that people would not normally be willing to discuss in other contexts such as in-street or over the telephone, where there is little opportunity for the interviewer to establish rapport and gain the trust of the respondent. One-to-ones may also be the only way of obtaining the views of specific key opinion leaders, such as company CEOs, who may not be willing to take part in other forms of research.

Group discussions enable the researcher to explore how people react in a group and how peer influence changes their behaviour or opinion towards a topic. They also allow the opportunity to gather information on a range of different experiences in a relatively short space of time. They may be the most appropriate way of interviewing children, since the group environment is less threatening.

The **clients can view** the proceedings, either as they take place behind a two-way mirror or by CCTV, or later on video. This enables clients to watch reactions first hand and this can help to make the research findings both richer and more convincing.

Finally, as mentioned in part (a), qualitative research is **relatively inexpensive** and relatively **quick** to conduct.

Limitations

In spite of the many advantages qualitative research is much more difficult to conduct well than quantitative research.

(1)   It **relies on the skills of the moderator or interviewer**, who must be adept at establishing good relationships with individuals and managing group dynamics and also highly trained and thoroughly briefed to ensure that observations and information are captured. Ill-trained or inexperienced moderators may miss important points.

(2)   The **moderator** may **bias** the responses and unwittingly influence the discussion, simply by virtue of being in the position of moderator and being perceived as an expert or as someone to impress.

(3)   The **moderator may not get on** with the individual or the group for reasons beyond his or her control: no matter how skilled he or she may be, it is a two-way process and a respondent may simply not be willing to co-operate. Dominant respondents can easily take over the proceedings, meaning that other respondents just agree to avoid an argument, whatever their true opinion, or else say nothing so that valuable information is lost.

(4)   **Logistics** may be an issue: for example, it is difficult and costly to conduct group discussions if the group needs to be drawn from widely different geographic areas. It is often hard to arrange interview times with certain respondents such as key opinion leaders because of their own work and time constraints.

(5)   It is **difficult to repeat** the same exercise, as all groups will be different. It is also harder to compare results across time because they may vary not merely as a result of the time passed but because of changes in the relationships.

(6)   Those who have not been involved in data collection may find it **harder to access** all the data: for example, they cannot make their own judgements about matters such as body language or the overall atmosphere of the discussion merely from a transcript of the conversation.

(7) Although the overall process is relatively quick, individual intervals may be lengthy and it may be **difficult** to find **respondents** who are willing to **give up the time**. Respondents may tire of a lengthy interview.

(8) The **data** that is collected **cannot be analysed statistically**, and the **small sample size** means that the **data may not be representative**.

(9) The **data** is **difficult** and **time-consuming to analyse**. Analysis is likely to be somewhat **subjective**, since it relies on human interpretation.

3

Tutorial note. Strong answers to part (i) will recognise the main issues, present a wide range of points about each method and develop a well thought-through recommendation. At pass level, a minimum of two strengths and two weaknesses should be identified, and some comparison should be made (ie an 'all I know about email surveys' is not sufficient to pass). Adequate rationale for the inclusion of each point needs to be given. A list of adjectives is not sufficient. Credit would be given for well-argued suggestions and for application to the particular scenario outlined. Our answer includes a lot of ideas and explanation to help with your revision: it is a good deal longer than you could have produced in the time available.

For part (ii) a good answer will offer a well thought out design, consider all the steps involved in setting up the survey, and provide a clear rationale for each point made. Ideally your answer should address some or all of the issues raised in the 'weaknesses' section of part (i). Again our answer is longer than you could have produced: it appears that many candidates had difficulty with this part of the question so if you also struggled you may find our answer helpful.

(i) **Advantages and disadvantages of the email approach compared to the postal method**

At its simplest an email survey may only differ from a postal one in terms of the **delivery mechanism** – a postal survey delivers a paper document, presumably via internal mail in this case; an email survey may merely deliver precisely the same document via the company's electronic messaging system as an attachment that needs to be printed out.

This is not the only way to conduct an email survey, however and, depending on the research needs, it is not necessarily the best use of the available technology.

Advantages of the email approach

Delivery is more certain. It is true that emails can get held up in cyberspace if there are problems with the organisation's mail servers, and this may be difficult to control in a very large, perhaps global, organisation, but they cannot get 'lost in the post' or physically damaged in the same way as they can if a postal system (even an internal one) is used. The email system is also likely to have mechanisms that enable the administrator to check receipt and check whether the mail has been read.

Delivery is also more certain in the sense that the recipient **cannot lose the questionnaire** once it is received, as they could with a postal questionnaire. Even if they print it out and then lose the hard copy they can always print out another copy.

The use of email is also preferable to post because it may make it **easier to reach** employees such as **on-the-road sales staff**, since they will be able to access their email remotely from wherever they happen to be at the time of the survey.

The email method is probably **cheaper** because there are no costs of printing and mailing the questionnaire (stamps or use of internal mail resources). If the responses can be made by electronic means this saves the costs of returning a paper questionnaire and the costs of entering data (see also below). It will also save some time, for the same reasons: all questionnaires are delivered in seconds and, after completion, returned in seconds.

The fact that the questionnaire is in electronic format offers many additional opportunities for administration and control (depending on the precise format used: see the answer to part (ii)) that are not available with paper documents.

(1) If it is in a format that can be completed electronically then **data entry** is done by the respondent, not by research staff, potentially saving a great deal of time and avoiding data entry errors, particularly in transcribing written responses.

(2) **Invalid responses** or **missing responses** can be **avoided** completely by means of computer checks that check consistency and completeness. There will be little or no need for editing.

(3) Much or all of the data can be **pre-coded** and coding can be applied automatically by computer, with great **savings in analysis time** compared with a manually completed paper questionnaire.

(4) **Routing** can be handled by computer so there should be no routing errors and respondents should be able to complete the questionnaire in a shorter space of time, attending only to questions that are relevant to their own work.

(5) The questionnaire itself could be **more 'fun'** to complete if it includes **interactive** elements and high-quality **stimulus** materials.

(6) Some respondents may perceive the exercise to be more anonymous, since their **handwriting cannot be recognised**. However, the opposite is more likely to be true: see below.

(7) It will be possible to **monitor** the progress of the project in **real time**, for example the researcher will be able to obtain an update at any time about how many responses have been received and possibly see an initial analysis of responses so far.

Finally, **response rates** may improve because receipt of the request to participate is more direct. Emails could be personalised to some extent, and could be sent as if from the address of a very senior manager in the organisation. The questionnaire is more likely to be perceived as a work activity to be completed in work time if it arrives through the same mechanism as other work. (This does not necessarily apply, of course – a paper questionnaire about work may equally be sent with a covering letter from a top manager and may equally be perceived as a work activity so long as it is delivered to the workplace, not the home.)

Disadvantages of the email approach

In spite of the delivery advantages above, it may be **easier to overlook** an email than it is a physical document, particularly for respondents who are away from the office (on holiday, sick) at the time it is delivered.

In spite of the cost savings it is possible that stationery costs will increase if employees need to print out the questionnaire and they do so several times. Likewise, if responses need to be printed out (due to the format of the questionnaire) there is no real saving in data entry and analysis time.

Delivery may also be problematic if there are **employees who do not usually or ever use a computer** in their work. This may be the case for shop-floor staff, factory staff, delivery staff and the like. Even if they have access to a computer they may not have the IT skills to respond. A paper-based, postal questionnaire may be the only feasible option for such staff.

There may be **differences in the software** used in different parts of the company: some branches may only be equipped to receive **text-based** email not HTML-based mails (and some individuals may have set up their system in that way), and some may have limited access to the **Internet** or company **intranet**. If the questionnaire is intended to be printed out some employees may not have the **appropriate package** (eg Word, Adobe Acrobat etc) to enable them to do this. Over-zealous **email scanning** programs may automatically remove attachments to emails, or prevent users from downloading attachments that are over a certain size.. All of this makes the choice of **format** of the questionnaire a much more complicated decision than it is in the case of a paper-based postal questionnaire.

Format is also an issue if the questionnaire has to be tailored in some way to facilitate electronic completion and recording. If so, the data collected may **not be comparable** with previous years' data.

Privacy could be a problem issue if the questionnaire is completed on-screen since a respondent's answers may be seen by other staff members (for example, other team members or managers about whom they are asked to comment). This could discourage respondents from expressing their true opinion. Such problems can be largely avoided with a postal questionnaire, except that hand-writing may be recognised.

Anonymity is perhaps the most serious drawback of the email approach compared with a postal questionnaire. If the responses are returned via email then the name of the respondent is inevitably returned. If responses are made via a website or intranet site it is still likely to be possible for the researcher to determine precisely who gave what responses, due to the way networks and web servers operate and log usage. The researcher need not record this information permanently, and can include assurances about anonymity, but employees cannot actually see that safeguards are operating and are still likely to be wary if confidentiality is an issue.

(ii) **How the email survey might be conducted and issues involved**

The fact that this survey is internal to the organisation helps to address some of the problems inherent in email surveys: the organisation should have a complete sampling frame and it should have information about the software available to its employees, which is very helpful for design purposes.

Format

As indicated in part (i) there is relatively little advantage in merely emailing a document that respondents have to print out and complete manually, and there are several possible drawbacks. Unless there are compelling reasons to do this (for example, if most employees do not have a computer) then an approach that takes advantage of the possibilities of **electronic completion** is recommended in this case.

Given the possible problems of document format and software compatibility (see part (i)) neither embedded questionnaires ((HTML based emails) nor attachments can be recommended. The most flexible approach is to create a questionnaire that can be read, completed and submitted via a **browser**.

Some enquiry will have to be made about **browser versions** in use in different parts of the company. Ideally all employees will have the latest version of the same browser (probably Microsoft Internet Explorer), but this is unlikely to be the case in a large company. The designer should either create a version that detects browser capability and displays and operates accordingly, or a version that only uses features that are available in all browsers.

On a further practical note the researcher should ensure in advance that the organisation's mail servers and software can **cope with mass-mailing** and that intranet servers and databases can cope with the **sudden increase in traffic** as people respond.

Design

All the usual **questionnaire design** principles apply – the questionnaire must be clear, easy to read, and well laid out. Important **additional considerations for on-screen questionnaires** are: the **landscape** format of computer screens, the need for **scrolling** (which can irritate users), and the need for clear **navigation** links, especially choices about whether users can go back and change answers, as well as forwards.

For **closed** questions (Yes/No and multiple choice) computers are ideal, but **open** questions requiring free-form answers are more problematic because decisions need to be made about the **size of text-box** to include. If a two-line box is used (perhaps to save space on screen) respondents may feel constrained to give briefer replies than they might have given otherwise, or they may be annoyed that a longer answer cannot be viewed in full. It is possible to restrict the number of characters that can be entered in a text box, but such decisions need to be made with great care: if the limit is set too low then valuable information may be lost, or the respondent may get frustrated and give up.

Decisions will also have to be made about the **amount of guidance** to give respondents. Some respondents may be far more IT-literate than others and the general level of IT literacy should be researched in advance. An instruction such as 'Control + click to select multiple items' may be second nature to some users but completely mystifying to others.

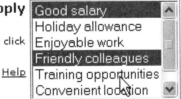

As in this illustration it may be necessary to include extra instruction in the form of **pop-up help** for the less IT-literate.

The usual issues apply regarding the **length** of the questionnaire: it should not be so long that employees tire of it, nor so short that it does not gather useful information and is not taken seriously. Some commentators recommend a maximum length of 15 minutes.

Setting up

The entire exercise should be **discussed with operational managers** who may not be willing to have employees distracted from their main work for long periods. It may be necessary to stagger the distribution of the questionnaire rather than sending a single mass mailing with the result that the entire company shuts down for half an hour one afternoon!

Decisions will need to be made about **sampling**. The ease of emailing and the reduction in cost over the postal approach may make it very tempting to send a questionnaire to all employees, but the consequences should be considered. The volume of responses could be overwhelming for the research department, especially if there are a lot of open-ended questions that require post-coding. On the other hand employees who are not included in the sample may find it objectionable that their views are not being taken into account. The decision may depend upon what has been done in previous years.

The issue of **anonymity** has been discussed in part (i). Given that the employer will already have a good deal of information about employees (age, address, position in company etc) it may be tempting to send questionnaires that have such details already completed, but this could make some employees suspicious about how their data will be treated.

Perhaps the best approach is to give appropriate assurances about confidentiality (and ensure that they are genuine, ie that responses are genuinely **not** logged in an identifiable way) and also to allow respondents to print out the questionnaire and fill it in manually if they prefer. Alternatively, or in addition, respondents could perhaps be given a choice on the questionnaire about whether they want their answers to be treated confidentially or not.

A further problem, connected with the above, is that without adequate safeguards it may be possible for the same individual to **reply more than once**, or for the questionnaire to be **completed by someone other** than the person it was sent to. The former can be prevented to some extent by the use of cookies (but only if the user has this technology enabled) or by the use of computer-generated URLs. The latter can be prevented to some extent by requiring people to log in with a password or a PIN, but these methods will at least appear to give the lie to assurances about anonymity. These issues must be considered, but current technology offers no ideal solution and some kind of compromise will be necessary.

Finally, as with all questionnaires, a **pilot exercise** should be conducted to ensure ease of use, check for software bugs, and to make sure that the questionnaire elicits the information required in a useable, analysable form.

4

Tutorial note. Strong answers will provide a clear description of each term with examples of where each might be used during the data analysis stage. Credit would be given for the accuracy of description and for the range and appropriateness of the uses suggested.

If you provide numerical examples in your answer use a calculator and make sure you get the numbers right. You may prefer to use Xs in place of numbers for speed. Numerical examples are very useful (we have used them quite extensively in our answer, but this is to make sure you understand the issues), but try to prepare them in advance, otherwise you could easily get bogged down if you spend too long trying to make the numbers you have invented work and then miss out on the (mark-earning) explanations. It is far more important to explain the terms in words and show your understanding of their relevance to market research than to demonstrate your numerical skills, however good they may be.

Questions like this tend to be unpopular, but if you know your stuff they are quite easy and you may score very highly if you can give some good explanations and examples.

(i) **Cross tabulations**

Cross-tabulations are tables that set out the responses to one question relative to the responses to one or more other questions. For example, initial questions may be about gender and age and a later question about shampoo usage. The resulting data could be cross tabulated as follows.

Which brand of shampoo do you use most often?						
	Men			Women		
	18 – 30	31 – 50	Over 50	18 – 30	31 – 50	Over 50
	%	%	%	%	%	%
L'Oréal	24	18	8	34	32	12
Pantene	27	26	6	34	31	16
Other	49	56	86	32	37	72

The convention is to use the **dependent variable** (the variable that the researcher is trying to describe or explain) for the **rows**, and the **independent variables** (the variables that are hypothesised to influence the dependent variable) as the **column** headings, as shown above.

Cross-tabulations are useful in analysis for **examining the relationships** between variables and **comparing responses** from different groups. The clearest conclusions that could be drawn from the (entirely fictional) cross-tabulation above is that people over 50 are less likely to use 'designer-label' shampoos than younger people and that men are less likely to use designer-label shampoos than women.

The number of ways in which variables can be cross-tabulated is almost endless in theory, but that **does not mean that all cross-tabulations will be relevant and meaningful**. For example, it may be possible to analyse a set of results and find that that 72% of people who use Pantene shampoo can also play a musical instrument, but (depending on the nature of the research, on what questions were asked, and on the criteria for choosing the sample) that information is probably not valid or reliable, nor is it likely to be relevant to the research objectives. On the face of it there is unlikely to be a correlation between hair product preferences and musical ability, and a different sample would probably have given entirely different results.

(ii) **Frequencies and percentages**

A **frequency** is a count of the number of times an answer appears, for example '300 out of 500 people surveyed preferred Brand X'. This is perhaps the **simplest form** of analysis that can be applied to survey data, but frequency analysis will very quickly highlight extreme responses or usual responses in the results, especially if displayed in graphical form, and it therefore helps to direct the analyst to areas that need further analysis.

A percentage expresses a frequency as a proportion of 100, for example '60% of people surveyed preferred Brand X'.

Frequencies give a clearer idea of the size of the sample, but **percentages** are easier to understand and compare, and therefore are **generally more informative**. For example, it is easier to understand '75%' than it is to understand '3,390 out of 4,520' (although they are the same) because most people cannot do the mental arithmetic unless the numbers are very easy.

Frequencies may nevertheless be important, especially if the total number of responses varies from question to question, as in the following example.

6. How often do you get paid by your employer?

Weekly (Go to question 7)	Monthly (Go to question 8)	Not applicable (Go to question 9)	Total
194	652	154	1,000
(19.40%)	(65.20%)	(15.40%)	(100.00%)

7. You are paid weekly. What weekly payment method does your employer use?

Cash	Cheque	BACS	Total
13	140	41	194
(6.70%)	(72.17%)	(21.13%)	(100%)

8. You are paid monthly. What monthly payment method does your employer use?

Cash	Cheque	BACS	Total
3	136	513	652
(0.46%)	(20.86%)	(78.68%)	(100%)

Percentages are still necessary to make valid comparisons. In the above example the frequencies indicate that, in absolute terms, about the same number of weekly-paid and monthly-paid people get paid by cheque. But no conclusions should be drawn from this without looking at the matter in relative terms: the percentages show that while cheque payment is the most popular method for the weekly-paid, it is BACS payment that is the most common method for the monthly-paid, and monthly payment is far more common than weekly payment.

(iii) **Measures of central tendency**

Central tendency is important in market research (and in statistics generally) because in real life a very large number of phenomena are distributed 'normally': in other words it is a proven fact that most people with similar characteristics do, or buy, or think (etc) the same thing.

Measures of central tendency are **measures of the 'average'** of a set of values. There are three measures of central tendency. For illustration we will imagine that the values recorded are the answers to a question posed to small and medium-sized businesses (SMEs) about how many desktop computers they own.

(1) The **mean** (the arithmetic mean) is what most people understand by the term 'average'. It is the figure calculated by adding up the individual values and dividing by the number of values, for example the average of the five values 10, 25, 25, 40 and 400 is (10 + 25 +25 + 40 + 400)/5 = 100. As this example shows, the mean will probably not correspond exactly to any of the actual recorded values, and it can easily be distorted by extreme values (400 in this case: the respondent is probably not a medium-sized business!). If the extreme value is omitted the mean is (10 + 25 + 25 + 40)/4 = 25, and that is clearly more representative of the sample of five businesses. The huge advantage of the mean over other averages is that it is suitable for further statistical analysis, but the values used for that purpose may well lack meaning if taken at face value. For example, the mean number of computers owned by SMEs may be 8.61, but that statistic is nonsense for most real life purposes,

where it is only meaningful to measure in terms of whole numbers of computers. (A more famous example is '2.4 children', the supposed average number of children in a family.)

(2) The **mode** is the most common value. In the example above (10, 25, 25, 40 and 400) the mode is 25 because this value occurs twice and all the others only occur once. There will not be a mode at all if all the values occur once only, but there may be several modes if particular values occur an equal number of times (for example 10, 10, 25, 25, 40, 40, 400). This might be useful information if, say, a software producer wanted to structure its prices and volume discounts on the typical number of computers owned by SMEs. Note that unlike the mean it will be a whole number that actually occurs in real life.

(3) The **median** is the middle value when the numbers are arranged in numerical order. In the example 10, 25, 25, 40 and 400 the mode is 25. If there are an even number of values the median is the average (mean) of the two middle values, for example the median of the six values 10, 11, 24, 26, 39, 40 is (24+26)/2 = 25. The median is not affected by extreme values so it is more representative of the population as a whole than the mean where the data includes such values.

(iv) **Measures of dispersion**

Measures of dispersion give an indication of how widely the data is spread about its average.

(1) The **range** is the difference between the highest value and the lowest value. For example, if the values are 10, 25, 25, 40 the range is (40 – 10) = 30. This sort of information is often used when comparing prices, for example it might be found that the hourly rates charged by freelance market researchers ranged from £40 per hour to £250 per hour, in other words there is a £210 difference (the range) between the cheapest and the most expensive freelancer.

(2) The **semi-interquartile range** may be a preferable measure if there are extreme highs or extreme lows. It is calculated in a similar way to the range but it only takes into account the middle portion of the data.

(3) The **variance** is one of several measures of variability that statisticians use to characterise the dispersion among the measures in a given population. To calculate the variance of a given population, it is necessary to first calculate the mean, then measure the amount that each score deviates from the mean and then square that deviation (to remove negative values). The variance is the average of the several squared deviations from the mean.

(4) The variance is used as one of the steps in calculating other statistics, but because it involves squaring deviations, it does not have the same unit of measurement as the original observations. For example, lengths measured in metres (m) have a variance measured in metres squared (m^2). Taking the square root of the variance gives us the units used in the original scale and this is the **standard deviation**. The standard deviation is the most commonly used measure of spread in statistics and is highly useful to the market researcher engaged in probability sampling because it can be proved that 68% of the values in a set of numbers will fall within one standard deviation of the mean, and 95% of the values in a set of numbers will fall within two standard deviations of the mean. This allows sample sizes to be determined and allows analysts to draw a variety of conclusions about the data collected.

5

(a) **Principles**

(i) **Informed consent**

Informed consent consists of two main elements:

Transparency: ensuring that individuals have a very clear and unambiguous understanding of the purpose(s) of collecting the data and how it will be used.

Consent: at the time that the data is collected, individuals agree to their data being collected, and have the opportunity to withhold their agreement to any subsequent use of data. In effect, researchers must always inform respondents about how their data is to be used, and give them the opportunity to refuse permission for the data to be used in this way.

Informed consent is necessary because research is founded upon the willing co-operation of the public and of business organisations. It depends upon their confidence that it is conducted honestly, objectively, without unwelcome intrusion and without harm to respondents.

(ii) **Anonymity and confidentiality**

Anonymity means that it must not be possible to identify a response with a specific respondent. All indications of the identity of respondents should be physically separated from the records of the information they have provided as soon as possible after the completion of any necessary fieldwork quality checks. Indications of identity include not only names and addresses but also any other information provided by or about them which could in practice identify them, such as their employer's name and their job title.

Confidentiality means that the researcher must ensure that any information which might identify respondents is stored securely, and separately from the other information they have provided and no unauthorised access should be allowed, in accordance with legislation such as the Data Protection Act 1998.

If the respondent has given permission for data to be passed on in a form which allows that respondent to be identified personally the respondent must first have been told to whom the information would be supplied and the purposes for which it will be used, and also the researcher must ensure that the information will not be used for any non-research purpose and that the recipient of the information has agreed to conform to the requirements of the MRS Code.

(iii) **Not deceiving respondents**

Respondents must not be misled when being asked for their co-operation. The principle of transparency referred to above is clearly of relevance here: respondents must not be misinformed about the purpose of collecting the data and what it will be used for.

Adherence to the principles outlined above should ensure that this does not happen, but not all organisations are members of the MRS and incidents of sugging (selling under the guise of market research) and frugging (fund raising under the guise of market research) are common.

There are several other points in the MRS code that are relevant under this heading.

(1) Respondents must be told (normally at the beginning of the interview) if observation techniques or recording equipment are used, except where these are used in a public place.

(2) Respondents must be enabled to check without difficulty the identity and *bona fides* of the Researcher. Researchers must not make false claims about their skills and experience or about those of their organisation.

(3) Wherever possible respondents must also be informed as to the likely length of time necessary for the collection of the information.

(b) Ethical considerations in conducting research among children aged 12 to 14

The MRS have issued a set of *Guidelines for Research among Children and Young People*, and the following answer is derived from those guidelines to the extent that they are relevant to the research study mentioned in the question.

Key among the aims of the guidelines are:

■   To protect the rights of children physically, mentally, ethically and emotionally and to ensure they are not exploited

■   To reassure parents and others concerned with their welfare and safety that research conducted under these guidelines is designed to protect the interests of children

The MRS Code of Conduct defines **children** as those aged under 16 years and young people as aged 16 and 17 years.

A **responsible adult** is an adult (someone aged 18 or over) responsible for the child's safety and welfare at the time of the research. In a protected environment, like a school, the responsible adult will be the person in authority, typically the teacher. In any other environment – like the street or in home – a responsible adult will be a parent, guardian or other person on whom a parent or guardian has conferred responsibility for the child.

Consent is the permission given by the **responsible adult** to the interviewer which allows the interviewer to **approach** the child. It is **not permission to interview** the child, as they must have their own opportunity to decline to take part.

Consent of a parent or responsible adult should be obtained for interviews with children under 16. Consent must be obtained under the following circumstances:

■   In home/at home (face-to-face and telephone interviewing)
■   Group discussions/depth interviews
■   Where interviewer and child are alone together

Where research is being conducted in schools with the consent of the responsible adult, the researcher or research agency should suggest to the school that consent is also sought from parents or guardians for in school interviews.

The responsible adult must be provided with sufficient information to enable them to provide **informed consent** as described in part (a) of this answer. This information should normally be provided in writing.

The opportunity to **opt out** of the research must be made clear to the child and to the responsible adult.

The **identity** (by name, relationship or role) of the **responsible adult** giving consent must be **recorded** but it is not normally necessary for this consent to be obtained in writing – certainly not in this case because the topic is not a sensitive one.

Quality validation must be carried out with the **responsible adult** who gave consent and not with the child respondent. Any quality validation carried out should therefore only cover the facts connected with the interview and not any of the responses or opinions given.

Responsible adults should be **told about any products** which the child may be asked to try or use and be given the opportunity to inspect or even try these, themselves. Where the research involves the testing of any products, as is quite possible in the case of research into use of mobile phones, special care must be taken to check that:

(i)   These are safe to handle. The researcher must confirm this with the supplier even though the latter may be legally liable for any adverse effects caused by the product

(ii)   There are no ethnic, religious or cultural barriers to the child handling the product

(iii)   The child is not asked to test a product which is illegal for the age group

If a **questionnaire** is used its content and language should be sensitive to the language, needs and feelings of the age group to be interviewed and their capabilities. The questionnaire language should be kept as simple as possible but not be patronising.

The research should avoid questions which might result in a child making unreasonable demands on a parent or guardian (again quite possibly very relevant in the case of research into mobile phones).

Research should only be conducted in **safe and appropriate environments**. The research agency must ensure that the responsible adult has full details of the research venue, name of moderator, finishing time etc.

If the research is conducted in the client's domain, the client must share equal responsibility with the researcher for providing a safe and appropriate venue.

It is advisable for research carried out in the home of the child, either in person or by telephone, that an adult remains on the premises – though not necessarily in the same room – throughout the interview.

Consent of the responsible adult must be sought for any **observation**, including one way mirror, audio or video recording. Any observation should be kept to a minimum and handled appropriately. Further informed consent must be sought for subsequent use or release of recorded material.

In interviews care must be taken to avoid any physical contact with the child. It is not normally necessary for the responsible adult to be present during **interviews**. Where their presence would be undesirable for technical reasons - eg if it could introduce bias – this must be explained and consent sought to interview the child alone. If a child is recruited in the street and taken into a central (hall test) location, there must always be **another adult** present in the same room throughout the interview.

Any gifts or incentives provided by the client or researcher must follow the same rules as those for products to be tested, in other words they should be safe, legal and acceptable to responsible adults. They must be suitable for the age of the child and fitting for the task required.

Any **refreshments** provided should be suitable and legal for the age group and care should be taken to avoid any products that are known to cause allergic problems.

An **MRS Thank You leaflet** must always be handed out at the end of the interview.

The research agency must take responsibility for **safely handing over the child** after a group discussion or depth interview or ensuring that arrangements for them to get home safely are in place.

6

Tutorial note To pass this question you should include points which refer to the research objectives, the clarity of the data/results provided and the level to which the interpretation given is convincing. You may have chosen to organise your answer in a number of ways, for example as an 'evaluation checklist' of actions or as a set of general principles. Our answer is a mixture of these approaches. Credit would be given for the range and validity of points made, and for the strength of the explanation given for each.

Evaluating the quality of research

The first step would be to find out what gave rise to the need for the research, in other words **what the original business problem was**. This may entail discussion with others in the business, given that you personally have only recently been appointed and may not be familiar with the issues and background. It will also be useful to have an **update** on the current status of the problem and to know whether **any actions have yet been taken** in response to the research, perhaps arising from preliminary or interim reporting by the research supplier.

Once the issues are understood the **research brief** should be consulted together with the researcher's **proposal**. It is possible that the problem was poorly defined and the research objectives were not clearly set out, or that the proposal indicates that the researcher did not understand the issues. In any of these cases the quality of the final research report will be impaired, but the problem has more to do with **communication problems** and the **commissioning process** than with the research abilities of the supplier. These are problems which you will have the opportunity to address in your new position so it will be as well to know about them from the outset.

Finally, before getting down to detail, you should determine whether the research was **delivered on time**, how much it **cost** and whether the cost was within **budget**. If the budget was low and/or the timescale was short this will naturally affect the research that was done and the quality of the results. If the cost was high in your judgement you will be looking for value for money, at the very least, and preferably lots of added value.

Turning to the report itself, you should get an **overview** of what it contains. It will hopefully have a **contents** page, an **executive summary** and a list of **conclusions and recommendations** (if not, and if the researcher's line of argument is in any way unclear that is the first negative point). Assuming these elements are present they should be read and compared with the brief and the proposal to see if the research actually does what it set out to do. Key points to check include the following.

- Does it address the research **objectives**?

- Is it clear what **action** now needs to be taken, and are the suggested actions sensible?

- Does it provide the **information** needed to make decisions about the business problem, given what you now know about the problem?

- Is the evidence **credible** and robust? Based on an overview would you have reached the same conclusions?

It may then be necessary to delve (selectively) into some of the detail of the report to check that the researcher's **summaries are consistent** with the detailed findings. Hopefully there will be footnotes and cross-references to help you. At this point you may also gain an initial impression of the quality and clarity of presentation of tables and so on, the use of graphics, the sophistication of analysis techniques used, and whether these are clearly explained for those who are unfamiliar with research methods and statistics.

If the answers to these initial questions are 'no' then it is possibly not worth wasting your own time by continuing the review exercise. All being well so far, however, it would be wise to keep a close eye out for **matters that may need immediate action** by you.

(a) Does the report concentrate narrowly on the research objectives or are **other explanations** or interpretations offered? Are all the **implications** recognised and drawn out? Might it be necessary to redefine what your organisation perceives as the problem?

(b) Does the report go beyond the brief, for example by suggesting new business solutions or **new opportunities** that have come to light as a result of the research, and had not previously been considered? Are the relevant operational managers in your organisation aware of this?

(c) Are there suggestions for **further research** and if so should these be followed up (and how urgently)?

The next step is to examine the detail of the research project: how well the research was **executed** and how well the project was **managed**. It will probably be necessary to look beyond the report itself and investigate **interim reports** if any, review **correspondence** files, and perhaps even talk to the supplier to access the full information. For example, the final report is unlikely to mention the problems that arose in the course of the research, what impact they had and how they were resolved. It may well not include raw data that may be meaningful to you but not to the original intended audience.

Questions that might be asked at this stage include the following.

(a) Was the research **design** suitable?

(b) Was efficient use made of **previous research**, if any was available?

(c) Was the **population of interest** appropriately defined? How did the researcher arrive at a sampling frame? Was the **sampling strategy** appropriate for the target population?

(d) Was there a **pilot** exercise and, if so, what modifications were made as a result of it?

(e) Were the methods of **data collection** appropriate and well-executed? You may wish to look at questionnaire design and review transcripts or footage of qualitative interviews. You would also consider whether in your experience other methods would have been preferable telephone rather than in-street, group discussions rather than one-to-ones and so on).

(f) What **response rate** was achieved?

(g) Was there an interviewer **briefing**? Was your organisation invited to take part?

(h) Is there any noticeable difference between the quality of the **qualitative** work and the **quantitative** work?

(i) What **controls** were operated to check on the quality of fieldwork and data processing? What type and number of errors arose and how were they dealt with?

(j)   How sophisticated is the **analysis** of the data? If analysis software was used are you just given standard reports, that anyone could produce at the touch of a button or has the researcher been more imaginative? Do they use their own proprietary techniques?

At the end of the review exercise you may be confident that the supplier's findings can be recommended to managers in your organisation and are likely to be considering this supplier for further work. If not, you may be busy chasing up the supplier to address the deficiencies or else may be commissioning further research from someone else.

Advanced Certificate in Market and Social Research Practice Examination

June 2004

TEST PAPER 2

Instructions for Candidates

Time allowed 2 hrs 30 minutes

Answer <u>ALL</u> questions in Section 1

Answer <u>TWO</u> questions from Section 2

Section 1 accounts for one third of the final result.

Section 2 accounts for two thirds of the final result.

Section 1: Compulsory question
(Recommended time: 50 minutes)

This section tests problem identification and problem solving using a number of skills. The answers in this section account for one-third of the total marks.

Read the following case study and answer ALL the questions below.

RenAid is a small charity which provides support for sufferers of kidney disease and raises money for research into new treatments. The charity employs a small number of staff and depends to a great extent on the support of volunteers to help it get its message over to the public. In order to secure public funding, RenAid must compete with other, better-resourced charities and, as a result, has received very little public money. The majority of its funding comes from donations contributed on a regular basis by individual donors.

RenAid now wishes to recruit more individual donors. However, before committing resources to a recruitment drive they want to better understand what motivates people to donate to charity. The charity's very limited budget means that they can not afford to employ a research agency to conduct the whole research project. However, one of RenAid's current individual supporters has offered to design a questionnaire and has suggested that the data collection be conducted by using the charity's volunteers to interview respondents face-to-face by door knocking.

You are a personal friend of the director of the charity and she has asked for your opinion about the proposed research.

1. What are the possible problems with the approach to research which has been suggested and what can be done to limit them?   **(Weighting: one-third of marks for Section 1)**

2. The following two questions are the last questions in the draft questionnaire which has been prepared for face-to-face interviewing. Discuss the problems which these questions present and give suggestions for how these problems might be overcome.
                                            (Weighting: one-third of marks for Section 1)

5. **How much money have you given to charity in the last year, including in street and door to door collections, regular donations and all other sources?**

....

6. **How much would you agree with the following statements which people have made about RenAid and about giving to charity?**

	1	2	3	4	5	6
It's a worthwhile charity and I would like to support it						
I have never heard of it						
I can't afford to support a charity						
I believe charity begins at home						
I only ever give money to charities through the National Lottery						
RenAid is doing a good job						

3. The charity's director is keen to explore possible alternative ways of collecting the required information. Discuss alternative methods which might be appropriate for this project and identify which you feel would be the best option for RenAid. Give reasons for your suggestions.

(Weighting: one-third of marks for Section 1)

Section 2: Optional questions
(Recommended time: 100 minutes)

The answers in this section account for two-thirds of the total marks.

Answer any TWO questions from the six listed below. Give a full answer to each of the questions you choose.

---

1   A local council has introduced a new scheme for recycling waste. It wishes to monitor the ongoing success of the scheme using quantitative methods. Three potential approaches have been suggested.

   (a)   Discuss the strengths and limitations of each of the approaches shown below.

(i)	an annual study	**(Weighting: 25%)**
(ii)	a monthly study	**(Weighting: 25%)**
(iii)	a continuous panel providing diary-based data	**(Weighting: 25%)**

   (b)   State which option you would recommend. Give reasons to justify your choice.
   (Weighting: 25%)

2   Outline the main benefits and difficulties of using the Internet to conduct the following types of research. Illustrate your answers with examples.

(i)	Secondary research	**(Weighting: one third of the total)**
(ii)	Quantitative research	**(Weighting: one third of the total)**
(iii)	Qualitative research	**(Weighting: one third of the total)**

3   The following methods of sampling or recruitment are commonly used in qualitative research.

   (a)   Describe what each method involves, giving examples of when and why it might be used.

(i)	List sampling	
(ii)	Snowball sampling	
(iii)	Convenience sampling (or 'lurk and grab')	**(Weighting: 50%)**

   (b)   Choose one of the methods you have described. Discuss its strengths and limitations, and give suggestions for overcoming the limitations. **(Weighting: 50%)**

4   Small firms, with fewer than 50 employees, currently make up over 90% of all businesses operating in the UK. The majority of these organisations do not have the resources to undertake primary research.

   (i)   Discuss the possible advantages and limitations of programmes of secondary research for small firms. Illustrate your answer with examples. **(Weighting: 50%)**

   (ii)   You have been asked by a small local firm for advice on setting up a programme of secondary research to help them understand better their current market (ie their competitors and their target market). Outline the steps they should take, giving reasons for the suggestions you make. **(Weighting: 50%)**

5   The following concepts are important when analysing quantitative data:

    (i)   a research hypothesis and a null hypothesis

    (ii)   inferential statistics

    (a)   Describe what is meant by each term.   **(Weighting: 50%)**

    (b)   Explain how the research hypothesis, the null hypothesis and inferential statistics are used in the data analysis process. Use examples to illustrate your answer. **(Weighting: 50%)**

6   Many of the problems which arise during a research project can be traced to poorly-set objectives.

    (a)   Discuss the potential problems which can arise at different stages in the research process when research objectives are not clearly defined. Illustrate your answer with examples.
        (Weighting: 50%)

    (b)   Describe the steps you would take to ensure that research objectives fully address the client's needs. Illustrate your answer with examples.   **(Weighting: 50%)**

Suggested answers

DO NOT TURN THIS PAGE UNTIL YOU
HAVE COMPLETED THE TEST PAPER

Section 1

ANSWER

> *Tutorial note.* The examiner commented that the main weakness of many Section 1 answers was a failure to set them in the context of the question. It is always important to relate what you say in your answer to the details you have in the question.
>
> In order to pass question 1 you need to include a minimum of two problems and at least one appropriate potential solution for each. A convincing rationale is required for each suggestion made. You would score better marks if you consider the overall approach, not just the data collection methods suggested in the question. We have included six suggestions: hopefully this covers any of the problems you may have chosen to write about.
>
> In question 2 you are again expected to include a minimum of two problems for each question, with a convincing solution for each. Most candidates do well on this type of question because there is something practical to get your teeth into.
>
> In question 3 you are specifically asked for a recommendation, so don't neglect this. At pass level you would be expected to include a minimum of one possible alternative with a very convincing rationale for its use, or two potential alternatives with a clear indication of which is more appropriate. (As usual we have covered several more than the minimum to help you mark your own answer).
>
> Solid and strong answers will offer a range of options with a convincing rationale for each and a well-argued, clear recommendation. For instance, you may also have included an Internet survey, although it would be difficult to achieve a representative sample and RenAid may not have the technical expertise.

1   **Problems with the approach to the research**

(a)   **Frugging**

The purpose of the research is said to be to understand what motivates people to donate to charity, but the business problem is the recruitment of donors. There is therefore a strong danger that the research will be seen by respondents as an attempt to obtain donations (**frugging – fund-raising under the guise of research**) and in fact it is not clear that RenAid does not have this in mind.

The MRS Code of Conduct states clearly that if fund-raising or list compilation is involved in, or forms part of, a project then the project lies outside the scope of confidential survey research and it must not be described or presented as such. They should be made to understand that this is as much in their own interests as it is in the interests of respondents, because people are more likely to participate in their research project if they are confident that it is being conducted honestly, objectively, without unwelcome intrusion and without harm to respondents.

If RenAid nevertheless wish to combine research activities with fund raising they must make it clear to respondents at the start of any data collection exercise what the purposes of the activity are and that the activity is **not** confidential survey research.

Interviewers should therefore be thoroughly briefed to make sure that they understand the **distinction**. It would be wise to write a script for interviewers to use at the beginning of any interview, which states the purposes of the interview and either gives appropriate assurances that the information they supply will not be used for any purposes other than research, or explains that respondents may be contacted again with a view to raising funds. In either case respondents should then be given the opportunity to decline to take part without further pressure.

(b) **Questionnaire design**

It may be that the supporter who has offered to design a questionnaire is a professional with experience in this area, but they may not be – most people think they can design a questionnaire but are unaware of the many pitfalls in framing questions and do not think through the entire process of data collection, data entry, data analysis and interpretation.

The designer's experience should be checked, and if it is wanting he or she should be referred to the MRS guidelines on questionnaire design (for general good practice) and to a good design guide that provides examples and explains what can go wrong.

It may be possible to obtain the services of an independent expert who would be willing to review the questionnaire for free or for a reduced fee. See also the point below about data analysis.

It is a highly advisable to conduct a pilot exercise before embarking on the full-scale project, to check that the questionnaire does indeed produce the information required in a form that is useful for subsequent analysis.

(c) **Interviews**

The volunteers are not trained interviewers and may not have the necessary skills either in questioning or recording results. Depending upon how widespread the exercise is it may be difficult to ensure that all interviewers are appropriately briefed: they may not be able or willing to travel to a central location.

Assuming that it is out of the questions to ask for professional help with interviewing there is a **limit to what RenAid can do here**. There are MRS guidelines on data collection and on the responsibilities of interviewers, and all interviewers should be asked to familiarise themselves with these. The questionnaire itself should be simple to administer and clear instructions should be issued about the recording of answers. It may be possible to conduct some pilot interviews that will highlight potential problems and allow RenAid to issue further guidance on these matters. Ideally returns should ideally be closely monitored for quality as the research progresses, and quality control procedures such as call-back may be used, although in both cases it is likely that the resources of RenAid are too limited for very extensive quality control.

(d) **Sampling**

It is not clear from the scenario how the sample will be selected. On the face of it, it appears that volunteers will knock on doors at random in their own vicinity, but this is too **haphazard** to produce results that are representative of the entire population of interest. In fact, the population of interest does not yet appear to have been clearly defined.

For more focused sampling RenAid presumably has its own list and that can be a starting point in developing a sampling frame. To expand this it could also obtain lists of charity donors from list brokers. However, it will also be interested in the views of non-givers and some form of quota sampling may be the best approach. In-street interviews (mall intercepts) would probably be quicker and easier than door-knocking for this purpose.

(e) **Other methods of data collection**

It appears that RenAid has not considered other methods of data collection such as a self-administered postal questionnaire or telephone interviewing both of which would probably be cheaper. This is the topic of **Question 3** so the point is not developed here.

(f) **Data input, analysis and interpretation**

It appears that RenAid have given no consideration to what they will do with their data once it has been collected. Given the lack of experience of interviewers the incidence of **completion errors** is likely to be high, but the issue of data editing has not been taken into account. Presumably, given the lack of resources, data will be collected on paper and it will need to be recorded on computer in some way. Depending on the length of the questionnaire and the size of the sample this could be a very time consuming task. There is no indication of how the data will be analysed once it has been input. No resources appear to have been set aside for this purpose and it is unlikely that RenAid has experience in this area.

It is possible that the **volunteers** will be willing to submit the data they have collected in computerised form, and a **simple data entry program** could be devised for them that would perform a certain amount of verification and validation, using a program such as **Access** or even **Excel**. Ideally this should be done at the time when the questionnaire is being piloted so that the program can be tested and debugged too.

Although the charity cannot afford to employ an agency for the whole project the **analysis and interpretation** of data would seem to be the part of the project that would most benefit from **professional help**. If commissioned early enough a professional is also likely to want have some input into the questionnaire design process (for example, advising on pre-coding), and into the data entry process, since they will want to be sure that they are not taking on an impossible task.

2 **Problems with draft questions**

Problems with Question 5

Most people would find this question very difficult to answer because it covers a very **long period of time** (a year) and several **different forms of giving**.

It also appears to ask respondents to give a **total**, so to answer accurately they will either need to perform mental arithmetic or they may not bother and give answers in a variety of forms (for example 'I give £5 per month to three different charities'). This will make it more difficult to record, input and analyse the data. In addition a considerable amount of potentially useful information is lost because the answers aggregate different types of giving.

The question is subject to what is known as **'prestige bias'**, in other words many people will be inclined to give what they see as a socially desirable answer and exaggerate the amount they have given.

It is more **intrusive** than it needs to be because it asks for a specific amount. People may be more inclined to refuse to answer.

It is somewhat vague because the word 'charity' may mean different things to different people. In particular the mention of in-street collection may lead some to include giving money to people who only represent themselves, such as the homeless or beggars.

Depending on other questions that may be included on the questionnaire, the focus on giving money may be inappropriate. People may give other things such as clothes or their own time, they may take part in sponsored runs and similar activities, and so on.

Overcoming these problems

The **question should be split into separate questions about each type of giving**. The more specific types of giving that can be mentioned the better to aid recall. For example, regular donations may be further split into different categories such as payroll giving as opposed to regular direct debits or standing orders. 'All other sources' may be made much more specific, for example raffle tickets, sponsored marathons, high-profile events like Comic Relief and Children in Need, and so on.

The period that people are asked to think back over should be **reduced** to three months or even one month.

A **set of options**, probably on a **show card**, will serve several purposes: it will avoid the need for people to perform arithmetic, it will ensure consistency of answer format, it is less intrusive and it will help to combat the problem of prestige bias, although people may still exaggerate.

The options might be:

- None
- Up to £5
- Between £5 and £10
- Over £10

and so on. These could all be pre-coded to aid later data entry and analysis.

The word 'charity' should be more clearly defined (although it may be that this was done at the outset of the questionnaire, since many questions will be about charities).

If questions on other forms of giving are not already included on the questionnaire then they probably should be.

Problems with Question 6

There is no indication of what the items in the scale mean: category 1 could be interpreted as either 'strongly agree' or 'strongly disagree' (although the wording of the question is biased because it only asks for degrees of agreement).

There is no 'don't know' option, although one might be needed, for example for the statement about RenAid doing a good job.

The question is about two different things, RenAid in particular and giving to charity in general. Three of the six statements are about Ren-Aid and the other three about giving in general but they are not in a logical order.

The first statement is also about two different things.

The ordering of the statements is illogical: the 'I have never heard of it' statement should come first or preferably be asked separately (since it is a Yes/No question, there can be no degrees of agreement). If the respondent has never heard of RenAid the other statements that assume that the respondent already knows about Ren-Aid should be skipped, or else they should be answered after the interviewer has given them some neutral information about Ren-Aid (prompted awareness).

This question should probably come before the previous one. For example, if the response to Question 5 is 'Nothing' then several of the statements in Question 6 may not apply and may merely irritate the respondent.

The quotation 'charity begins at home' (ie help the needy in your own environment before helping others) is clearly relevant to a survey that aims to understand what motivates people to donate to charity, but expressed like this it may not be understood by some respondents.

There are no statements to cover those who prefer to give to charity in forms other than money.

Overcoming these problems

The question should be reworded to **remove bias**: 'How much would you agree or disagree ...?'. The scale should then be labelled, ranging from 'Strongly Agree' to 'Strongly Disagree', and a 'Don't Know' option should be provided.

The **question** should either be **split into two questions**, one about RenAid and the other about giving to charity in general, **or** at least the statements should be **re-ordered** along these lines. The statement 'I have never heard of it' does not belong here at all: it should be a yes/no question and should have been asked earlier in the questionnaire, with appropriate routing instructions for respondents who are unaware of RenAid, perhaps also with instructions for interviewers about prompting.

The first statement should be split into two: 'RenAid is a worthwhile charity' and 'I would like to support RenAid'.

The quotation 'charity begins at home' should be reworded so that the meaning is clear.

Additional statements, or a separate question should be added to cover those who give to charity in forms other than money.

Finally consideration should be given to the order of this question relative to other questions.

3   **Alternative ways of collecting the required information**

Secondary research

Research will undoubtedly have been done by other charities, and by research agencies, with greater resources than RenAid, into what motivates people to donate. Organisations such as the Charities Commission (in the UK) and the Charities Aid Foundation also conduct research that may be of help. The UK National Centre for Social Research conducts an annual British Social Attitudes Survey which includes data on charitable giving.

Whatever other options RenAid chooses it should begin by obtaining copies of such publications, and it could do so at a fraction of the cost of conducting its own survey. Even if the secondary data does not answer all of the questions that RenAid wishes to research, and is not as up-to-date as RenAid would like, it may save them a considerable amount of work and help to guide them in their approach to their own data collection.

Postal survey

A postal survey would be cheaper (at least in terms of time) than face-to-face interviews, and could achieve wider coverage of the population of interest. This assumes that a sampling frame can be constructed as explained in the answer to question 1, and it would be more difficult to contact non givers by this means.

The drawbacks with this approach are that the response rate is likely to be much lower than it would be with face-to-face interviews. RenAid is unlikely to be able to include the sort of incentives that would improve response rate, except perhaps a very low value prize draw. Questionnaire design would need even more care, since there will be no interviewer to guide respondents, and questionnaire design is already a problem for RenAid, as indicated in the answers to Questions 1 and 2.

Response rate could possibly be improved if questionnaires are dropped off by volunteers and then collected at a later date, but then the advantages of wider geographical coverage and the time savings would be lost.

Telephone research

This is similar to the door knocking approach except that it places less burden upon the volunteers. It would be quicker to complete and a wider spread of respondents could be reached.

If volunteers used their own telephones, however, there would be limited opportunity for central control, usually one of the main advantages of telephone research. A central facility with CATI software and so on is probably beyond the resources of RenAid.

Omnibus survey

An omnibus survey is one conducted by a major agency which covers a number of topics for different clients. RenAid would buy space on such a survey – possibly at lower overall cost than conducting its own research – and the agency would help with matters such as design of questions and would handle data collection, data entry and data analysis, using professional methods. Depending on cost and on restrictions imposed by the agency it may only be possible to ask a very limited number of questions, so great care would be needed in the choice of questions that focused very clearly on the research objectives: hopefully guidance would be provided by the survey operator. The sample would be larger and wider than RenAid could manage on its own, and the agency would attempt to ensure that it was representative of RenAid's population of interest.

There could be some drawbacks. RenAid would have no control over what kind of other questions appeared in the survey or where in the survey its questions appeared (for example, if they were tacked on at the end of the survey respondents may be more inclined to answer 'don't know' because of fatigue and lack of interest).

Qualitative research

A small number of qualitative interviews may provide richer detail and greater understanding than a larger quantitative survey. This may be more appropriate given that RenAid's aim is to understand motivation.

Problems include recruiting a representative sample who will be willing to give up their time, finding appropriate venues, devising an interview guide, and actually conducting the interviews, given that this requires skill and experience that RenAid do not seem to possess. It would probably be necessary to employ trained interviewers to get the best results and trained analysts to interpret them, neither of which would be cheap.

Recommendation

Secondary research should certainly be conducted in all circumstances: it may be that RenAid does not need to do additional research of its own at all.

If that is not adequate a carefully chosen **omnibus** survey is the approach most likely to provide useful and useable information at lowest cost, and it addresses not only the data collection problem but also all of the problems that RenAid faces with data entry, analysis and interpretation.

Section 2

(Remember — in the examination answer TWO questions only from Section 2)

1

Tutorial note. This is an unusually weak question and not surprisingly it was one of the less popular questions on the paper when it was set. It is a shame that the term 'success' is not more clearly defined: on the face of it surely success can be measured most accurately in terms of tonnes of materials collected, not by means of market research.

To pass in part (a) you should identify a minimum of two strengths and one limitation for each option. The best answers will offer a comprehensive evaluation of the options (taking note of the context) and a well-argued rationale for the recommendation with suggestions for overcoming limitations. It appears that it does not matter which option you recommend, so long as you justify your choice. The examiner's answer does not provide a recommendation at all.

(a) **Strengths and limitations**

(i) **Annual study**

Strengths

An annual study would be **less costly** to conduct than the other potential approaches mentioned, and this would free up financial resources for **development of the questionnaire**, for collecting data from a **larger, more representative sample**, and for **in-depth analysis** of results.

Limitations

The council wishes to monitor ongoing success, but there will be a very long period between one survey and the next. An annual survey may not reflect the ups and downs in opinions over the year due that may occur due to factors such as adverse weather, strikes or under-manning at holiday periods.

An annual survey is very dependent upon timing: it should be done at the same time each year, but the time chosen may not be typical of the year as a whole. If the survey itself has to be delayed one year then it will not be possible to compare like with like.

Whatever type of survey is used respondents are likely to base their opinions on the current situation: it is unlikely that they will have sufficient recall to give a balanced opinion based on an entire year's experience.

Finally it may be problematic to recruit matching samples from year to year: again this means that results may not be truly comparable.

(ii) **Monthly study**

Strengths

A monthly study will take more account of the **ups and downs** in opinion, and it will be much easier for respondents to recall the standard of service they have received over the period

It will also be easier to **link** the findings both to specific changes in the scheme itself and to particular uncontrollable external events.

Although once again the precise timing of each study is a factor and specific factors could distort the results in particular months it is more likely that the aggregate picture will be a reasonably typical one.

Limitations

Repeating the work every month is likely to be more **costly** than an annual study. Presumably the sample size will be smaller to keep down data collection costs and subsequent analysis costs and this will make each study less representative. It may also be necessary to reduce the size of the questionnaire, so less data will be collected than might be possible with an annual study.

More care will have to taken over the choice of the sample each month to ensure that the components of the sample are well matched from month to month.

Some management procedures will have to be done irrespective of the size of the sample, and it is obviously more costly and time consuming to do them twelve times a year than once only.

(iii)   **Continuous panels**

Strengths

A panel involves a fixed sample of respondents whose opinions are measured repeatedly over a period of time and the results provide management with a picture of changing views. Because the sample is fixed the **risk of sample variation is eliminated**. It is common practice when setting up such a service to have, for example, three panels of identical composition. These will be rotated to minimise respondent fatigue.

The use of diaries should mean that much **more accurate and detailed data** can be recorded than is possible with annual or monthly studies which rely on memory.

The results can be mapped closely to changes in the scheme and to external events.

Limitations

This option is the most **expensive**, partly because more data will be generated and will need to be analysed, partly because panel members are likely to want rewards or incentives for their continued co-operation, and partly because the council will need to make extra effort (via newsletters and so on) to maintain interest in the scheme.

The initial **recruitment** of the sample will be **no easier** than it is for other approaches and it can be very difficult to maintain the integrity of the panel over time. Panel replacement, for example because of illness or boredom, is an ongoing concern. Ideally, the newcomer should really be a clone of the 'drop-out' in every way. This is not easy to achieve.

Another problem is the degree of **bias** that creeps in over time when people are consciously recording their behaviour. Validity of the data depends on the participants being no different to non-participants, but the participants' raised level of awareness of the matters that are being tracked means that a certain distortion may occur over time. On the other hand there is evidence that newly recruited panel members tend to behave differently from longer-established members and need a kind of 'running-in period', such that their data will be discarded for the first few reporting periods. Necessary though this may be it is wasteful.

Finally, the very fact that much more and more detailed data will be collected may present problems. The sheer volume of data may be difficult to manage for analysis purposes.

(b) Recommended option

To some extent the 'ongoing success' of the scheme can surely be monitored by analysing operational data that the council will have to collect in any case, for management and accounting purposes, for example physical volumes of different types of items collected (paper, glass etc), volume of material rejected, and the costs of running the scheme as against the income earned by it.

In view of this it seems excessive to consider the additional cost and considerable management time that would be needed to operate a continuous panel. Council tax payers might legitimately argue that the money would be better spent on improving the scheme rather than just measuring it. Further, it seems fairly unlikely that opinions on a subject such as a recycling scheme will be so volatile that continuous measurement would be justified.

Although an annual study is the least costly option, there is a good deal of risk that it may be thwarted by external events and it will only ever be a snapshot at one point in time: data could be too inaccurate and unrepresentative to be of use. The requirement is to measure ongoing success

A **monthly** study is therefore the most appropriate of the three options suggested and the data collected from this should be mapped to data that is collected for operational purposes.

2

> *Tutorial note.* You are expected to identify a minimum of two benefits and two limitations within each section (as ever, our answer provides more than this to help you mark your own). A shortfall in one section may be compensated for by greater depth in another. At pass level, you are expected to provide adequate description or illustration to demonstrate awareness of the practical application of the Internet in all three areas.
>
> We very strongly recommend that you register with yougov.com and participate as fully as you can while you are studying. Not only will you earn at least £1 for free, but this will keep you aware of many current issues, and (perhaps more importantly) of how they might be researched.

Strictly speaking the Internet is a global computer network that supports a number of applications for information sharing and retrieval including (amongst others) email services and HTML pages. The term is commonly used synonymously with the **world wide web**, accessed via a web browser, and that is how it will be interpreted in this answer.

(i) Secondary research

Benefits

The Internet provides researchers with a **colossal amount of secondary data** at their fingertips, on any subject they might think of and on many that they might never think of.

Data publishers range from interested individuals, through corporations of all sizes, specialist information providers like LexisNexis, professional and academic institutions, and governments, and this enables the researcher to obtain a **wide variety of perspectives** on a subject.

Access to much of this data is **free** (apart from hardware, software and telecommunications costs) and information is available **24 hours a day**. Data on the Internet can also be **updated** by information providers far more **quickly** (even in real time), than it can be by other means.

Tools such as search engines and directories enable highly specific topics to be researched more **quickly** than might be the case using other means such as libraries. Research can be conducted by **relatively inexpert staff**.

Difficulties

The sheer **volume** of information available is also the biggest drawback of the Internet. Searching for secondary data on the Internet can be **time consuming** unless searchers are trained in the use of the most productive search engines and have the skills and knowledge to focus on the subject of the research. It is very easy to get sided-tracked when looking for relevant secondary data.

Another major problem is assessing the **quality** of the data found. If the subject is an unfamiliar one the researcher may not know whether he or she is reading an authoritative source, or the minority views of a fanatic, or even a spoof. Much data is provided for marketing purposes and individual sites may well give a biased or incomplete picture, designed to show the site owner in a favourable light.

Many sites require the user to **login** to access the most valuable data, and this will require either a product purchase or a subscription, either of which may be very expensive. Such data will typically be stored in a database that cannot be accessed by unauthorised users or indexed by search engines – some estimates suggest that there is now at least 500 times more material in this form than there is on the conventional web, so it is possible that search engines give a misleading view of what is really available.

Finally, although data **can** be updated very quickly that **does not mean that it is up-to-date**. It is often unclear from a website when the material was written. The researcher needs be on guard against this and compare information from a variety of sources, thus increasing the time required to research the topic thoroughly.

All of these difficulties can be overcome by an experienced web researcher with good background knowledge of the subject under research and resources to subscribe to high quality information services.

(ii) **Quantitative research**

From initially being used in desk research, the Internet is being applied increasingly in both quantitative and qualitative research. Survey tools are now available which allow sophisticated **CAI (Computer Aided Interviewing) questionnaires to be executed online** and some researchers are using the Internet to carry out **group discussions over the web**.

Benefits

Internet surveys are **quick** to administer and **cost less** than other means of data collection such as postal and telephone surveys.

Data is entered by the respondent, which **saves on data processing costs**, and it can be **verified and validated** to a considerable extent at the **time of entry**, which **cuts down on errors** of various kinds. Responses can be obtained **without postal delays**.

The respondent can **answer** at any time, **24-7**, from **any location**, which is both more convenient for them and may help the researcher to achieve a wider geographical spread and get the views of hard-to-reach individuals.

Routing can be handled by computer, making questionnaire completion quicker and easier and more relevant for the respondent, and again helping to avoid response errors. The researcher has control over the order in which questions are seen and answered. The time taken to provide a response can easily be monitored if that is of interest.

High-quality stimulus materials such as sounds, pictures, movies, and interactive multimedia presentations can be **provided** with no need for printing or reproduction costs.

Awareness of the survey can be raised by sending **emails** and response rate can perhaps be improved by email reminders, especially if the organisation conducting the survey is in regular contact with potential respondents for other reasons (for example, if they subscribe to a weekly email newsletter).

Difficulties

Questionnaire design has all the normal difficulties and the designer also has to take account of factors such as **screen layout** and **incompatibilities between different browsers and different operating systems**. To compound the problems an increasing number of people access the web via devices other than computers such as mobile phones and television. This could add considerably to the overall time required for design.

The designer is also reliant upon the **IT skills of respondents**. It may be necessary to include extra help for users and in some cases it may be necessary to make compromises with question format that would not have been necessary with a paper-based questionnaire or one administered face-to-face.

Automated features such as pre-coding, routing and data recording may be difficult and time-consuming to program and need to be very thoroughly tested to ensure, for example, that respondents do not get stuck in a loop and cannot give inconsistent answers.

Other **technical issues** include the reliability of web servers and the availability of sufficient bandwidth and web server processing power to cope with varying levels of web traffic. If the site is off-line for some reason when respondents attempt to reply their contributions may be lost forever; likewise if the server and its underlying database can only cope with a limited number of simultaneous submissions of data.

The **sample is limited to those who have access to a computer and the Internet**, and this may not be appropriate for some types of research, nor properly representative of the population of interest. Even if the required respondents can be reached it is more difficult to be sure that the person who completed the survey was the person the researcher intended to target than it is with telephone or face-to-face interviewing.

Response rate depends on respondents being aware of the survey. A link on a website may be ignored or mistrusted (once common techniques such as pop-up surveys are now defeated by modern browsers and security software, and in any case are regarded as irritating and intrusive by most web users).

Stimulus materials that cannot be rendered in digital format – in other words tastes, smells and textures – cannot be used. Materials that rely on plug-ins such as 3D viewers may be ignored because the user does not want to download the relevant software.

Finally the researcher needs to be careful not to breach **privacy legislation** such as anti-spam laws, and this varies considerably from country to country. **Confidentiality** is also an issue: some respondents may be unwilling to provide the kind of information the researcher needs because of worries about Internet security.

(iii) **Qualitative research**

Online collection of qualitative data can be done by a variety of means, the most common of which are **bulletin-board discussions** (which may last several days or even weeks) and **chat room discussions**, conducted in real time. One-to-one qualitative research might sometimes be done by an exchange of freeform e-mails rather than in a web-based form.

Benefits

The Internet has hundreds of millions of users worldwide and this potentially gives the researcher **access to communities** that would and could not have formed otherwise. Many of the usual problems of qualitative research such as finding a suitable venue and time can be overcome by conducting the research online. Online qualitative research can be conducted **across time zones in multiple countries** and possibly in **multiple languages**. Respondents can review the moderator's questions and post their answers at their convenience. As with quantitative research there are **savings in data entry costs** because verbatim responses are ready transcribed in computer format.

Samples may **better represent** the target audience because they can include rural areas and smaller cities. (Most in-person groups are conducted in a few major urban markets.)

Peer pressure is **minimal** in online qualitative research. The absence of real-time interaction in asynchronous communication methods like bulletin boards also removes the conventions of turn-taking and interruptions, and may lead to a more democratic view of the subject under discussion.

An **anonymous environment** can be created online that may lead to greater openness and honesty in discussing sensitive topics, such as money, sex, politically incorrect views, and so on.

A **moderator can screen messages**, if necessary, to keep the discussion focused on the matter in hand and to avoid offence to others.

Respondents have **more time to reflect** on their answers and can, therefore, produce more thoughtful and in-depth comments than they might in other forms of qualitative research.

Certain qualitative techniques such as **word association** and **sentence completion** lend themselves well to an online format and, as with quantitative research, it is possible to use **multimedia stimulus materials**. The researcher has more control over how often and for how long such material is viewed before a response has to be given, which may be important in researching the impact of promotional materials.

Some aspects of **behaviour** can be **observed** and **monitored** – this is limited to the way users interact with their computers, but that may be very important information for software designers and website designers.

Difficulties

Many of the difficulties that apply to quantitative research also apply to qualitative research, such as browser differences, the device used to connect, web server reliability, bandwidth issues, limitation of participants to those with Internet access, worries about confidentiality and so on.

Some potential respondents may have **limited keyboard skills** making it more difficult for them to provide lengthy text-based responses. This is a particular problem in a real-time chat room environment. Moreover chat rooms have their own **jargon** and **conventions** which may mystify or even offend those who are not familiar with them, such as IMHO (in my humble opinion); IRL (in real life); PMFJIB (pardon me for jumping in but); ::POOF:: (Goodbye, used when leaving the chat room).

Privacy is an important issue. There are a large number of easily accessible pre-existing groups online and transcripts of their past communications can be obtained very simply, but it is particularly important to obtain appropriate permission before recruiting participants for studies or using comments that were not made in the context of the researcher's own project.

The **anonymity** of this method of research can create problems. In theory, participation can be restricted to those who match the required profile (by requiring a login), but in practice there is no foolproof way of checking that respondents are who they say they are.

An **online moderator** requires different **skills** to those of a face-to-face moderator, but must be equally expert, especially in live discussions. The participants have not met one another or the moderator, so it is difficult to establish rapport and trust, let alone be authoritative enough to control the discussion. Some participants may use foul language that offends others (although software controls can prevent this to some extent). Flaming – posting deliberately insulting messages to the writer of an earlier post – is not uncommon.

The **nature of communication** itself is limiting because it is void of visual and aural cues – for example, an ironic comment cannot be accompanied by a certain tone of voice or a smile. Many forums use emoticons to try to overcome these limitations, but used to excess they can be very irritating, and in some contexts users may find them frivolous and childish.

Finally, there is **no opportunity** for the researcher to **observe non-verbal behaviour** such as body language.

3

> *Tutorial note.* A good answer would offer detailed descriptions of each sampling method, relevant practical examples, and comprehensive accounts of the advantages and limitations of the sampling option chosen. Note that the question specifies qualitative research.
>
> In part (b) you are expected to focus on one area only, and to provide evidence that you understand the practical application of the area. Credit would be given for both the range of strengths/limitations identified and for the clarity of suggestions given for overcoming limitations.

(a) **Sampling and recruitment methods**

(i) **List sampling**

This method involves choosing names of potential respondents from a pre-existing list or sampling frame. For example, the list may be a list of contacts supplied by the client, such as its customer database, or it may be purchased specially for the purpose from a list broker, or it may be one that the researcher has developed having undertaken similar research in the past.

List sampling is appropriate if an accurate, up-to-date list exists and if it is feasible to contact a sufficient number of respondents, given the nature of the research problem, the timescale and budget and practical considerations such as the geographical spread of the list members.

(ii) **Snowball sampling**

Snowball sampling is the selection of sampling units recommended by initial sampling units. For example, the researcher may be interested in selecting potential purchasers of a specialist design software package for the sample. The sample required is 20 and the researcher only has four or five names of potential respondents. The researcher will ask these first few respondents if they have the names and contact details of other purchasers of the design software. These names will then be added to the sample list until 20 respondents have been contacted.

As indicated by the example this is most appropriate when very little is known in advance about the population of interest and information cannot be obtained by other means. It is more common in business to business situations.

(iii) **Convenience sampling**

Convenience sampling involves taking as the sample those units which are easiest to access. For example, a small shop owner may ask a researcher to spend one day selecting members of the public outside the shop who are willing to answer a few questions (hence the expression 'lurk and grab'). Another example is to invite visitors to a website to take part in a survey.

Convenience sampling may have to be used when no appropriate sample frame exists for the group(s) in question, but when it is reasonable to expect that suitable respondents will be encountered in particular locations. It may also be an acceptable method for initial research when the aim is to uncover prevailing trends in thought and opinion as quickly as possible.

(b) **Strengths and limitations of these methods and suggestions for overcoming the limitations**

> *Tutorial note.* We tackle all three methods but you should only have dealt with one of them.

List sampling

Strengths

If a suitable list exists it is obviously much **quicker** and easier to find people with the required characteristics than it is with other methods, where the researcher has to make active efforts to search for them and there is every chance that many contacts made will not be representative, wasting time and resources.

A very wide range of lists is available from **list-brokers**

A full list allows the widest range of sampling techniques, from probability based methods suitable for detailed statistical analysis, such as simple random sampling and stratified random sampling, to cheaper to administer non-probability methods such as quota sampling. This means that the researcher can choose whichever approach best satisfies the research requirements.

The very fact that someone is on a list is likely to mean that the researcher already has a certain amount of data about them, and this could save a good deal of time in the data collection process. For example, if names are drawn from a customer database the researcher will also have data about their spending habits. If names are drawn from a list of subscribers to a magazine this indicates that the potential respondents have certain interests. For consumers it will also be possible to superimpose geo-demographic data, assuming postcodes are known.

Finally, once it is developed, a list may be a valuable resource in itself and it may be possible to **sell it to others**.

Limitations

The problem with list sampling is that a **completely suitable list rarely exists**. Ideally the list should have the following **characteristics**.

(i)   It should include all members of the defined population.

(ii)   The frame should be a complete, up-to-date list of the defined population.

(iii)   No population member should be listed more than once.

(iv)   The list should contain information about each individual that could be used for satisfying the sample.

In practice it is likely that any list will be **out of date**, at least to some extent. A list of a company's customers does not include potential new customers, so it must be **incomplete**. However, it will include lapsed customers, so it is **not accurate**.

As mentioned in part (a) a further problem may be the **geographical spread** of the list members, especially as qualitative research is involved and especially if it is desirable to assemble focus groups.

The development of a suitable sampling frame can be costly and time-consuming. An out-of-date list may need to be **updated extensively**, which will undermine the advantage of the speed of this method. If two or more lists have to be combined the data will need to be cleaned by **removing duplicates** and ensuring that data is complete in both cases and in a consistent format: again this could take a considerable time.

The **cost of buying lists** from other sources may also be considerable, especially if it is a non-standard lists that the broker needs to tailor to certain requirements. Budget limitations may mean that it is only possible to buy so many thousand names from the full list, so the list will not be complete. For instance, a full list of Head Teachers in the UK might cost over £20,000.

Overcoming the limitations

Every effort should be made to clean the list and ensure that it is accurate, up-to-date and as complete as possible. Lists of potential purchasers might be obtained in some cases from other surveys or the general household survey (which asks questions such as 'Are you considering purchasing a new car/DVD recorder/etc in the next six months?'.)

If list brokers are used they should be reputable ones who are willing to give verifiable information about their sources and offer guarantees.

It is unlikely that the limitations can be fully overcome, however. The researcher will have to make certain **compromises** and ensure that any reporting of results makes it clear that there is a margin of error.

Snowball sampling

Strengths

Snowball sampling may be the only feasible option for recruiting a sample **when the desired sample characteristic is rare** and especially if it is something that respondents would not wish to be known about them, for example involvement in crime or drug taking.

Sample recruitment requires little effort on the part of the researcher, it is inexpensive compared to developing a list, and it should be very quick unless self-completion questionnaires are used (less likely in the context of this question, given that the research in question is qualitative) and there are delays in returning them.

In theory the method has **great potential power**. Studies of social networks have revealed that even in a population as large and as geographically spread as that of the US, every member is indirectly associated with every other member through approximately six intermediaries, so that even the most socially isolated individuals can be reached through the sixth wave of a referral chain, beginning with any arbitrarily chosen individual (although that individual would have to chose absolutely everyone he or she knows).

Limitations

The key limitation of snowball sampling is that it is **likely to result in a biased sample**. This is for several reasons.

(i)   The initial sample usually cannot be drawn randomly. Inferences about individuals must rely mainly on the initial sample, since additional individuals found by tracing chains are never found randomly, or even with known biases.

(ii)   Samples tend to be biased towards the more co-operative subjects who agree to participate; this problem is aggravated when the initial sample are volunteers, because in terms of co-operation they are outliers.

(iii) Samples may be biased because of masking, that is, protecting friends by not referring them, an important problem when a population has strong privacy concerns. On the other hand, an initial respondent is most likely to have contacts amongst and influence with others who share his or her views, not with those who oppose them.

(iv)   Referrals occur through network links, so subject with larger personal networks will be over-sampled, and socially isolated individuals will be excluded.

Overcoming the limitations

Because of its potential power various methods may be employed to attempt to overcome its limitations.

(i)   The contacts obtained can be assembled into a **frame** from which members of the 'rare' population can be **randomly selected**, reducing bias. For construction of the frame, a list of members of this population should be created to the point at which no new members are identified. Obviously, however, this greatly increases the cost and time taken.

(ii)   **Key informant sampling** is designed to overcome response biases by selecting especially knowledgeable respondents and asking them about others' behaviour rather then their own. For example, social workers might be asked to report on patterns of drug use.

(iii)   **Respondent-driven sampling** involves asking respondents to recruit their peers personally into the study rather than asking them to identify them. It also entails offering respondents two incentives, one for participating themselves and a second for the participation they elicit from the persons that whose names they supply. The principle here is that those who may not have be tempted to take part by the first incentive may nevertheless be recruited by others who are, because they are more likely to respond if the pressure to take part comes from one of their peers.

Convenience sampling

Strengths

The very name suggests the main strength: it is convenient in the sense that **sample recruitment entails very little effort on the part of the researcher** (apart from choosing where to place the interviewer), and less pressure on the interviewer to secure the co-operation of respondents.

It is a useful approach if the population of interest is geographically-bound in some way, or if there is a reason for members of the population to gather in a particular place, such as bus users would at bus stops.

The method may be the only feasible one for researchers with very restricted time and resources.

It may be a useful approach for highly exploratory research where the research topic is so new or unusual that it is difficult for the researcher to know where to being. A quick convenience sample may at least provide some direction for more scientific approaches once detailed research begins.

Limitations

The likelihood of bias with this method is very high: the day and time chosen for the interviews may have been unrepresentative due to a wide variety of uncontrollable factors. Results may vary widely depending on the location chosen. It is therefore not possible to draw any inferences from the results obtained.

Because stopping people the street is an extremely haphazard approach it may be **mistaken for a type of random sampling** – an unscrupulous researcher might portray it as such to an unsuspecting client – but of course it is not random because the researcher has little control over whether the persons who pass by belong to the actual population of interest.

Overcoming the limitations

The problem of bias might be overcome by discarding the responses of those who were not representative of the population of interest, but in the worst case this could mean that all responses have to be disregarded.

A more practical and efficient answer is for the interviewers to 'lurk' in the same way as they might in a convenience sampling exercise, but to 'grab' in a far more discriminating manner.

(i)   **Quota sampling** identifies the total number of units to sample and the **specific characteristics** of sections of the sample, although it does not select each individual unit in advance. The actual unit selection is carried out by the field worker, who will ask an initial set of questions to determine whether the person chosen is suitable. The population of interest is divided into segments (cells) via certain control characteristics: eg age, gender, level of education. The number of units to be selected is determined by the expert judgement of the researcher. Interviewers are then instructed to fill quotas assigned to the cells.

(ii) **Judgement sampling** is selecting units to collect data based on the expert opinion of the researcher. Great care is needed with this approach because any preconceptions the researcher may have will be reflected in the sample, and if these preconceptions are inaccurate then even larger biases can be introduced than with convenience sampling. However, this is a more usual method of sampling in business and industrial markets, particularly for exploratory research projects, when the researcher is actively looking for specific people, eg opinion leaders or experts in a particular field.

4

Tutorial note. This question was not popular when it was set – perhaps because it had limited relevance to market research students, who presumably know more about the clients that do require their services than those that don't! Very unusually, the question mentions the UK specifically, and that may also have helped to put off non-UK-based students, even though the real issue is the limited resources of small businesses wherever in the world they may be.

Even in some otherwise adequate answers there was little or no acknowledgement of the setting of the question – small businesses. This is becoming a regular complaint by the examiner, so you would be well advised to make every attempt to apply your knowledge to the business situation in the questions you answer. Don't just write down everything you know about the first term you recognise.

In part (i) at pass level, you are expected to identify a minimum of two advantages and two limitations (our answer gives you several more to choose from), and to provide clear examples for the points you make. In part (ii) you should provide a brief plan, with clear stages outlined. The plan should be convincing in that it should demonstrate a logical progression and a clear rationale for each stage included.

Our answer to part (ii) is longer than you could have managed in the time available. This is to cover the full range of points that you might have made and also because it includes some extra information – we have noticed that many students very wrongly assume that clients can freely re-analyse existing company records for research purposes … without customers' informed consent! That is not so, of course: if you suggest this course of action make sure you also mention the ethical/Code of Conduct/data protection issues.

You should not be afraid to point out difficulties in the question itself (see our answer) – the question may be (deliberately?) carelessly worded, as this one appears to be – but please don't take that to mean that you can rewrite the question to suit yourself. You must answer the question set, not the one you would have liked to have been set!

(i) **Secondary research for small firms**

Features of secondary research that make it especially **advantageous** for small firms with limited resources include the following.

(1) It is **quick** to obtain and it is relatively **cheap**, or even free. If the research needed has been done by someone else already and the results are available at reasonable cost, are up-to-date, and are relevant to the firm's particular problem there is no point in repeating it. (This applies to all businesses, of course, not only small ones.)

(2) In the UK at least (and the UK is specifically mentioned in the question), there is a **huge range of sources** of very high quality secondary information, ranging from freely available UK government information and information from the BBC, to syndicated English-language sources such as Mintel reports, to quite expensive reports from very highly respected information providers such as the Economist Intelligence Unit.

(3) Unlike primary research, which may require specialist skills in sample design, data collection, interviewing, and analysis, secondary research can be conducted by persons who have **no formal research experience or qualifications**, so long as they understand the research problem and/or are given clear instructions on the information required.

(4) Small firms, lacking resources, tend to focus on immediate and local issues and may easily miss the bigger picture. A regular programme of secondary research may help to identify **new opportunities** or **upcoming problems** that managers would otherwise have missed due to the pressure of dealing with everyday affairs.

Researchers should always begin with secondary research to make sure that they are not reinventing the wheel, but they must recognise that it also has **limitations** such as the following.

(1) By its very nature it could be **out of date** and **unrepresentative** of the current situation, because it has been done already.

(2) It may be difficult to obtain details of the research **methodology** used, including **sampling** details and the scope of the research. It may be that an entirely different approach would be needed to help with the particular problem that the small firm faces, for example a much broader sample or a much narrower one. In other words it could be **wrong** to assume that research results collected for one client, in one set of circumstances, are **representative, reliable and valid** in all other circumstances.

(3) If it is free or very cheap the research may only have been published to **advertise the skills of the researcher** and promote more comprehensive research studies that must either be paid for, or are not publicly available at all. This is obviously true of private sector agencies but it may also apply to government studies produced by government agencies that are required to operate on a commercial basis.

(4) The published research results may be **biased** in various ways depending upon **who commissioned it**. For example, research commissioned by a competitor X plc is likely to have asked questions specific to X plc customers' views of the precise services provided by X plc. It may not be possible to extrapolate from those results and assume that they also apply to the customers of a small firm competitor of X plc – the small firm may offer an entirely different type and level of service and have a totally different customer profile.

(5) Different data providers may publish research results in widely different ways and this may make it very **difficult to combine data from different sources**.

(6) Thanks to the Internet and search engines, secondary research appears to be very easy for anyone, but **amateur** researchers may very **easily miss valuable sources of information** entirely (for example, if they happen not to pick the right combination of keywords in an Internet search, or don't appreciate what may lie within a web database) or at least they may **take a very long time** to track down the best sources.

(ii) **Programme of secondary research**

Existing data

We will assume that the firm has recognised that the data that is contained in its **own information systems** – in particular accounting data – is very valuable and can probably be explored in various ways to provide new insights, albeit strictly subject to **data protection legislation** and **individuals' privacy rights**.

It can be argued that this is a form of secondary research, but given that the data may **not have been collected for research purposes**, that informed consent may need to be obtained to use it in another way, and that extensive and expensive re-analysis may be necessary, the exercise may well have **more in common with primary research**, and primary research is not the subject of this question.

New data

The **objectives** of the research, as stated **in the question**, are for the firm 'to understand better their current market (ie their competitors and their target market)'.

Step 1, as in any research project, should be to **define** these **very vague objectives** as clearly as possible.

(1) The objectives themselves are **ambiguous** as stated: does the firm want to understand its **current** market (existing customers) or its **target** market (existing and potential customers)? We will assume in what follows that both the existing and the potential market need to be researched, since that would be the most usual aim.

(2) What does 'better understand' actually mean? In other words what **information** is **known already** and what additional information is **required**? How is it expected that this new information will **benefit** the business?

(3) What is the **target market**? For a conventional business such as a firm of plumbers the target market may be defined in geographical terms (this town only, or the next nearest one too?) and/or in terms of type and scale of work and customer (domestic work or business premises too?). For a producer of an innovative new product or service the potential market might be worldwide in theory, but the ability to supply worldwide would be restricted by **available resources** of staff, time, finance and so on. There is little point in a small business spending time researching new markets if the business cannot realistically expect to have the resources to support them.

(4) Who are the **competitors** in the target market, as it has now been defined (or is it one of the aims of the research to find out)? What **information** about them is needed? Likely topics include size, market share, financial information, strengths and weaknesses, and so on. The questions to be answered need to be clearly defined in advance so that the same information is collected on each competitor, in a form that is **comparable**, both between competitors and with information that is available about the firm conducting the research.

(5) Does the market also need to be defined in terms of **other key players** such as suppliers, government, or regulatory bodies, and/or other **political** and **environmental issues** such as new technology, influential pressure groups and so on.

Step 2 is to decide on the **resources** that can be spared to conduct the research. A one-person business, for example, may decide to spend one hour per evening for two weeks only, using free material on the Internet as its only source. A larger firm may ask one or more members of staff to conduct the research and may set a **budget** (for example, to subscribe to information services like LexisNexis or buy Mintel reports) and **deadlines** by which reports should be delivered that address the questions set at Step 1. The detailed objectives set at Step 1 may need to be redefined if adequate resources are not available. The firm may decide that the research should be **ongoing** (done at a specific time each month, say) or it may be a **one-off** exercise.

Step 3 is to draw up a list of **information sources**. This would either be done by the person appointed to conduct the actual research or it might be pre-defined, on quality or date grounds, in order to limit the amount of work done. As examples of the latter the firm may specify that Internet searching should be limited to the first thirty results turned up (by Google, say, or by a metasearch engine such as Ixquick), or that information should only be gathered if it is dated in the current year, or that only specific information services, such as an Internet portal devoted to the industry in question, should be searched. The firm might specify specific sources that MUST be searched, such as the website and publications of a professional body to which it belongs or the information resources available from its own bank.

Step 4 is to conduct the research itself and record the results, subject to all of the above, and bearing in mind difficulties that may be encountered at the analysis and reporting stages. In very small businesses the remaining stages may be done by more senior persons (who have a better understanding of the business issues), so it is very important that the data is recorded in a way that is manageable for subsequent collation and analysis.

Step 5 is to collate the data collected and analyse it in useful ways, bearing in mind the questions that need to be answered, as defined at the outset. This requires a very good understanding of the business problem or opportunity and the potential value of information collected so responsibility for this step may well be handed over to someone more senior than the initial researcher.

Step 6 may be to produce a report – the level of sophistication will depend on the skill of the researcher, the size of the business, the complexity of the issues and the regularity of reporting. It may range from a mere list of links covering the latest relevant news stories to a full-scale report with background details, pivot tables and graphs showing market share, seasonal factors, forecasts and so on, quotes from media commentary, analyses of implications of secondary findings and so on.

Step 7, finally, is for the firm to consider what action needs to be taken as a result of the data collected and analysed.

Step 6 (the report) may well be omitted by smaller businesses if the scope of the research does not justify it, and steps 5 (analysis) and 7 (action) may be combined, since the analysis and interpretation of data collected and the decision making will be done directly by senior managers.

If this is a continuous cycle (as it probably should be), the firm should then return to the initial problem (or the problem as redefined as a result of the research) and the process should begin again, perhaps at the same time next month.

5

(a) **Meaning of terms**

(i) **Research hypothesis and null hypothesis**

A **null hypothesis** is a hypothesis that is presumed true until statistical evidence, in the form of a hypothesis test, indicates that an alternative hypothesis – the **research hypothesis** in this case – is true. The hypothesis is a statement about a parameter that is a property of a population of interest such as the average value (the mean, μ) and this is tested based on the results from a random sample from the population (whose mean would be notated as μ_0).

As a simple example, the researcher may believe that:

Washing powder X washes whiter than washing powder Y.

This would be the research hypothesis (often abbreviated as H_1), which is typically the idea formulated at the beginning of the research process that there is some form of link between two or more concepts.

However, it is easier to test a null hypothesis (H_0), framed in the form:

*There is **no difference** between the whiteness of the wash obtained from powders X and Y*

It is easier to test the null hypothesis (ie to test how probable it is that the sample average whiteness is the **same as** the population average) than it is to test whether there is a difference, because many factors may contribute to that difference. In notational form, it is easier to test H_0 – whether it is likely that $\mu = \mu_0$ – than it is to test an alternative hypothesis – whether $\mu \neq \mu_0$ or whether $\mu > \mu_0$ or $\mu < \mu_0$. The latter cannot be proved with 100% certainty, but the former can be disproved on the basis of sample evidence.

The usual **process of hypothesis** testing consists of **four steps**.

1 Formulate the null hypothesis (commonly, that the observations are the result of pure chance) and the alternative hypothesis (commonly, that the observations show a real effect combined with a component of chance variation).

2 Identify a test statistic that can be used to assess the truth of the null hypothesis.

3 Compute the probability (which we will call p) that a test statistic at least as significant as the one observed would be obtained assuming that the null hypothesis were true. The smaller the value of p, the stronger the evidence against the null hypothesis.

4   Compare the probability to an acceptable significance value which we will call α. If p is less than α, the null hypothesis is ruled out, and the alternative hypothesis is valid.

(ii)   **Inferential statistics**

Whereas **descriptive** statistics such as the mean and the standard variation merely describe the characteristics of a population, **inferential statistics** are used to draw conclusions (make inferences) about the entire population of interest based on the sample results. Thus inferential statistics allow the researcher to determine if the relationships between variables, or the differences between proportions or percentages, are real or if they have occurred by chance.

There are two main methods used in inferential statistics: hypothesis testing (as explained above) and estimation. In estimation, the sample is used to estimate a parameter and a confidence interval about the estimate is constructed. A parameter is a numerical quantity measuring some aspect of a population of scores, for example, the mean, measuring central tendency. A confidence interval is a range of values that has a specified probability of containing the parameter being estimated. The 95% and 99% confidence intervals which have .95 and .99 probabilities of containing the parameter respectively are most commonly used.

(b)   **Using the research hypothesis, the null hypothesis and inferential statistics in the data analysis process**

At the start of the analysis process the data that has been collected will be organised into a suitable format, for example into cross-tabulations with independent variables relating to the research hypothesis as column headings. For example if the hypothesis is that women are more likely than men to buy a certain type of car then men and women would be the independent variables and the various questions asked to determine preferences would be the dependent variables.

The next step is to decide what type of statistics can be derived from the data and therefore what type of tests can be used.

(i)   With **nominal data** (identification labels such as 1 for men and 2 for women) the only quantification possible is to count up numbers and calculate percentages, and statistics are limited to the calculation of the mode (the most frequent value or values), a binomial test, which examines the relative proportions of a dichotomous variable such as male or female (for example, a researcher may want to check that the proportions of men and women in a sample don't deviate significantly from what would be expected by chance) and the chi-squared test, which looks at the difference between observed values and expected values (for example, if the researcher wants to check whether the level of variation in results is greater than would be expected by chance).

(ii)   With **ordinal** data (data that is ranked on a scale of say, 1 to 5) it is useful to calculate descriptive statistics such as the mode (the most frequent value or values) and the median (the central value when all the values are arranged in ascending order). Neither of these are suitable for further statistical analysis however, and there is no way of knowing the degree of difference between the item ranked 1 and the items ranked 2, 3, 4, and 5. However, the Spearman rank-order coefficient of correlation might be calculated to see if there is a positive correlation between two variables such as advertising expenditure and turnover.

(iii)   **Interval data** is similar to ordinal data, but the intervals between each item in the scale are intended to be equal, although there is no zero value that clearly defines the starting point. **Ratio data** is data that consists of real numbers starting from zero. Many kinds of arithmetic can be performed with such data and all manner of testing may be done, such as hypothesis testing or measurement of relationships by examining correlation and simple regression or by using multivariate techniques.

(1)   A **t-test** might be used to determine whether there is a difference between two separate groups by looking at their sample means.

(2)   The **paired t-test** determines whether there is a difference between measurements taken on a single group at two separate time points. The test operates on the mean of the differences between the two time points.

(3)   **Analysis of Variance** tests determine whether there are differences between three or more separate groups by looking at their sample means.

(4)   The **Pearson correlation coefficient** allows the researcher to quantify the degree by which two variables are related in a linear fashion and simple regression can generate an equation linking those variables.

(5)   **Factor analysis** aims to discover patterns among variations in the values of multiple variables by generating artificial dimensions (called factors) that correlate highly with the real variables.

Once the appropriate test or tests have been chosen and applied (typically using some kind of **statistical software package** such as SPSS, especially in the case of the more complex techniques) the results will need to be **interpreted** in the context of the research objectives and in a way that will be meaningful to the client, who may not be expert in statistics. For example, if the results show that the null hypothesis should be rejected then the research hypothesis can be accepted, and this can be couched in the same language as the original objectives.

6

Tutorial note. Questions that assert that such and such has some sort of effect on 'the research process' are not uncommon, so make sure that you know all the stages of the research process off by heart and can list them in your sleep. This basic knowledge gives you a ready-made structure for your answer to questions like this one.

At pass level in part (a) you are expected to identify problems at a minimum of three stages and provide some illustration of those problems. Candidates who identify problems at only two stages are expected to provide thorough explanation and illustration of those problems in order to pass. Stronger candidates may provide a wider range of points across the various stages of the research project and/or more convincing description of the practical implications of the problems.

In part (b) at pass level you should provide enough evidence to show that you are aware of the importance of checking the client's needs and carrying out research into the background of the problem.

(a)   **Research objectives and the research process**

Research objectives

The **general objective** of a research project states what researchers expect to achieve by the study in general terms. However, it is advisable to break down a general objective into smaller parts. These are normally referred to as **specific objectives**. Specific objectives should **systematically address the various aspects of the problem** and the key **factors** that are assumed to **influence** or **cause** the problem: the detailed questions to be answered by the research are framed in terms of: 'Who?', 'What?', 'How?' (and often 'How many?'), 'Why?', 'When?', 'Where?'.

To put it more briefly, research objectives set out **what it is that the client needs to know** to solve a specific **problem**. If this is not clearly defined, in the way indicated above, it is not likely that the research findings will help the client to make the necessary decisions about the problem that gave rise to the research in the first place.

Types of research

There are three basic **types** of research: in reverse alphabetical order (EDC) exploratory, descriptive and causal.

(i) **Exploratory** research projects are designed to identify problems, clarify their nature and define their scope.

(ii) In **descriptive** research the researcher has an idea of the nature and scope of the problem and designs the research project to find the answers to more clearly defined questions. For example, the answer to a 'Who?' question in exploratory research might be 'people in socio-economic groups ABC1', and descriptive research would attempt to draw that out into richer detail – age, gender, precise income bracket, educational background and so on.

(iii) **Causal** research projects are designed to identify causes of behaviour: why do people of a certain age behave differently to younger or older people?

If the research objectives are not defined clearly enough the researcher might well undertake exploratory research when descriptive research is needed, or descriptive research when causal research is required.

Moreover, each of these types of research may involve **qualitative** and **quantitative** data. Poorly defined objectives may not make it clear whether one or the other or both are wanted. For example, causal research that delivers the qualitative answer 'Some people do X because of Y and others do it because of Z' may be useful but it would probably be more useful if 'some' and 'others' were quantified. However, quantification would require more work at the data collection and analysis stages: if it were not clear from the objectives that 'How many?' answers were needed as well as 'Why?' answers the required data may not have been collected.

Research design

There are four main types of research design, cross-sectional, longitudinal, experimental and case study.

(i) **Cross-sectional research** collects data at **one point in time** from a sample or, if it is repeated at intervals, it collects that data from a **fresh sample** on each subsequent occasion. This type of design is suitable for exploratory or descriptive research and it may also provide initial data for causal research, although it can only indicate causal direction, not prove cause.

(ii) **Longitudinal research** collects data from the **same sample** of respondents on **more than one occasion**. This type of research is suitable if the impact of the passage of time is important, either because external events may change views or because the client has changed something and wants to measure changes in views.

Once again this type of design is suitable for exploratory or descriptive research and it may also indicate causal direction, though not prove cause.

(iii) **Experimental research** is used to find out if causal relationships exist. Variables other than those being tested are removed or controlled and this allows the researcher to draw more robust conclusions about causality.

(iv) **Case studies** involve in-depth exploration of, say, particular households or particular organisations. Very rich data can be obtained for exploratory, descriptive or causal research purposes but if the intention is to make inferences about the population(s) to which the cases belong great care is needed in the selection of truly representative cases.

Quite clearly the choice of design is somewhat influenced by the type of research required and it in turn influences **sample selection** and **data collection** methods. If the original objectives are not clearly defined the researcher may, for example, conduct a cross-sectional study when a longitudinal one was needed (because it was not clear that the impact of time was important), or conduct unrepresentative case studies because the research objectives seemed to require rich data but did not make it clear that it should be possible to extrapolate from this data to the population as a whole.

Data collection

Poorly defined objectives are likely to mean that data that should have been collected is not collected, because the question that would have yielded the required data is not included in questionnaires or interviews, or that data is collected that is not necessary, at needless cost of time and money. Questions may include some bias that could have been eliminated if the objectives had been clearer, or interviewer guides may include some prompting when the client is not interested in prompted awareness of issues.

Data analysis

Research objectives should determine the variables that need to be explored. Unclear objectives may not have defined these variables in enough detail and that will mean that the results will not be analysed appropriately, even if the necessary information has been collected, or that it is not possible to analyse the collected data in the appropriate way, if not. For example, vague objectives may distinguish between 'younger people' and 'older people', but if this was not more clearly defined (for example, in specific age bands), the results will depend on the research agency's understanding of these terms (which may in turn depend on fieldworkers, who judged entirely on appearances). The client may have meant something quite different.

Data interpretation

If objectives are not clearly defined the researcher may not focus upon issues that are really important to the client when interpreting the data, even though sufficient data may have been collected to make other or more detailed interpretations possible. Typically research results will confirm much of what the client already knows, but if the researcher is not on alert for new information or contradictory information (because that is not part of the brief), it may easily be missed. For example, if the objective is merely to 'confirm such and such' the research may either confirm it or not; if the objective is to 'confirm such and such or suggest alternative explanations' then the researcher is compelled to think outside the box.

Reporting results

The final report will reflect the researcher's interpretation of the objectives, but if the objectives were not clearly defined there is every chance that the actual business problem will not be addressed at all, or not in enough detail to provide useful information for decision making. In the worst case the report may even reach conclusions that are incorrect and recommend a course of action that is actually the wrong thing for the client to do.

(b) **Steps to ensure that research objectives fully address the client's needs**

Problems with poorly defined objectives are most likely to arise when the client is not used to research, when the researcher is inexperienced (either generally or in the specific type of research or research topic), in new client/agency relationships, and when projects have tight deadlines. The researcher should be on extra alert if any of these apply.

(i) Above all it is essential to remain in good **communication** with the client, not just at the beginning and end of the project but throughout, so that the client's needs and the decisions that need to be made can be clarified when necessary and the research can be refined and adapted in the light of findings. The researcher should be aware of who is involved at the client's organisation in the various stages of the research and know what are they looking to get out of the research.

(ii) The **brief** should be studied in detail and if it is vague the researcher should hold further discussions with the client to seek confirmation of their understanding and clarify uncertain matters. If the client is new to research then the researcher should make extra effort to help them by explaining in detail the types of research that could be conducted.

(iii) The researchers should ensure that they understand the business problem in its context. A important step that should not be neglected is **background research**. For example, the researchers may think that they already understand the business and the industry it is in – they may even have been appointed as a result of previous experience in that industry – but that does not automatically mean that they understand the particular client's problems.

(iv) Further rounds of discussions may be needed to ensure that the client and researcher see the **business problem** in the same way and that the researcher understands what **decisions** will be made as a result of the research: this should make it clear what **information** is required and in what form the client expects to receive that information.

(v) It may be possible to refine the objectives still further at later stages of the research. For example, when a questionnaire has been designed the client should have the opportunity to review it, because it may be only when they have something concrete to look at that they realise that further questions should be asked or that questions should be asked in a different way.

(vi) At the analysis and interpretation stages it should be possible to produce some kind of preliminary report for the client, once again to check that information needs are likely to be addressed and to clarify the format that the client requires.

REVIEW FORM

Name: _____   Address: _____

_____

_____

How have you used this Kit?
(Tick one box only)

☐ With BPP distance learning programme

☐ In conjunction with programme run by employer

☐ On a course: college_____

☐ Other _____

Why did you decide to purchase this Kit?
(Tick one box only)

☐ Have used BPP's distance learning material

☐ Recommendation by friend/colleague

☐ Recommendation by a lecturer at college

☐ Saw advertising in journals

☐ Saw website

☐ Other _____

Do you intend to use the new Passcards for this subject?　　☐ Yes　　☐ No

Your ratings, comments and suggestions would be appreciated on the following areas.

	Very useful	*Useful*	*Not useful*
Introductory section (Study advice, question and answer checklist etc)	☐	☐	☐
Tutorial questions	☐	☐	☐
Exam-standard questions	☐	☐	☐
Content of suggested answers	☐	☐	☐
Tutorial notes	☐	☐	☐
Structure and presentation	☐	☐	☐

	Excellent	*Good*	*Adequate*	*Poor*
Overall opinion of this Kit	☐	☐	☐	☐

Please note any further comments and suggestions/errors on the reverse of this page.

 Please return to: Alison McHugh, MRS Course Manager, BPP Professional Education, FREEPOST, London, W12 8BR

REVIEW FORM (continued)

Please note any further comments and suggestions/errors below.

See overleaf for information on other
BPP products and how to order

MRS ORDER

To: MRS course administrator, BPP Professional Education, Aldine Place, London W12 8AA

Tel: 020 8740 2211

Email: mrs@bpp.com

Distance learning programme – materials only   £452.37 (incl VAT)

Your distance learning programme consists of study material (which covers the whole syllabus and provides activities and learning tools to help you acquire the necessary knowledge), a Practice & Revision Kit and Passcards (available Spring 2005, see below). We provide you with a personalised study timetable that guides you through the course, ensuring that you have enough time for revision. You submit your Integrated Assignment to BPP for assessment and you sit the exam at an MRS-designated centre. **Please complete the registration form on the next page and submit it with your payment.**

Distance learning programme – materials plus e-tutor support
£822.50 (incl VAT)

As well as receiving the materials and study timetable mentioned above, you have email access to a tutor who will offer invaluable advice on the preparation of your Integrated Assignment. As you work through the material in line with recommended completion dates, you submit each stage of your Integrated Assignment via email to your designated e-tutor. Your e-tutor will review your submissions and offer constructive feedback. The programme also includes a mock exam (see below). **Please complete the registration form on the next page and submit it with your payment.**

Passcards   £14.95

Available Spring 2005, these pocket-size, spiral-bound cards provide revision notes in a user-friendly format.

Mock exam   £117.50 (incl VAT)

Your answers to this will be marked and returned to you with vital feedback on areas for improvement.

To download a brochure/order form, please visit our website at www.bpp.com/mrs. Alternatively email your MRS queries to mrs@bpp.com

---

Grand Total (Cheques to BPP Professional Education) I enclose a cheque for
Or charge to Access/Visa/Switch   £

Card Number

Expiry Date   Start Date

Issue Number (Switch Only)

Signature

PRIORITY
registration form

BPP MRS ADVANCED CERTIFICATE DISTANCE LEARNING COURSE

PERSONAL

Title   Surname

Forename(s)

Address for delivery / correspondence

Postcode   Country

Daytime tel   Mobile tel

Email address   Date of birth

YOUR COURSE

Please indicate the type of course you require   ☐ Materials only   ☐ Materials plus e-tutor support

Please indicate which course you you require
☐ February 2005 sitting   ☐ June 2005 sitting   ☐ October 2005 sitting   ☐ February 2006 sitting
(Registration open till 17/11/04)   (Registration open till 23/3/05)   (Registration open till 20/7/05)   (Registration open till November 05)
(E-tutor access from 11/8/04)   (E-tutor access from 15/12/04)   (E-tutor access from 13/4/05)   (E-tutor access from August 05)

PAYMENT DETAILS

	Price	VAT	Total	Quantity	Cost
Distance learning materials only	£385.00	£67.37	£452.37	_____	_____
e-tutor support purchased separately You must already have purchased the materials	£400.00	£70.00	£470.00	_____	_____
Distance learning materials and e-tutor support	£700.00	£122.50	£822.50	_____	_____

TOTAL COST   _____
The cost includes registration and assessment

Cheque enclosed (payable to BPP Professional Education) or Charge to Visa / Mastercard / Solo / Switch

Card number ☐☐☐☐ ☐☐☐☐ ☐☐☐☐ ☐☐☐☐ ☐☐☐☐ ☐☐

Valid from   Expires end   Issue no. (Solo/Switch)   ‡CV2 no.

‡Last three digits on signature strip on reverse of credit card

EMPLOYER'S DETAILS (If sponsoring)

Name and address of company to be invoiced

Postcode   Company VAT number

Telephone   Contact email

Authorisation signature   Print name

CONTINUED OVER PAGE

ENTRY REQUIREMENTS

Required qualifications / experience

You are expected to have one or more of the following qualifications / experience to enable you to enter for the Advanced Certificate qualification.
Please indicate clearly and give details of all those you possess.

☐ One or more years of relevant experience in market or social research
Describe this experience, including details of organisations for whom you have worked.

_____

_____

_____

_____

_____

☐ The MRS Foundation Course Certificate

Your MRS candidate number _____

Centre at which you studied _____

Date certificate awarded _____

☐ The MRS Introductory Certificate

Your MRS candidate number _____

Centre at which you studied _____

Date certificate awarded _____

☐ Satisfactory nomination by employer
Name and address of employer, and nature of employer's business

_____

_____

_____

_____

☐ Satisfactory nomination by course tutor
(where the Advanced Certificate is being taken alongside an undergraduate degree or CIM Certificate)

Name of course tutor _____

Name and address of establishment at which you are studying

_____

_____

_____

Details of course _____

_____

_____

_____

_____

☐ 2 A Levels (or equivalent)

Subject _____

Grade _____ Year _____

Subject _____

Grade _____ Year _____

☐ None of the above

If you are unable to fulfill these entry requirements, we will contact you to discuss your application further.

Recommended qualifications

Please indicate clearly which of the following recommended qualifications you possess.

☐ Mathematics GCSE at grade C or above, or equivalent

☐ English GCSE at grade C or above, or equivalent

If you do not possess the above qualifications, we will contact you to discuss your application further.

Proficiency in English language

You are expected to have an appropriate level of language competence in English to allow you to undertake and complete the assessed components of the qualification.

If English is NOT your first language, please indicate clearly which of the following English language certificates you hold, and provide details of score / grade and date of award.

☐ Cambridge Proficiency in English, grade C or above

Score / grade _____ Date of award _____

☐ Cambridge Advanced Certificate in English, grade B or above

Score / grade _____ Date of award _____

☐ IELTS (6.0 or above)

Score / grade _____ Date of award _____

☐ TOEIC (880 or above)

Score / grade _____ Date of award _____

☐ None of the above

If English is not your first language and you do not hold any of the above certificates, we will contact you to discuss your application further.

BPP reserves the right to request documentary evidence of any qualifications, experience or proficiency.

Data protection requirements

May BPP pass your contact details to the MRS to add you to the MRS Qualifications Database?　　　　☐ Yes　　　☐ No

May BPP and / or the MRS use this information to tell you about its products and services?　　　☐ Yes　　　☐ No

May BPP and / or MRS pass your details to third parties that may wish to send you details about their products and services?
　　　　　　　　　　　　　　　　☐ Yes　　　☐ No

Signature _____

Date _____

Declaration

The information I have given in this Registration Form is correct to the best of my knowledge and belief.

Signature _____

Date _____

Please return to: Alison McHugh, BPP Professional Education, BPP House, Aldine Place, London W12 8AA, UK. Or fax to 020 8740 2239.

BPP
PROFESSIONAL EDUCATION®